What others have said about *Income without taxes*

"This is a valuable, clearly written introduction for anyone interested in investing in municipal bonds."—*Publishers Weekly*

"The authors' practical and methodical presentation provides valuable and easily understood information on all aspects of these instruments, including tax advantages, municipal trusts and mutual funds, bond ratings, investment risk and investment strategies. Recommended . . ."—*Library Journal*

"A good buy for self-education in the amazingly versatile world of municipals."—*"Bank Notes," Law Office, Economics & Managements*

". . . handy guidebook to the market and a book to make Jim Lebenthal's heart glad."—*Credit Markets*

"The Richelsons have written an excellent no nonsense primer on investing in bonds. . . . This work is informative, well written, and highly recommended for the libraries of investors and advisors alike."—*Tax Management Financial Planning Journal*

INCOME WITHOUT TAXES

AN INSIDER'S GUIDE TO TAX-EXEMPT BONDS

REVISED
AND
UPDATED TO
INCORPORATE
THE NEW
TAX REFORM
ACT.

HILDY & STAN RICHELSON

Carroll & Graf Publishers, Inc.
New York

*To our children,
Jolie and Scott
and
to our parents*

Copyright © 1986 by Hildy and Stan Richelson

All rights reserved. No part of this book may be reproduced in any way or by any means without the written permission of the publisher.

First Carroll & Graf edition 1985
First Carroll & Graf paperback edition 1987

Carroll & Graf Publishers, Inc.
260 Fifth Avenue
New York, NY 10001

ISBN 0-88184-278-8

The selection that appears on p. 211 appears with the kind permission of The Wall Street Journal, © Dow Jones & Company, Inc. (1983). All rights reserved.

Manufactured in the United States of America

Table of Contents

ACKNOWLEDGMENTS　　vii

PREFACE　　ix

PART I

CHAPTER
- I: Why You Should Buy Municipal Bonds　　3
- II: So You Want to Be Rich . . .　　13
- III: Municipal Bonds Will Solve Your Financial Problems　　19
- IV: Ready-Set-Go　　31

PART II

CHAPTER
- I: What Is A Municipal Bond?　　37
- II: Special Features of Certain Municipal Bonds　　53
- III: A Comparison of Municipal Bond Trusts and Funds　　67
- IV: Evaluation of A Trust　　77
- V: Evaluation of A Fund　　89
- VI: Evaluation and Credit Analysis of General Obligation and Revenue Bonds　　109
- VII: The Rating Agencies and Methods Used To Improve Ratings　　127
- VIII: Risks of Investing in Municipal Bonds and How to Avoid Them　　147
- IX: The Proper and Improper Uses of Municipal Bonds　　167
- X: How and From Whom to Buy Municipals　　176
- XI: Selling Strategies and Techniques　　189

XII:	Market Strategies	199
XIII:	Tax Aspects of Municipal Bonds	217
XIV:	The New York City Story	235
XV:	The Washington Public Power Supply System (WPPSS)	249

POSTSCRIPT 267

GLOSSARY 269

INDEX 271

Acknowledgements

We wish to acknowledge use of material from the following sources. There are a few standard reference books in municipal bonds. The simplest overview is found in *Fundamentals of Municipal Bonds*, published by the Public Securities Association. For a technical understanding of the risk factors, good sources include *Municipal Bonds* by Robert Lamb and Stephen P. Rappaport and *The Appraisal of Municipal Credit Risk* by Wade S. Smith. Finally, for an in-depth and most recent discussion of municipals there is the two-volume set entitled *The Municipal Bond Handbook*, edited by Fabozzi, Feldstein, Pollack, and Zarb. More informal sources include witty newsletters from Lebenthal and the thoughtful commentary of Steve Hueglin of Gabriele, Hueglin & Cashman. Merrill Lynch's *Fixed Income Strategy* is also useful. On the dilemma of the Washington Public Supply System, the articles in *Current Municipal Defaults and Bankruptcy*, a Practicing Law Institute chaired by James E. Spiotto, summarize the legal issues. For the New York City default dilemma, the *Securities and Exchange Commission Staff Report on Transaction in Securities of the City of New York* provides information not widely available. *The Rating Game*, published by the Twentieth Century Fund in 1974, offers a good overview of the rating process. For the definitive work to date on the history of municipal bond defaults, we read George Hempel's book *The Post War Quality of State and Local Debt*.

In addition to the few books available on the subject, we have drawn from articles published in *The New York Times* and *The Wall Street Journal*. Numerous periodical publications have provided insights; they include *Business Week, Forbes, Institutional Investor, Credit Markets, Fortune, Barron's, The Journal of Taxation, The Economist, Government Finance, The Journal of Portfolio Management, Hospital Financial Management, National Tax*

Journal, Yale Law Journal, National Law Journal, Review of Business and Economic Research, Journal of Bank Research, Financial Analysts Journal, Newsweek, Value Line, New York Law Journal, Financial Executive, Dun's Business Month, Dun's Review, National Real Estate Investor, Daily Tax Reports, Savings and Loan News, Texas Business Review, Journal of Financial and Qualitative Analysis, Journal of Corporation Law, Bankers Monthly Magazine, The Bankers Magazine, Illinois Business Review, Legal Times of Washington, The New Leader, Pension and Investment Age, Medical Economics, Real Estate Law and Practice, ABA Banking Journal, New England Economic Journal, Journal of Corporation Law, Federal Reserve Bulletin, Nebraska Journal of Economics and Business, Public Finance Quarterly, Harvard Journal on Legislation, Review of Business and Economic Research, Journal of Accounting, Auditing and Finance, Journal of Bank Research, Fixed Income Investor, CPA Journal, The Practical Accountant, Engineering News Record, and *Investment Analysis and Portfolio Management.* Nancy Solomon, vice president of Security Pacific, Merchant Banking Group, kindly agreed to read selected sections of the book. Mitchell Martin did an excellent job in editing the manuscript.

We wish to thank James O. Smith, librarian of the Legal Services Group of W. R. Grace & Co., for doing much of the research for the background of this book. Most of the books and articles were located in the Brooklyn Business Library. We wish to thank Peter Christus of Gabriele, Hueglin & Cashman, and Jeff Sena of Paine, Webber, Jackson & Curtis Incorporated, for their insights and suggestions. We also wish to thank our children Jolie and Scott for their patience and our friends for their forbearance as we discussed the unfolding of this book. We especially appreciate the work of Daisy Hein in typing the myraid drafts of this manuscript.

Preface

Income Without Taxes grew out of a luncheon meeting between Stan Richelson and Richard Gallen, President of Richard Gallen & Company. After a discussion of municipal bonds Richard asked whether there was any book which spoke directly to you, the individual investor, about the purchase and sale of municipal bonds. To our surprise, there was no such practical handbook for those who wish to become knowledgeable and comfortable enough with the subject to buy municipal bonds.

Investment decisions are frequently based on casual conversations with friends, family, and account executives. Too often the decisions are made on the basis of incomplete information. For example, a salesman calls to promote one investment over another and argues persuasively that you should purchase a particular financial product. Do you freeze and make no investment decisions, allowing inflation to gobble up your underused savings? Do you jump ahead eagerly but later regret your hasty decision?

Municipal bond investments can provide a secure and profitable return for you. Unlike many other investments, filled with unmarked potholes that jolt and jounce your equilibrium, municipal bonds offer comfortable returns and smooth sailing if you are a knowledgeable purchaser. *Income Without Taxes* represents a guide to decision-making with respect to municipal bonds.

While it is our conclusion that purchasing the actual municipal bonds themselves is generally desirable, there are situations where you may desire to buy a mutual fund or a unit investment trust that holds municipal bonds. This book will describe these vehicles and discuss their relative advantages and disadvantages. It will explain the methods and techniques of buying bonds and the pitfalls that might be encountered along the way. It will be your own personal investment advisor in the field of municipal bonds.

This book is a complete revision of the original hardcover version of *Income Without Taxes*. This 1987 edition brings the original book up to date and includes the changes necessary to reflect the dramatic impact of the Tax Reform Act of 1986.

Dr. Hildy Richelson is a Registered Investment Advisor and is president of The Scarsdale Investment Group, Ltd., which is located in Scarsdale, New York. Hildy specializes in helping people buy and sell municipal bonds. This book presents the practical knowledge of the municipal market and how to buy and sell bonds which she has gained through her business activities. Stan Richelson is a senior tax counsel for W. R. Grace & Co. in New York City.

PART I

CHAPTER I

Why You Should Buy Municipal Bonds

A. Why Municipal Bonds
B. Comparison of Municipal Bonds to Other Tax-Favored Investments
    1. Rental Real Estate that You Directly Own
    2. Tax Qualified Plans
    3. Income-shifting Techniques
    4. Common Stock

A. Why Municipal Bonds

MUNICIPAL BONDS ARE THE BEST AFTER-TAX INVESTMENT AVAILABLE TODAY! This is a strong statement. Read this chapter and see if you don't agree. This book was written for you, people who have family income of $25,000 or more and are intelligent enough to guide their own investment decisions. If you identify with this description, some part of your investment portfolio should be in municipal bonds.

Municipal bonds will provide you with

—High after-tax return
—A high degree of safety
—Marketability if you wish to sell them
—Flexible investment planning
—Safety from an IRS challenge

Does this sound too good to be true? Despite all the advertising, municipal bonds are still a mystery to almost all investors, even those of you who own them. This book was written to lift the veil and provide an insider's view of the municipal market. This is the best book on municipal bonds written for you, the high-income, intelligent investor.

The concept of a municipal bond is simplicity itself. A municipal bond is proof of money owed to you where the interest earned is exempt from federal income tax. Everyone knows this. This book will fill in the details. Part I will explain municipals in a general way with many specific examples. Part II will expand the general principles and be your handbook of knowledge on the subject of municipals.

After reading Part I, you will understand why individuals like yourself have been exploring the world of municipals in greater and greater numbers. You will also learn how to go about buying municipal bonds for yourself.

Municipals have been around for more than a hundred years. Why do individuals now purchase 87% of all municipal bonds rather than the historic 30%? Here are the reasons:

Times have changed. Many families now are in high tax brackets when paying their federal, state, and local income taxes. This means that municipal interest is worth a great deal more than other sources of income. For example, if a Treasury bond yields 7%, you will only keep 4.69% if you are in the 33% federal incremental tax bracket. In 1987, the top federal tax bracket is 38-½%. In 1988, the top federal tax bracket is 28%. However, if your taxable income is at least $71,900 but less than $149,250 (and you are married, filing jointly), your federal tax bracket will be 33%. Your overall bracket could increase to more than 40% if you live in a state with high taxes. Table I summarizes marginal federal tax brackets.

TABLE I
FEDERAL TAX RATES 1988

Single		Married	
$17,850 – 43,150	28%	$29,750 –71,900	28%
$43,150 – 89,560	33%	$71,900 – 149,250	33%
over $89,560	28%	over $149,250	28%

By comparison, a 7% municipal bond is exempt from federal income tax and will thus yield 7% after federal income tax, 33% more to you than the Treasury bond. Stated another way, you would have to receive a 10.45% return on a Treasury bond to match a 7% return on a municipal bond if you are in the 33% federal tax bracket. Treasury bonds do not yield 10.45%. What secure investment will provide a 10.45% after-tax return? The answer is easy; there is no such investment.

Municipals have recently become of great interest to individuals such as you because of the 1982, 1984 and 1986 changes in the federal tax laws and the strident and aggressive attack by the Internal Revenue Service (IRS) on tax shelters. These tax acts have finally provided the IRS with the weapons needed to attack tax shelters, and the IRS has done so with a vengeance.

Prior to 1986, individuals were properly fearful of the IRS invading and upsetting their financial lives and intruding on their private lives. Tax shelter investments became very risky. Promoters and some investors were jailed. Other tax shelter investors were hit with large deficiencies, penalties, and interest two or three times the size of their investments! In addition, many tax shelters have provided no cash return, ever.

In the Tax Reform Act of 1986, with very limited exceptions, the government has effectively closed down all tax shelters by providing that losses and credits from passive investments may not offset income from salaries, active business income or portfolio income (viz. interest, dividends, and royalties).

As tax shelters have been eliminated, municipals have come to the fore. More individuals wish to be in control of their investments. They want to have the power to turn their investments into cash at will.

Many investors have abandoned the stock market.

They have become fearful of violent price changes. On September 11, 1986, the Dow Jones industrial average fell 86 points, followed the next day by a 36-point decline. As a consequence, many investors have decided that they want a secure source of income, payable without fail. They want to be able to count on a predictable high after-tax return.

Individuals have also lost interest in trading commodities such as gold, silver, and soybeans. They have become aware that commodities trading is a sucker's game if you are not a professional trader, since 90% of the nonprofessional traders lose!

In summary, if you are a conservative, high-bracket taxpayer, what investments make sense to you? The tax shelter game is over. Stocks provide an uncertain return, at best. Commodities are for suckers. Thus, you are left with bonds. If you are in a high tax bracket, municipal bonds, are a premier investment!

If this analysis makes sense to you, keep reading. We will teach you all you need to know to become a savvy investor in municipals. But first let us compare municipal bonds to other investments such as rental real estate, tax qualified plans, income shifting techniques, and common stocks.

B. Comparison of Municipal Bonds to Other Tax-Favored Investments

In order to determine the true return from an investment and to compare investment returns, all investments should be viewed on an after-tax basis.

Municipal bonds are not the only tax-favored investment. The other tax-favored alternatives or investments which used to be tax-favored, considered by knowledgeable investors and their advisers are (1) rental real estate, (2) tax qualified plans, (3) income-shifting techniques, and (4) common stocks. In our view, qualified plans make sense in certain circumstances. The other three categories generally do not make sense today for high tax bracket individuals.

1. Rental Real Estate That You Directly Own

While real estate investments used to be tax-favored, the Tax Reform Act of 1986 has adversely affected real estate in the following ways:

• Capital gains on real estate investments are taxed at ordinary income rates while net capital losses can only be deducted up to a maximum of $3,000 per year. However, for 1987 only, the top rate for capital gains may not exceed 28%.
• In 1981, real estate could be depreciated on an accelerated basis over a 15-year life. However, the depreciable life on residential rental property is now 27½ years, and 31½ years for commercial real estate. In addition, straight line depreciation rather than accelerated depreciation must now be used.
• Net losses from real estate activities are treated as passive losses. Thus, except for a limited exception for certain active

rental real estate activities, such losses may only be deducted against income from passive investments. The exception is that losses up to $25,000 per year may be used to offset salary income and other income if (a) the taxpayer actively participates in the rental activity and (b) the taxpayer's adjusted gross income is below $100,000. This amount of $25,000 is phased down to zero for taxpayers whose adjusted gross incomes are between $100,000 and $150,000.

As a result of the foregoing tax changes, there is little tax incentive left to real estate investments. In addition, there are many other disadvantages to the average investor who has little knowledge of the real estate business, including the following:

Despite what you may have heard, real estate may *permanently* decline in value. By comparison, a municipal bond will come due at its face value. Before maturity, short-to intermediate-term bonds will not suffer much decline in market value in the face of rising interest rates.

Real estate can be quite illiquid, particularly in bad economic times when you may really need your money or when interest rates are high. We personally purchased some land in Vermont at $300 per acre. Although we planned a quick resale, we actually had to hold the land for 18 years before we could sell all of it. And we thought, "How can you lose money at $300 an acre?" By comparison, municipal bonds rated A or better are readily salable in the market. Even if you must sell at a loss, you can still sell. We could not even find anyone to look at our land for three years!

Real estate generally requires a large investment of funds and/or large indebtedness. By contrast, municipal bonds may be purchased in units as small as $5,000.

Real estate investments generally require management time, skill, and the possible exposure of having to invest substantial additional funds. By contrast, an investment in muncipal bonds does not require additional investment or management time.

Real estate investments may not generate current cash returns, while municipal bonds pay tax-free interest every six months.

If you have successfully invested in real estate, municipal bonds can balance your investment portfolio by providing a safe, high-yielding haven for your excess cash. An investment in bonds with staggered maturities provides a return of capital on a regular basis in case a good investment opportunity presents itself, while providing a high rate of return on your investment.

2. Tax Qualified Plans

Tax qualified plans include individual retirement accounts, pension and profit-sharing plans, and salary reduction plans. The advantage of these plans is that they enable you to invest your income before you pay taxes to Uncle Sam. Because the funds are for your retirement years, the government waits until you withdraw the money before taking its share. While a certain portion of your savings should be invested in one or more of these favorably taxed plans, they are not appropriate for the bulk of your holdings because:

• The funds are illiquid and generally cannot be used without penalty or sometimes not at all unless you lose or quit your job or retire. Thus, funds invested in these plans cannot generally be used without penalty as a vehicle to save funds for college expenses, a house, or other large expenditures. Municipal bonds, on the other hand, are liquid and flexible.

• Qualified plans generally have unfavorable tax consequences when the funds are distributed to you. In most plans, you are taxed at ordinary income rates if the funds are withdrawn over a period of years. In some cases, five-year averaging is available to soften the tax bite on a lump-sum distribution. However, even if five-year averaging is available, it may still result in a heavy tax if a large distribution is involved.

The deduction for contributions to IRA's has been curtailed or eliminated for taxpayers whose income exceeds $40,000 or who have other qualified retirement plans. Nondeductible contributions may still be made to IRA's. However, taxpayers are required to keep records tracking their nondeductible contributions and report this information annually on their tax returns. Attempting to keep track of withdrawal allocations will mean headaches for IRA contributors.

3. Income-Shifting Techniques

Up until July 1984, a favorite tax planning maneuver of high tax bracket investors was to make an interest-free loan to a child or other low tax bracket relative. The child or relative would invest the loan proceeds in a high-yielding investment.

The Tax Reform Act of 1984 ended such tax maneuvers for interest-free or low interest loans by providing that interest income will be imputed to the lender (the high tax bracket investor) at market rates.

Other income shifting techniques have been terminated by the 1986 Tax Reform Act. The investment income (e.g. dividends and interest) of children under 14 is taxed at their parent's tax rates if it is in excess of $1,000. In addition, the income shifting techniques of the Clifford Trust (10-year trust) and spousal remainder trusts have been eliminated for trusts created after March 1, 1986.

4. Common Stock

Under prior law, investments in common stock had two aspects. First, dividends were taxed as ordinary income, which is unfavorable compared to interest on municipal bonds. Second, gain on stock held for more than six months was taxed as a capital gain. However, under the Tax Reform Act of 1986, the 60% capital gains deduction has been eliminated so that beginning in 1988, capital gains will be taxed at the same rate as ordinary income. In addition, common stock may decline in value and never be worth the amount originally paid. By contrast, a municipal bond will always repay its face value when it comes due. This is the ultimate distinction between a bond (which is a debt owed to the holder of the bond) and a stock (which is an equity ownership in a corporation).

CHAPTER II

So You Want to be Rich . . .

A. An Investment Philosophy
B. Richelsons' Investment Rules Applied to Municipal Bonds and Other Investments

A. An Investment Philosophy

It is well known that you can never be too thin or too rich. This book will not make you thin. However, if you follow our conservative investment advice, it may make you rich. Being rich is advocated by many sages and in many sources.

That well-known twentieth-century New York philosopher, Sofie Tucker, advised: "I've been rich and I've been poor; rich is better." Sound advice, old girl. But before the wise Miss Tucker there spoke the Holy Bible:

> A feast is made for laughter, and wine maketh merry: but money answereth all things. *Ecc. 10:19*

Other sages of the ages have offered their views on the desirability of money: Charles Dickens said that "money and goods are certainly the best of references." And Benjamin Franklin in *Poor Richard's Almanac* offered the view that "there are three faithful friends—an old wife, an old dog, and ready money." Finally the jurist Oliver Wendell Holmes opined: "Put not your trust in money, but put your money in trust."

Case closed; we all desire money. Now, how to achieve wealth without risk. If you are already rich, we wish to convey our compliments. This book will teach you how to conservatively preserve and increase your capital. Another great philosopher (who was not a great grammarian) said: "More is better."

Everyone wants to be rich. However, most methods of getting rich require either that you take substantial risks with your money or that you spend a great deal of time.

An example of a high-risk, high-reward investment is commodities trading. No one afraid to lose will play this game of chance for very long since 90% of the nonprofessional investors lose at commodities trading. They are no match for the top professionals who have deep pockets and win the game in the long run.

An example of a potentially good investment is the purchase and servicing of real estate. However, as discussed above, there are many skills to be mastered and a lot of time is required.

Our investment philosophy does not require either substantial risk or a large expenditure of time. It does, however, take patience and relies upon the old virtue of thrift. This is not a get-rich-quick book because to get rich quick involves substantial risk. It is, however, a book that will help you preserve and increase your capital. All things considered, municipal bonds are today the best investment for people who earn more than $25,000 per year.

We believe that one of an investor's principal goals should be to achieve financial security. Financial security softens or eliminates two of life's significant concerns: unemployment and disability caused by sickness or accident. For most investors, municipal bonds are the best way to achieve financial security. This book will provide the required knowledge and the tools to enable you to confidently make investments in municipal bonds.

In June 1984, an investor could earn 9.3% tax free on a highly rated municipal bond. The combined magic of tax-free income and compound interest is truly amazing. At a 9.3% tax-free yield, an investment will double every 7-1/2 years. Thus, $50,000 will become $400,000 in about 22 years. If additional funds are added each year, the goal of financial security can be achieved and wealth without risk can be a reality.

If you are interested, keep reading. If not, give up on wealth and try a diet book. At least you can become thin.

B. Richelsons' Investment Rules Applied to Municipal Bonds and Other Investments

If you are not yet convinced that municipal bonds are the best conservative after-tax investment, we shall at this point introduce you to "Richelsons' Investment Rules" and apply these rules to evaluate and compare municipal bonds and other favorably taxed investments. The rules were developed over many years and reflect our experience in investing in many different vehicles.

Rule #1—Specify your objectives precisely and define the risks you are willing to take. Your objectives should depend on your age, net worth, family requirements, and current income. The risks that you take will depend on financial factors and the strength of your stomach. The risks and rewards inherent in municipal bonds can be evaluated better than those in many other investments.

Rule #2—The potential yield from an investment is *always* proportionate to its risk. There is no free lunch. Insider tips are often illegal, usually old, and generally unreliable. Get-rich quick schemes are always risky. You can make a bundle by investing in commodities or options because of high leverage (borrowed funds). However, the leverage cuts both ways and can easily wipe you out.

The yield on a municipal bond is precisely known from the date of investment and is generally proportionate to its rating. A bond rated AAA always yields less than a bond rated BB. Other factors influencing a bond's yield are the number of years to maturity and general economic conditions affecting interest rates and market demand for a particular issue.

Rule #3—*Don't lose money!* This is not said in jest. Fifteen years ago we invested in a portfolio of no-load mutual funds holding common stocks. We bought when we thought the stock market was going up and sold when we thought the market was going down. After three years we added up the gains and losses and found we were about even. Much ado about nothing. We could have lost a bundle. People only talk about their winners, whether at the race track or in the stock market. You will come out way ahead if you never lose money, compared to investors who win some and lose some. Investments in municipal bonds can be essentially risk-free if you learn about them and follow the simple rules discussed in this book. Read on.

Rule #4—Evaluate all investment yields *after* tax. Don't compare apples to oranges. This principle was discussed above.

Rule #5—Don't invest unless you completely understand the economic, tax, and other aspects of the investment. Tax shelters are generally not understandable to the average investor. A warning flag should be raised when you register MEGO (My Eyes Glaze Over). Promoters love to tell you about the front-end tax benefits of an investment, but they rarely tell you what happens when an investment terminates—recaptures, penalties, and cash calls (Oh, God!). By this time you should know what to do when a promoter says, "Trust me."

This book is intended to teach you all you need to know to make an intelligent investment in municipal bonds so the only person you need to trust is yourself.

Rule #6—Be in control of the investment. Liquidity and flexibility are as important as yield. Know how to get out. A bond can be sold at any time with settlement in five days. Real estate and oil and gas (like diamonds) may be forever.

Rule #7—The economics of an investment are paramount. There are no good investments solely for tax purposes. Municipal bonds enable you to get a precise after-tax yield that has little downside risk if you invest prudently.

Rule #8—Look for the promoter's potential conflict of interest and try to determine whether this affects his investment advice. For example, a broker generally gets a larger commission on stocks than on bonds. Do you think this affects his advice when he suggests a stock investment?

Richelsons' Investment Rules were developed over many years to assist in the evaluation of proposed investments. They advise (1) honestly define the risks that you as an investor are willing to undertake; (2) recognize that financial return is *always* proportionate to risk; (3) don't lose money; (4) compare investments on an after-tax basis; (5) invest only in projects you can understand; (6) be in control of your investment; (7) know that good tax breaks are not sufficient reason for investing if you cannot anticipate return of principal; and (8) always look for a promoter's conflict of interest. Applying these rules indicates municipal bonds are a premier investment.

CHAPTER III

Municipal Bonds Will Solve Your Financial Problems

A. Desirable Features of Municipal Bonds
    1. High After-Tax Yields Compared to Taxable Bonds
    2. Safety
    3. Marketability
    4. Flexibility

B. Specific Examples of Financial Solutions Using Municipal Bonds
    1. Example 1—Mr. A Gressive
    2. Example 2—Mr. and Mrs. Y. G. Suburban
    3. Example 3—Mr. Yuppy and Ms. Preppy
    4. Example 4—Ms. G. T. Success
    5. Example 5—Mr. Win Baron

C. Misconceptions about Municipals
    1. You Are Locked In—Wrong
    2. You Need to Invest at least $25,000—Wrong
    3. Municipals Are Difficult to Buy—Wrong

Are municipal bonds for you? Bracket creep, the hidden tax increase caused by inflation which silently pushes you into a higher tax bracket, has attracted millions of people like you to municipal bonds. In 1982, sales of new municipal bonds broke records. About $75 billion in new municipal bonds were put on the market in that year, more than one and a half times the record set in 1980.

Who was buying all those bonds? John Q. Public purchased a whopping 87% of new municipal long-term bonds in 1982 and 1983, through outright purchases of bonds and through the purchase of interests in municipal bond funds and unit investment trusts. The lure of tax-free income, the privacy accorded the transactions, and the income from the bonds have made municipal bonds particularly attractive.

A. Desirable Features of Municipal Bonds

For investors with more than $25,000 per year in taxable income, municipal bonds are the best after-tax investment available today, considering their
1. High after-tax yields,
2. Comparative safety,
3. Marketability, and
4. Flexibility.

All of these features of municipal bonds are discussed in detail in later chapters. At this point a summary may be useful.

1. High After-Tax Yields Compared to Taxable Bonds

All investments should be evaluated on an after-tax basis. Thus, an investment in a *taxable* bond that yields 10% is worth only 6.7% to an investor in the 33% tax bracket or 7.2% to an investor in the 28% tax bracket. Viewed another way, if you can achieve a 10% return from a municipal bond, you would have to receive a 14.93% return from a taxable bond if you are in the 33% tax bracket or 13.89% if you are in the 28% tax bracket. This comparison is not just between municipal and taxable bonds, but applies to a comparison of municipal bonds and any other taxable investment, such as dividends on stock, royalties, rents, or capital gains.

Table 1 shows the effect of federal income taxes on the following:

—Investment in a municipal bond yielding 10%
—Investment in a taxable bond yielding 13%
—Investment in a stock paying an 8% dividend

As you can see, a couple filing a joint return, who are in the 33% tax bracket and who invest $30,000 in a municipal bond, earn $3,000 a year and do not pay federal tax on that income. The same investment in a taxable bond yielding 13% would return only $2,613 a year after federal income taxes—a yield on the investment of only 8.7%. An investment in a stock paying an 8% dividend would return only $1,608 a year after federal taxes—a yield of only 5.4%.

2. Safety

Municipal bonds have historically been very low-risk investments. Even when there have been defaults, most were cured, so no principal was lost. Recent examples of such cures are the New York City default (see Part II, Chapter XIV) and the Cleveland default. Virtually complete safety can be achieved by investing in certain United States Government-escrowed municipal bonds. Alternatively, a high degree of safety can also be achieved by (a)

TABLE 1
EFFECT OF FEDERAL INCOME TAXES ON YIELDS OF MUNICIPAL BONDS, TAXABLE BONDS, AND STOCK

	MUNICIPAL BOND YIELDING 10%	TAXABLE BOND YIELDING 13%	STOCK PAYING AN 8% DIVIDEND
Cash investment	$30,000	$30,000	$30,000
Interest or dividend income	3,000	3,900	2,400
Federal income tax in the 33% tax bracket	-0-	1,287	792
Net after-tax return	3,000	2,613	1,608
Yield on investment after tax	10%	8.7%	5.4%

investing in bonds guaranteed by a large bank or by insurance companies; (b) purchasing portfolio insurance; or (c) purchasing highly rated bonds.

3. Marketability

All major brokerage firms make markets in and trade municipal bonds. This means that they hold bonds in their inventories for sale to the public and will offer to purchase bonds from you at a competitive price. In addition, there are numerous small firms that deal exclusively in municipal bonds. Many banks have municipal bond departments, including most major New York City commercial banks. Investors can buy and sell quality bonds without much trouble in this active market. The names of major regional underwriters for bonds can be found by examining the announcements of new bond issues in the financial newspapers.

It should be clearly understood that all municipal bond dealers, including banks, buy and sell municipal bonds for their own accounts as principals rather than as brokers. This means that they do not charge a commission, but instead they make their profit on the spread between the price they pay for the bonds and the price at which they sell the bonds to you. The amount of the spread will not be disclosed to you. By comparison, when you buy shares of stock which are listed on a stock exchange from a brokerage firm, they will disclose to you the precise amount of their commission. As with most other purchases, you should comparison-shop to establish that the bonds are offered for sale at a reasonable price.

4. Flexibility

As a result of the large number of municipal bond issues available at all times, including new bonds coming to market and the trading of previously issued bonds, you have a wide choice. This flexibility results from the variety of maturity dates, the kinds of bonds available, and a ready resale market. Below are some examples of flexibility.

- You can invest in a three-to-six month municipal note, five-year, 10-year, or all the way out to 40-year municipal bonds or any year in between. The year you select will be based on your own particular investment plans.
- You can buy bonds that are guaranteed by an agency of the U.S. government; such bonds are as safe as money in a savings bank. Or you can buy bonds that are issued by states or other municipalities rated AAA and thus are essentially risk-free. If you wish to take on more risk in order to increase your rate of return, you can invest in many grades of lower-rated municipal bonds.
- A selection can be made from bonds with variable interest rates, bonds that can be sold back to the issuer at the holder's option (so-called put bonds), zero-coupon bonds sold for very low prices, bonds with coupons that are not registered, and bonds that are registered as to principal and interest. Each type of bond has features that make it attractive to certain buyers. All of the above possibilities are discussed in detail in Part II, Chapter II.
- You can select whether more of your dollars are returned in the form of interest payments or in a lump sum at maturity. A discount bond is one that sells for less than $1,000 but which is redeemed for its face value of $1,000. You can buy a low-coupon bond at a substantial discount from face value in order to realize a large capital gain when the bond comes due. For example, a New

York State bond with a 3% coupon and a face value of $1,000 coming due in the year 2019 and which sold at $380 in November 1983 will return $1,000 when it comes due. Similarly, an investor might buy a $1,000 14% coupon bond coming due in the year 2000 at a price of $1,300 and receive $1,000 when it comes due. The $300 premium is returned in higher annual interest payments.

B. Specific Examples of Financial Solutions Using Municipal Bonds

In the course of our investment advisory business, clients have sought the answers to goal-oriented financial problems. Because of the features discussed above, municipal bonds, in one form or another, presented the best solution to their problems. Here are some examples:

Example 1—Mr. A. Gressive, an executive, aged sixty, plans to retire in five years. He is earning a high salary but has always had some trouble saving money. He has in the past invested in stock and commodities with mixed results. His income will drop substantially when he retires, so he will be in a low tax bracket. He intends to move from New York to Florida after retirement and thus will pay no state or local income tax. His specific financial goal is to accumulate substantial additional capital during the five-year period before his retirement, while he is in a high tax bracket, without taking any further risks.

We devised the following financial plan for Mr. A. Gressive.

Advice: Sell all of the common stock and close the commodity positions.

Reason: At age sixty, when assets must be accumulated for future needs, the risk of capital losses prior to retirement could not be tolerated.

Advice: Invest the proceeds from the sale of stock and commodities in municipal bonds that meet the following profile. The municipals would be a diversified group of general obligation bonds of states that are selling at discounts (i.e., below face value) and which come due in five years.

Reason: The municipal bonds would provide tax-free income

while Mr. A. Gressive is in a high tax bracket. General obligation bonds issued by states have historically been easy to identify as very safe investments. Diversity of holdings provide additional safety. Bonds selling at a discount provide guaranteed appreciation during the five-year period since they come due at their face value. The term of the bonds should be five years because at that time Mr. A. Gressive would be in a lower tax bracket, so he may wish to buy Treasury bonds, which are taxable but which may yield more after-tax income because of Mr. A. Gressive's new low tax bracket. Finally, Mr. A. Gressive may wish to buy a house, car, or other large item after retirement.

Example 2—Mr. and Mrs. Y. G. Suburban have a daughter who will be of college age in 1988. They wished to provide for her college expenses without any legal complications such as trusts and without taking any risks. They are in a high tax bracket and have $22,000 to invest. They also desire some current return on their $22,000 to pay current expenses.

We devised the following financial plan for Mr. and Mrs. Y. G. Suburban:

Advice: Purchase $40,000 face amount of municipal bonds in 1980 for $22,000, which come due as follows to cover the four years of their daughter Debbie's years at college:

Face Amount of Bond	Amount Paid for Bond	Due Date of Bond	Daughter's Age at Due Date
$10,000	$6,000	1988	18
10,000	6,000	1989	19
10,000	5,000	1990	20
10,000	5,000	1991	21
$40,000	$22,000		

Reason: Highly rated municipal discount bonds were recommended in this case because the added value of the bonds would be realized when Debbie needs the money. Four different issues give diversity. $10,000 will come due in each of the years 1988 to 1991 to help pay college expenses. The tax-exempt income generated during the 11-year period can be used for current living expenses while the family's income improves over the years.

Example 3—Mr. Yuppy and Ms. Preppy are a young upwardly

mobile married couple living in New York City. They each earn a good salary, so they are in a high tax bracket. They wish to have a family in the future, and their goal is to save enough money for a down payment on a suitable house in an expensive location near New York City. Because of their high present expenses they do not know when their goal will be achieved.

We devised the following financial plan for this couple:

Advice: Purchase put bonds, which can be sold back to the issuer each year for a full return of principal. Certain put bonds would provide a current tax-free return plus the option to resell such bonds at a predetermined price in years 1, 3, 5, or any year thereafter.

Reason: A put bond will protect the principal value of the bonds even if interest rates were to rise prior to the maturity of the bonds. The put would enable this couple to regain their invested principal at the end of years 1, 3, 5 or any year thereafter so that they would have the equivalent of a short-term bond but would obtain a higher after-tax return than they otherwise could on a short-term investment. The tax-free income would currently help with their savings plan.

Example 4—Ms. G. T. Success is a vice chairman of a company that sells computers. After retirement she will be retained as a consultant to her company. To supplement her income, she would like to invest the $400,000 she expects to receive from the sale of company stock in income-producing securities. Due to her continuing high tax bracket, Ms. Success decided to invest in tax-exempt securities. Ms. Success asked us whether she should invest in municipal bond trusts, funds, or purchase the individual bonds.

We made the following recommendations:

Advice: Purchase the individual bonds instead of either unit investment trusts or municipal bond funds.

Reason: The individually selected bonds would return a better yield than either trusts or funds. Due to the large amounts of money controlled by the funds, it is difficult for them to take advantage of swings in interest rates since all bonds of the same rating tend to move as a herd. As prices of bonds held by a fund fluctuates, so does the fund's net asset value, the amount you would be paid if you were to sell your shares. The longer the maturity of bonds held by a fund, the wider the price fluctuations of the fund. You are not guaranteed a return of principal on a fund as you are with the individual bonds. You must also pay management fees and, in some cases, advertising fees.

The trusts offer a fixed portfolio and small yearly management fees. They collect their selling fees when you invest. This is called a front-end load. A load generally ranges from 3% to 6% of the amount invested, and such load is an added cost of purchasing the bonds. Trusts also have a back-end charge of 4% to 8% if the trust is sold, although it is not called a load. It is called a spread between the buy and sell price. You can determine for yourself what the spread is by asking how much you would have to pay for the trust if you bought it in the morning and how much they would pay you for your shares at the end of the same day. The promised diversification can easily be achieved by purchasing the same ten or twelve bonds as offered by the trusts, if you thought they were of sufficient quality.

You get what you pay for. If you buy a trust or fund you have to expect a smaller return on your investment after the salesman's fees and the packaging and advertising costs have been subtracted.

In our experience, only the inexperienced investor chooses to purchase bond funds or trusts rather than the individual bonds. Bond salesmen and traders do not purchase trusts or funds for their own accounts.

Advice: We advised Ms. Success to buy intermediate-term bonds with a maximum 8- to 13-year life for her portfolio. This will generally earn the investor half a percentage point more than buying funds or trusts. In order to earn such higher return on a fund or trust, she would generally have to purchase a *long-term* bond fund or trust.

Reason: Though Ms. Success did not plan on selling the municipals and planned only to live off the interest, the intermediate-term bonds would enable her to better protect the principal against the possibility of inflation and rising interest rates. If inflation continued to result in increased interest rates, Ms. Success would have the opportunity to reinvest the principal of her intermediate term bonds when they came due at the then higher rates, rather than sitting with low-yielding devalued long-term municipal bonds.

Example 5—Mr. Win Baron is a builder who invests heavily in real estate. His business is forming syndicated real estate partnerships in which he serves as general partner. He is always on the lookout for good investment possibilities and must therefore keep large amounts of cash in liquid investments to enable him to take advantage of the next investment opportunity.

Mr. Baron kept his liquid assets in a tax-free money market fund which yielded about 4% in tax-exempt income. Despite all the tax benefits from his real estate deals, he is still in the 33% federal tax bracket and in the 13% New York State tax bracket.

Mr. Baron asked us whether he could increase the yield on his liquid assets. We made the following recommendations:

Advice: We advised Mr. Baron to keep some money in a tax-exempt money market fund to enable him to have some ready cash and invest the remainder in municipals coming due in 12 to 18 months.

Reason: Compared to the 4% return on the money market fund, the municipals would yield about 5½%. Short-term municipals are very salable in case the hoped-for golden opportunity arises, and yet the money would be earning 1½ percentage points more than in the fund. As an alternative, Mr. Baron might borrow money from a bank or broker and secure such loan with the short-term municipals. Note that the IRS would disallow his interest deduction.

Advice: Invest the money to come due over a number of months rather than all at one time.

Reason: The longer the maturity of a bond, the more interest it generally pays. By spreading the money out over a period of time, some money is always coming due and readily available for other investments, yet the money still outstanding is earning the highest interest rates possible.

C. Misconceptions About Municipals

In the course of our advisory activities we have found that many investors have rejected municipal bonds as an investment for the wrong reasons. Let us review some common misconceptions with you:

Misconception 1—"Municipal bonds lock me into an investment for a long time."

This is completely wrong. Municipals can be sold at any time. However, due to interest rate fluctuations, you may receive more or less for your bonds. With some planning, however, municipal bonds can be purchased to come due in a particular month and year when you anticipate a need for your invested money. If you have a need for short-term liquidity, you can buy municipals which come due in one year or less. Finally, you can invest in a municipal bond money market fund and write a check on your investment at any time.

Misconception 2—"I cannot invest in municipal bonds because you need to invest at least $25,000."

This is completely wrong. Municipal bonds are sold in denominations as small as $5,000. You can invest in a municipal bond trust with as little as $1,000. You can buy low-coupon municipal bonds at a large discount. Thus, a $5,000 face value municipal bond with a 2% coupon coming due in 10 years may sell for $3,000 or less, providing almost the same rapid compounding as zero-coupon bonds.

Misconception 3—"Municipal bonds are difficult to buy."

Like stocks, the purchase of muncipal bonds is a phone call away. Municipals can be bought in many forms and from many sellers. Your stockbroker can sell you municipal bonds. In addition, you can purchase municipal bonds from specialized municipal bond houses. Finally, you can invest in one of many types of municipal bond funds or trusts, which are discussed in Chapters III, IV and V of Part II.

Municipal bonds are a safe, secure, and fairly liquid investment providing attractive tax-free returns for you. They are easy to purchase and easy to manage. All that you need is to see to it that the bonds are kept safely in either a safety-deposit box or in your account at a bank or brokerage house.

CHAPTER IV

Ready—Set—Go

Having read this far, you are convinced, we hope, of the safety and substantial rewards you can gain by investing in municipal bonds. On an after-tax basis they will generally provide a predictably higher return than any other investment. Municipal bonds are a safe haven for your money when it should be sheltered. Yet you can easily turn your municipals into cash by selling them or by using them as collateral for a loan. In addition, the maturity dates for your municipals can be tailored to your needs, thus providing you with ready capital when you need it.

All right, you say! You have convinced me to purchase municipals, but how should I proceed?

The first step is to call brokerage houses and ask them for material on municipal bonds. Though the presentations from many of the sellers are very similar, you will benefit by reading the material and talking to the bond sellers.

Second, it would be helpful to familiarize yourself with the columns in newspapers and magazines dealing with municipals. This is not a big task because little is written about them. You should check out Ben Weberman's column in *Forbes* and the daily columns on bonds in *The Wall Street Journal* and *The New York Times*.

Third, you should have a serious conversation with the interested parties in this investment and decide how much you have to invest and how soon you would like the principal returned. Do you anticipate early retirement, children going off to school, the purchase of a new home, car, or boat, or perhaps an expensive trip overseas?

Fourth, decide how many issues you would like to have in your portfolio. Bonds are usually sold in minimum lots of $5,000.

Before you pick up the phone, write the following information on the top of a piece of paper:

Rating & No. of Bonds	Coupon	Issuer	Date of Maturity	Yield After Tax	Current Yield	Unit Price

Now you are all set. You are ready to write down information about bonds sold by the brokerage houses. You have prepared yourself to be a knowledgeable investor.

When the broker asks you what kind of bonds you are looking for, tell him you would like a plain vanilla bond—one with no frills, just good solid value. That should help you avoid many pitfalls and provide you with a very successful investment in municipal bonds.

Your conversation and agreement to purchase bonds will be verified by a written confirmation. Review the confirmation carefully to verify that it conforms to the bond you purchased. If you have any question, call the seller of the bonds and ask for clarification. Once you are satisfied, you must immediately send payment to the seller. Payment for the bonds is due within five business days after you orally agree to purchase. Once payment is received, the bonds will be sent to you.

Place your confirmation slips in a safeguarded place. You will need them if you ever decide to sell your bonds to prove ownership and for tax purposes. Enjoy the tax-free interest you receive twice a year and keep smiling on April 15th!

If you wish to engage in more sophisticated municipal bond purchases or if you wish to have a deeper understanding of municipals, you should read Part II of this book. If you have specific questions you can write to us care of The Scarsdale Investment Group, Ltd., P.O. Box 454, Scarsdale, New York 10583.

PART II

CHAPTER I

What Is a Municipal Bond?

A. Municipal Bonds—A Definition
B. Types of Municipal Bonds
C. Short-Term Tax-Free Instruments
D. Common Features of All Bonds
    1. Name
    2. Date
    3. Maturity Date
    4. Basis Point
    5. Bond Pricing—Par, Premium, and Discount
    6. Interest Rate
    7. Interest Payments
    8. Accrued Interest Charges
    9. Registered Versus Unregistered Bonds
    10. Call and Redemption Options
    11. Rating
    12. CUSIP Number
    13. Bond Certificate Number
    14. Legal Opinion
    15. Trustee
    16. Yield Computations
        (a) Current Yield
        (b) Yield-to-Maturity
        (c) Yield-to-Maturity after tax on Capital Gains
        (d) Yield-to-Call

A. Municipal Bonds—A Definition

A bond is written evidence of its issuer's promise to repay a loan to the bondholder at a specified time, with interest, which is generally payable every six months. A municipal bond is issued by a state, a state agency, or a subdivision of a state such as a city or a county. What is special about municipal bonds is that they are generally exempt from federal income tax and certain state and city taxes as well. This key concept is the basis of a $75 billion-a-year industry and is the reason why you are reading this book. A good quality municipal bond is one of today's most secure and high yielding after-tax investments.

As we said above, a bond is evidence of the debt owed by the municipality to the bondholders. Some municipal debt is not evidenced by a bond certificate but is instead recorded merely by a "book entry." In this case the purchaser of the debt (that is, the bond buyer) receives a statement from the issuer's agent that describes the debt and indicates that the purchaser has the right to receive payments of principal and interest.

Bonds may be thought of as marketable packages that enable an issuer to borrow money from many people at the same time and allow the lenders (the bond buyers) to conveniently resell their investments.

Bonds are negotiable (easily salable) and can be bought and sold many times before they are finally redeemed, which usually occurs when the debt is paid off by the issuer at maturity. Fortunately, there is an active marketplace of investors and dealers selling and buying bonds every day.

Below is a nitty gritty description of the basics of bonds. As you concentrate on the basic concepts, remember that you are anticipating and arming yourself against the despicable month of April. Doing your homework now will alleviate the painful exercise of putting your hand in your pocket on that dreaded day, the 15th of April.

B. Types of Municipal Bonds

Municipal bonds may be divided into two general categories: general obligation bonds and revenue bonds. The main difference between a general obligation bond (known as a G.O.) and a revenue bond is the source of funds used by the issuer to pay the bond's principal and interest. A general obligation bond is backed by the issuer's full faith and credit. Thus, a G.O. bond is backed by all the resources of the state or municipality that issued it. General obligation bonds are usually paid off with receipts from real estate taxes, although sales taxes, income taxes, and other taxes are also important sources of support.

Revenue bonds, by comparison, are supported only by the stream of income of a particular bond issuer under the auspices of a municipality or a municipal agency. The municipality under whose auspices the revenue bonds are issued has no legal responsibility for them. As a result of the 1986 Tax Reform Act, municipal revenue bonds may be subject to the alternative minimum tax or may be issued as taxable municipal bonds. (See Part II, Chapter XIII.)

Revenue bonds generally fall within one of the following categories:

—Electric utility bonds
—Water system and sewer bonds
—Toll road, bridge, and port authority bonds
—Airport bonds
—Hospital bonds
—Housing bonds
—Industrial development bonds
—Pollution-control bonds
—Student loan bonds
—University bonds

These bonds are described in detail in Part II, Chapter VI.

C. Short-Term Tax-Free Instruments

A state, municipality, or agency wishing to borrow funds for periods of less than two years can choose to issue either notes or commercial paper. Tax-free commercial paper is a relatively new means of municipal borrowing. It is either an unsecured I.O.U. or secured by a bank letter of credit for periods of 15 to 45 days. These instruments are not widely available to small investors.

There are three major kinds of notes: bond anticipation notes, revenue anticipation notes, and tax anticipation notes. They are referred to as BANs, RANs, and TANs, respectively. They are issued for periods ranging from six months to one year. All short-term notes do not have the same collateral. BANs are repaid by revenue obtained from a new bond issue. RANs are repaid from revenue, usually aid expected from a state or the federal government. TANs are repaid with taxes and unencumbered revenue of the municipality.

D. Common Features of All Bonds

Before you purchase a bond, it is important to understand all of its features. This will enable you to obtain a replacement if you lose the bond, or if you wish to sell it.

1. Name

All bonds have an official name. There are over 40,000 municipalities that have issued municipal bonds, and many of them have multiple bond issues outstanding. Bonds might have a simple name such as Hawaii G.O. or a more complicated name such as Frisco, Colorado Sales Tax Revenue, Registered, MBIA Insured. In the latter instance, the fact that the bond is registered and insured is an integral part of the information you need to know about this particular bond.

2. Date

All bonds are dated when they are issued. The "dated date" is the date from which the bond begins to pay interest. The dated date also helps identify one particular bond issue from another.

3. Maturity Date

All bonds have a maturity date when they must be redeemed at their face value, ending the loan from the bondholder to the issuer. Although two bonds may have the same name and dated date, they might have different maturities. If a bond issue has multiple maturity dates, the non-callable bonds are known as serial bonds and the longer callable maturities are known as term bonds.

4. Basis Point

A basis point is a measure used to indicate percentage changes in the yield you receive when the bond's price changes. One basis point is equivalent to one hundredth of one percent (.01%). For example, if a bond's yield-to-maturity increased from 8% to 9.25% there is an increase of 125 basis points. Thus, on a bond with a face value of $10,000, a 125 basis point improvement in return would be in the amount of $125 ($10,000 × .0125).

5. Bond Pricing—Par, Premium, and Discount

Most bonds issued by corporations and municipalities are sold in five bond units with a face value of $5,000, although there are some old issues sold at $1,000 per bond. The price that bonds will bring at any time depends upon what another buyer is willing to pay. If a bond is sold at the price stated on its face, it is said to be sold *at par*. If a bond is sold at a price in excess of its face value, it is said to be sold at a *premium*. If a bond is sold at less than face value, it is said to be sold at a *discount*. If the bond has a face value of $1,000 and is selling at par, the price quotation from the broker is 100, or at par. A bond that is quoted at 99 means that the cost is $990 per each $1,000 and it is a discount bond. Similarly, a $1,000 bond priced at 108 would sell at $1,080 and is a premium bond.

The price at which a bond is sold changes as a result of the rise and fall of interest rates. With slight variations, bonds of the same quality and type move in unison. As interest rates rise, bond prices fall, and when interest rates fall, bond prices increase. Though the interest coupon (the amount of interest received every six months) and redemption value (the face value of the bond) remain the same, the change in the price of the bond has the effect of adjusting the effective rate of interest the buyer receives on the bonds purchased. For example, if a $1,000 face value bond coming due in five years has a 10% coupon and sells at *par*, the buyer receives interest income of $100 a year for a 10% return. If the buyer pays $900 for the same $1,000 bond, the buyer would still receive $100 a year of interest income, but because he paid only $900 for the bond, his "yield-to-maturity" (discussed below) would be 12.77%. This computation takes into account that in addition to receiving $100 interest each year, the investor would also have a gain of $100 when the bond comes due in five years ($1,000 face received less $900 original purchase price). If the same bond is purchased by the buyer at a premium of $1,100, the buyer would still receive $100 interest income each year, but receive only $1,000 (its face value) when the bond is redeemed, resulting in a yield-to-maturity of 7.56%.

6. Interest Rate

All bonds are assigned a stated interest rate when they are issued. This is sometimes called the coupon referring to a time when most municipal bonds were unregistered and had coupons attached. The amount of interest due is printed on each coupon. A bond's interest rate is decided upon at the time the bond is sold, based upon competitive bidding among the underwriters or upon a negotiated agreement between the underwriters and the issuer.

7. Interest Payments

Interest payments are made to a bondholder in one of two ways. If you hold a bond with coupons attached, you would cut off a coupon every six months. You can present the coupon directly to the paying agent of the issuer for cash. The paying agent is usually a designated bank or the treasurer's office of the issuer. Alternatively, the usual procedure is to deposit the coupon into your checking account. Most banks charge a fee for cashing coupons. If you hold registered bonds, the issuer or its paying agent will send you a check every six months. If you deposit your unregistered bonds with a brokerage firm, coupons will be clipped automatically and credited to your account. Similarly, interest checks received by your broker for registered bonds will be credited to your account.

The interest payment dates occur twice a year. They are as follows:

> January—July
> February—August
> March—September
> April—October
> May—November
> June—December

In 1986, some issuers began selling newly issued bonds with a "long first coupon." That means that no interest is paid out for one year from the date of issue instead of after the traditional six months.

The interest payments are generally made on either the first or the fifteenth of the month.

8. Accrued Interest Charges

Interest on a bond accrues or accumulates daily. However, the interest is paid only twice a year. Thus, if you do not purchase a bond on a date at which it pays interest, you will be required to pay to the seller of the bond the interest that has accrued between the last payment and the settlement date (the date you become the owner of the bond). On the next semiannual interest payment date, you will be paid the full six months interest. For example, assume you buy a $10,000 face bond at par ($10,000), which pays $1,000 interest per year, $500 on January 1, and $500 on July 1. If the settlement date is April 1, you will pay $250 in accrued interest to the seller of the bond in addition to the $10,000 purchase price. However, on July 1 you will collect the full $500 semiannual interest payment, thus recouping the $250 interest which you previously paid. Accordingly, the amount of accrued interest should not be a factor in deciding whether to buy a particular bond.

9. Registered Versus Unregistered Bonds

Bonds are either registered or unregistered. If a bond is registered, the agent of the issuer records the purchase and mails the bondholder interest checks. If the bond is lost, stolen or destroyed, a replacement bond will be provided to the owner.

Unregistered bonds are known as bearer bonds. Coupons for each interest payment are attached to unregistered bonds. Such coupons are clipped and cashed as they come due. There is no official record of who owns bearer bonds and if they are lost, stolen, or destroyed, replacement is difficult and sometimes impossible. The federal government claims that unregistered bonds have been used to evade the payment of taxes by laundering illegal funds through the purchase of municipal bonds, or transferring of funds to the younger generation without payment of inheritance taxes. Opponents of registration claim that registering all bonds will substantially slow the trading of municipals. Currently all new issues must be registered, but a number of states are appealing the recent federal regulation that requires it.

There is some anticipation that coupon bonds may eventually be more valuable than registered bonds if registration is not overturned.

10. Call and Redemption Options

A common municipal bond provision permits an issuer to call or redeem part or all of an issue before its stated maturity date. Issuers prefer to sell bonds with call provisions because the practice enables them to retrieve a high-yielding issue before it matures and replace it with a lower-yielding issue if interest rates fall. This is precisely why investors prefer buying bonds that do not have call features.

Bonds are called either at par or at a slight premium. For example, a bond might pay 103 (i.e., $1,030 for each $1,000 bond) if it is called before its maturity date, or it might be called at par. If you ask, your broker will tell you if a bond has a call provision.

Frequently, a mandatory call or extraordinary call feature is not mentioned by a broker when a bond is sold, either because there is no fixed date when the bond may be called or the broker does not know of the call provision. Mandatory or extraordinary call features may be buried in the bond's fine print. Housing bonds frequently have such provisions, requiring that some or all of the bonds issued be called if the mortgages that are held by the issuer are prepaid more quickly than expected, or if the money raised from the sale of the bonds is not borrowed. There is no premium paid on bonds redeemed pursuant to a mandatory call. Housing bonds are frequently called soon after a drop in interest rates. A pool of money collects because people refinance their mortgages at lower interest rates. Such calls were very common in 1986.

11. Rating

A rating is an estimation, by a rating service, of the issuer's ability to pay interest and principal when due. The best known rating services for municipal bonds are Moody's Investors Service and Standard & Poor's Corp. Fitch Investors Service Inc. also rate municipal bonds.

When an issuer plans to sell bonds, it pays one or more of the rating agencies to rate them. The higher the rating, the less interest the issuer will generally have to offer the investors to entice them to purchase the bonds.

Some bonds are unrated because the issuers plan to sell them to local buyers such as banks. Other bonds are unrated because the issuer anticipates that the rating will be low.

Once an issuer's bond is rated, the rating is periodically reviewed, with special attention given to a new issue or an area with a changing situation.

Standard & Poor's highest rating of an issue is AAA, and its lowest rating is D for default. Moody's highest rating is Aaa, and its lowest rating is C. So-called investment-grade bonds, which are the only bonds that can be purchased by banks without special justification, must be rated AAA, AA, A, or BBB by Standard & Poor's or Aaa, Aa, Aa, or Baa by Moody's. Both Moody's and Standard & Poor's use similar rating systems, though Moody's is generally considered the more conservative of the two. The rating agencies differ on about 20% of those issues rated by both and then only slightly.

12. CUSIP Number

Each bond has a separate identification number which is called a CUSIP number. CUSIP is an acronym for Committee on Uniform Securities Identification Procedures. An example of a CUSIP number that might be listed on a confirmation is CU. 664176X5. It is essential to know the CUSIP numbers when you plan to sell your bonds. The CUSIP number is the fingerprint of the bond, which enables the dealers to specifically identify it and thereby determine the value of your bond.

13. Bond Certificate Number

This is a number that identifies the particular bond you own. This number appears on the front of each certificate with a matching number on every coupon if it is a coupon bond. If you take possession of your bonds, you should keep a separate record of these numbers. The record will help you replace the bonds if they are lost, stolen, or destroyed.

14. Legal Opinion

All municipal bonds are sold with a legal opinion attached or printed on the bond certificate. The opinion is that of a lawyer specializing in bond law, and it states that the bond is indeed exempt from federal income tax and that the bond is a legally binding obligation of the issuer.

15. Trustee

The Trustee is the custodian of all debt services and reserve funds and sometimes of construction and operating accounts. A trust company or a commercial bank is usually appointed to insure compliance with the contract and represent bondholders to enforce their contract with the issuer. The trustee will call bonds at designated periods and disburse interest and principal payments.

16. Yield Computations

Read this section at least twice and make sure you understand the difference between the different kinds of yields discussed below. This is a dollars-and-cents issue.

Municipal bonds are generally sold on the basis of yield or financial return, calculated to the date the bond comes due or matures. The yield of a bond is the amount that can be expected to be earned over the period of time starting from the date the bond is purchased and ending when the bond comes due. There are different kinds of calculations for yield. The four yield concepts that you must understand are: current yield, yield-to-maturity, yield-to-maturity after tax on capital gains (for discount bonds), and yield-to-call (if bonds are callable).

(a) Current Yield

The current yield is a ratio of the annual interest to the amount paid for the bond. The current yield does not take into account reinvestment of the income earned from the bond. The current yield also does not *fully* take into account the discount or premium originally paid for the bond. This means that the loss of $100 that you incur when you receive $1,000 at maturity for a bond originally costing $1,100 is not fully considered by this calculation. The formula to compute current yield is:

$$\text{Current yield} = \frac{\text{coupon interest for the year}}{\text{amount paid for the bond}}$$

For example, assume you buy a 10%, $1,000 face value bond for $1,100, which comes due in 10 years. The current yield is computed as follows:

$$\frac{\$100 \text{ (coupon interest for the year)}}{\$1,100 \text{ (amount paid for the bond)}} = 9.09\% \text{ Current yield}$$

Current yield can be a quite misleading measure of return if the bond is purchased at a substantial premium or discount and matures in a relatively short time. If the bond is long-term or is purchased near par, the current yield is a relatively good measure of true return.

(b) Yield-to-Maturity

The yield-to-maturity calculation is the key rate used by professionals when they trade municipal bonds. Unlike current yield, the yield-to-maturity considers both reinvestment of the interest and the discount or premium paid for the bond.

The concept of yield-to-maturity includes the notion that time adds value to money. Money has time value because it can earn interest at a compounded rate over time and grow into a larger amount in the future. A dollar received in the future is less valuable than a dollar received today because of the "magic" of compound interest.

The general concept of compound interest is simple. Interest is earned on an initial investment during the first interest payment period. In subsequent periods, interest is earned not only on the original principal, but also on the interest earned in previous periods. Thus, the first dollar of interest is more valuable than the last dollar because interest will be earned on the first dollar of interest for most of the life of the bond.

The yield-to-maturity computation takes into account the time value of money (the reinvestment of coupon interest). It combines in one rate the coupon interest and the fact that although the bond was purchased at a discount or a premium, it will be redeemed at maturity at par (its face value). The yield-to-maturity on a bond with an 8% coupon bought at par is 8%. If an 8% bond is bought at 90 (i.e., $900) and comes due at $1,000 in 10 years, the yield-to-maturity would be 9.57%.

Two assumptions are made in the yield-to-maturity computation: that the investor will keep the bond until it matures and that the investor can reinvest the interest payments *at the same rate as the yield-to-maturity*. If the current return on a bond can be reinvested at a higher rate than the stated yield-to-maturity, then the original yield-to-maturity rate is understated (i.e. too low). If the current return can be reinvested only at a lower rate, the original yield-to-maturity is overstated (i.e. too high). Thus, in the example given above, for a bond with an 8% coupon bought at 90 ($900) that comes due in 10 years at $1,000, the investor would receive $80 each year for 10 years in coupon interest plus an additional $100 gain in year 10. The combination of such amounts combined with the time value of money works out to a 9.57% yield-to-maturity if the $80 each year can be reinvested at 9.57%.

Yield-to-maturity calculations can be made using calculators that perform financial functions, such as the Hewlett-Packard HP12C, which can be purchased for less than $100. Alternatively, you can buy a "basis book," which contains mathematical tables of yields and equivalent rates and maturity dates. The *Expanded Bond Values Tables* can be purchased from the Financial Publishing Company at 92 Brookline Avenue, Boston., Mass. 02215.

(c) Yield-to-Maturity after Tax on Capital Gains

If a bond is bought for less than par but is redeemed at par, the difference between the purchase price and redemption price is a capital gain that is subject to tax. Beginning in 1988, the favorable treatment of long-term capital gains will be eliminated, and such gains will be taxed as ordinary income. The yield-to-maturity after the tax on capital gains computation is the same as the regular yield-to-maturity computation except that the redemption price used is not par but par minus the amount of tax on the discount.

(d) Yield-to-Call

If a bond has a call feature (which allows the issuer to buy it back from the investor before maturity at a pre-determined price), the calculation of yield-to-maturity will not be accurate if the call occurs. The yield-to-call computation is the same as the yield-to-maturity computation except that the amount used when the bond comes due is the call price and it is assumed that the number of years the bond will be outstanding is only to the first call date. When a bond has a mandatory call if certain conditions occur, yield-to-call cannot be calculated because the call date is unknown.

CHAPTER II

Special Features Of Certain Municipal Bonds

A. Put Option
B. Warrants
C. Floating or Variable Rate
D. Minicoupon and Zero-Coupon
E. FDIC and FSLIC Insurance
F. Refunding
G. Sinking Fund
H. Supersinkers
I. Private Insurance
J. Bond Bank Backing
K. Letter-of-Credit (LOC)
L. Moral Obligation Security
M. Book-Entry Bonds

The previous chapter introduced you to the buzz words and gave you an understanding of the features common to all municipal bonds. This chapter will complete the basic description by describing the special features of some municipal bonds.

Various techniques are used to sell bonds and make them more attractive to investors. These features include puts, warrants, floating rates, minicoupons and zero coupons, FDIC and FSLIC insurance, sinking funds, supersinkers, pre-refunding, bond bank backing, letters-of-credit, moral obligations and book-entry bonds. Each feature presents a potential advantage for you to consider and to compare to a "plain vanilla" bond (the usual bond described in Part II, Chapter I). Most of these special features are used when issuers are having trouble selling their bonds because of unsettled or adverse financial conditions. In 1982, for example, inflation was running wild and issuers were having marketing problems. Accordingly, many of the special techniques and features discussed in this chapter were found in bonds issued in that year.

A. Put Option

A put feature provides you with the right to sell the bond back to the issuer at a specified price (generally at par) at one specific date in the future or at stated intervals until the bond matures. Let's compare two similar bonds, both due in 30 years. One bond has a put feature that enables you to sell the bond back to the issuer at par after five years and every year thereafter. The other bond is exactly the same but has no put feature. Assume interest rates rise for each of three consecutive years. As rates go up, the price of the bond *without* the put feature will fall. However, the price of the put bond will remain close to par because you can tender the bond to the issuer at par in year five. In this instance, the put bond performs like a short-term bond.

Put bonds always come in different variations. Take the 7.10's of 2018, notes recently issued by the New Jersey Turnpike Authority. The buyer can either put the bonds in 1990, or keep them to maturity. The hitch is that the issuer has the option to retire the $2 billion issue if interest rates on 30-year revenue bonds drop below 7%.

Some words of warning: Put bonds require that holders notify the issuer that the bonds will be tendered for redemption at a specified time. It could be one to three months before the put date. There is no leeway for error.

A new municipal bond product was introduced in May 1984 called Tender Option Puts or "TOPs" for short. TOPs are low coupon, long-term bonds with put features. The put feature enables a holder on the bond to sell it back to the issuer of the TOPs at par (i.e. face value) at a specified date. The put feature was guaranteed by a letter-of-credit issued by a major bank.

TOPs were created to allow major holders of long-term, low coupon municipal bonds whose tax situations change to sell their bonds at higher-than-market prices. The sellers can then reinvest the proceeds in taxable bonds that will provide them with higher net returns. The put option guarantees a set price for the bonds on the put date, regardless of possible interest rate increases or other circumstances that would otherwise reduce the securities' value.

Make sure you understand any new products that you buy. A product sold by one group may appear to be just like one you investigated, but it has a twist. Tender Option Puts were followed by Collateralized Option Puts (COPs). The names sound similar, but the COPs were a much weaker security than the TOPs.

B. Warrants

A bond may be issued with warrants attached. A warrant generally allows you to purchase additional bonds at your option at a similar yield, within a given period of time. If interest rates drop before the warrants expire, you will benefit because you can either

Special Features of Certain Municipal Bonds 57

sell the warrants and make a profit or use the warrants to buy bonds with higher interest rates than those generally available in the market.

In 1981, warrants were used by the New York State Municipal Assistance Corporation (MAC) to help sell an issue. These MAC bonds carried a 12¾% coupon and warrants that entitled the bearer to purchase an equal number of bonds at the same yield within a specified period of time. Interest rates dropped for equivalent bonds, to 10¾% within the life of the warrant, costing MAC more than $1 million annually for the new bonds issued at 12¾% to exercisers of the warrants. However, some of these extra costs were offset by a reduced interest cost to MAC on the original sale of the bonds, and the savings in investment banking fees when the holders exercised their warrants.

Warrant holders do not always come out ahead. In 1981, MAC sold a $100 million issue of 10⅝% bonds with attached warrants expiring in January 1982. During the life of the warrant, similar MAC issues were yielding more than 10⅝%, making the warrant valueless. In this case the warrant holders lost money if they accepted a lower interest rate on their MAC bonds in order to receive the warrants.

C. Floating or Variable Rate

A floating rate or variable rate allows a bond's interest rate to change as market rates fluctuate. Interest on floating rate bonds is usually set at some percentage of the Bond Buyer Index of Treasury Bond yields (for example, 65% of the yield on 90-day Treasury bills). An occasional floater is tied to the higher of the Bond Buyer's 20-Bond Index of long-term municipal bonds or the 90-day Treasury bill rate. This gives an added hedge because both short-term and long-term rates are used as a formula to peg the interest rate of the bond. The theory here is that if the yield on the bond approaches current returns, the price of the bond will remain around par.

Another feature that is sometimes available to make floaters more attractive is the ability to convert a floating rate bond into a 20- or 30-year bond that pays a fixed rate of interest. If interest rates fall substantially, the convertible feature can price floating-rate bonds at a premium.

Although floating rate bonds help protect a bondholder against rising interest rates, they have a number of disadvantages:

• If interest rates drop, a bondholder's return will decline. By comparison, the usual municipal bond pays a fixed rate of interest, so that as market rates drop, the price of the bond will increase.

• Floaters may sell at a discount of 85% to 90% of their face values. For example, if the floater is pegged to 65% of a 10-year Treasury bond, it will sell at a discount from par if the spread between Treasury bond interest and municipal bond interest is less than 35%, as it was in 1983.

• Floaters usually have an interest-rate ceiling so that they are only a partial hedge against a big jump in the rates. For example, if the 90-day Treasury bill rate shoots up to 20%, and a floater's rate is set at 65% of that, the bond should pay 13%. However, a ceiling might limit the interest rate to only 12%, which would lead to a drop in the price of the bond. Although floaters generally also have floor rates of 6% to 7%, below which the interest rate may not fall, these may be too low to be of substantial value.

• If the floater is tied to the 90-day Treasury bill rate, it will provide little protection if long-term rates rise faster than short-term rates.

Jane Bryant Quinn, the syndicated financial columnist, views large-scale issuance of floating rate bonds, as an indication that issuers think interest rates are about to peak. For example, taxable floaters were issued in 1974 by Citicorp one month before interest rates began to decline. There were no floating rate bonds again until the summer of 1978. At that time their issuance was premature because interest rates did not peak for almost a year. No one can accurately predict the actions of the market, but the appearance of floating-rate bonds indicates that the issuers are betting on a drop in interest rates.

D. Minicoupon and Zero-Coupon

As its name indicates, a zero-coupon bond does not pay interest. Because of this feature, it is sold at a substantial discount from its face value. For example, a zero-coupon bond with a face value of

Special Features of Certain Municipal Bonds

$10,000 might be sold for $3,000. The difference between par ($10,000) and the selling price ($3,000) is called "original issue discount" (OID). At maturity, you would receive $10,000. The amount of OID on non-taxable municipal bonds is not subject to federal income tax.

A minicoupon bond is similar to zero-coupon bond in that it is sold at a fraction of its face value. However, a small amount of interest is paid each year. Like zero-coupon bonds, the difference between the original issue discount price and par value generally is not subject to federal income tax.

Zero-coupon bonds, and to a lesser extent minicoupon bonds, protect you against a decline in interest rates on the reinvestment of the bond's current return. For example, if you buy a regular $10,000 face bond yielding 12% currently, you would receive $1,200 each year, and must reinvest the $1,200 at a 12% return to make a 12% yield-to-maturity. In contrast, a zero-coupon bond automatically provides the stated yield-to-maturity for the life of the bond.

Beginning September 1, 1984, the Municipal Securities Rule Making Board required specific information on confirmation slips for purchasers of zero-coupon bonds. Confirmation slips have to state that no interest payments will be received and that no notification will be given if bearer zero-coupon bonds are called. If a zero-coupon bond is callable, it will not be a good hedge against declining interest rates since the issuer will probably call the bond if interest rates drop.

Zero-coupon and minicoupon bonds have certain disadvantages. First, they generally are issued at a below-market yield-to-maturity rate of interest. Second, they are unusual and thus there are not many buyers who will bid on the bonds if you decide to sell them before maturity. Third and most important, if inflation boosts interest rates, your yield is locked in at a lower rate, with no possibility of reinvesting the interest at a higher rate.

E. FDIC and FSLIC Insurance

One innovation (which is now rare) in improving bond ratings and marketability is using a "back door" route to obtain federal government insurance. Here is how it works. The proceeds from a municipal issue are used to purchase bank certificates of deposit

(CDs). Since the Federal Deposit Insurance Corporation (FDIC) insures the CDs, federal agency backing is thus provided for the municipal securities. The bank borrows against the CDs and lends the money to a borrower at a higher rate of interest. This is beneficial to you because the bonds are federally insured up to $100,000 per bondholder and beneficial to the issuer because it reduces the interest rate necessary to make a successful public offering.

For example, the sale of a long-term bond issue to raise money to finance a garden-apartment complex for moderate income families in Tulsa, Oklahoma, would ordinarily have required a coupon of 11.25% and have received an A rating when it was issued in 1983. However, due to the federal guarantees provided through the purchase of certificates of deposit with bond proceeds at a savings and loan association, the bonds were rated AAA and carried an 8.75% coupon. The bank pays the bond interest of 8.75% and lends money to the builder at a higher rate. The bonds are guaranteed by the certificates of deposit and the bank assumes the risk if the builder defaults. That is, the bank pays the interest on the certificates of deposit that back the bonds whether or not the builder can meet the interest payments on the loan.

Under present law, the FDIC and the FSLIC guarantee principal of up to $100,000 per bondholder. If the bank fails, the CD holders and bank depositors will be paid by the FSLIC or FDIC. At that time the bonds would be called. Another possible scenario might be that the failed bank would merge with another bank with the latter assuming its obligations. In that event, the previously insured CDs and deposits would continue to enjoy federal agency insurance.

The FDIC and FSLIC bonds are sold in book-entry form. This means that the purchaser never gets a bond certificate, but instead receives ledger statements to the effect that he owns a bond. Treasury notes and bills are dealt with in the same fashion.

The issuance of new bonds of this sort was banned after April 15, 1983, unless a binding agreement for sale was effective before March 4, 1983. Housing agencies rushed to sell these issues to make the deadline, bringing to market both rated and unrated bonds. However, FDIC and FSLIC bonds issued before April 15, 1983, still provide to bondholders federal agency insurance.

F. Refunding

Refunding occurs when U.S. government obligations, or other obligations are purchased by a municipal issuer and placed in an escrow account at a bank for the sole purpose of meeting the interest and principal requirements of outstanding municipal bonds. A municipal obligation so backed by Treasury bonds is the safest municipal bond investment available.

Bonds are refunded for one of three reasons:

- To Refinance Debt. When interest rates decline by more than 200 basis points (2 percentage points) it may be worthwhile for an issuer to refund oustanding bonds.

The issuer sells new bonds at the lower rates. The proceeds from the new issue are used to buy Treasury bonds. The Treasury bonds are tailored to provide the interest and principal payments needed to pay off the outstanding bond issue. The Treasury bonds are placed in escrow to ensure that they will be used only to pay off the old bonds that are then traded on a yield-to-call basis instead of a yield-to-maturity basis because they must be redeemed on the call date.

- Changing the Repayment Schedule. If an issuer discovers that many bonds are coming due at the same time, it may prefer to stretch out repayment by refunding one issue and floating another. The refunded bonds may have a lower coupon than the new securities if the objective is to restructure debt payments.

- Removing Restrictive Bond Covenants. Many revenue bonds include limitations on the utilization of the funds, restrictions on rate changes, requirements for expenditure of funds for special purposes, or special tests for the issue of new bonds. Refunding takes the old bonds off the books and releases the issuer from the restrictive covenants.

In summary, bonds identified for refunding include those that are: more than 200 basis points higher than current interest rates; high-coupon revenue bonds such as hospital or electric power revenue bonds; high-coupon moral obligation bonds, only if the issuer is not a heavy borrower; mortgage revenue bonds due to mortgage refinancing; and part of a cluster of bonds due in the same year for the same issuer.

There is no central clearing house for information about refunding though refundings are often announced in *The Bond Buyer* or in other newspapers, especially those serving the issuer's areas.

If you are holding a recently refunded bond you are going to be pleasantly surprised because the bond rating and thus your bond price will increase. For example, in 1982, Platte River Power Authority in Colorado issued term bonds maturing in 2002 and 2012 with coupons of 14% and 14½% rated A-1 by Moody's and A plus by Standard & Poor's with first call in 1992. One year later, Platte River refunded the more costly issues by offering a new series with a coupon of 9.75% due to a decline in interest rates. As a result of the refunding, the price of the Platte River bonds increased 11 points, from 121 to 132 because the refunded Platte River bonds were now backed with the collateral of U.S. Treasury bonds.

The only negative aspect of refunding is that in certain situations it may reduce the length of time the bondholder can receive high-coupon interest because of call features. This is especially important if the bond was originally sold at a premium. In this case, the premium or the amount of the price in excess of 100, must be amortized over fewer years thereby reducing the yield-to-maturity. For example, assume you purchase a 20-year bond with a 14% coupon, which is callable in 10 years at a price of 120 ($1,200). In this case, the 20 premium is amortized over 20 years. However, if your bonds are prerefunded to the 10 year call date, the premium you paid must now be amortized over 10 years rather than 20 years, thereby reducing your yield-to-maturity. Assuming the bonds are refunded at 103 ($1,030), the yield on your refunded bond would be 10.85% because of the reduction in the life of the bond from 20 years to 10 years. If the bond had not been called, the effective yield-to-maturity would have been 11.44% if the bonds remained outstanding for 20 years.

In the fall of 1986, municipal bond dealers began purchasing large blocks of prerefunded bonds in order to strip the coupons from the principal payments. These bonds were then sold either as zero coupon bonds, or bonds with only one coupon payment per year. The coupons themselves which were removed from the bonds were sold separately. This activity has dramatically increased the value of large blocks of prerefunded bonds.

G. Sinking Fund

A sinking fund consists of money regularly set aside in a special account for the periodic retirement of a certain portion of a bond issue. It adds security to the bond issue by providing a reserve out of which to repay the bonds.

When the sinking fund is active it reduces the number of bonds outstanding, increasing the safety of the remaining bonds. The issuer first buys bonds available in the open market if the price is attractive, raising the price of the bonds that remain outstanding. Issuers might also call for bond tenders by advertising in a newspaper. Your response to a bond tender could be to offer to sell the bonds at a stated price. The issuer buys the bonds tendered at the lowest price. If funds still remain, the bonds must be called by lot and are usually redeemed at par. If the issuer is actively retiring bonds, sinking-fund bonds can be very profitable to bondholders because their securities maintain their price better than other bonds in the face of rising interest rates. However, if the sinking fund is inactive, this feature offers no additional protection. Moreover, a sinking fund may be costly if your bonds are called away when interest rates are falling.

Sinking fund provisions on some issues may not help you very much if the provisions do not require bond retirement to begin until 20 to 25 years after the bonds are issued. Often only a small portion of the issue is retired by the sinker, with the majority of the bonds being retired at maturity. If bond retirement is not mandatory, the bonds will be retired only if it is advantageous to the issuer.

H. Supersinkers

Supersinkers are single-family mortgage revenue bonds with maturities of between 20 and 30 years that are expected to be redeemed within 10 years. Supersinkers are always part of a larger housing bond issue. The redemption of the supersinkers depends on prepayment of the mortgages. All funds from early mortgage retirements must be used to redeem the supersinker bonds.

First issued in 1980, supersinkers are attractive to investors who prefer the high yield of long-term bonds, while desiring the possible protection of short-term maturities. Compared to other bonds with 5-to-10-year maturities, supersinkers have higher yields. However, there is no guarantee that they will actually be called within that period of time. As a rule of thumb, it appears that the higher the mortgage rate, the faster the rate of prepayment; however, there is no firm data to support this contention. Thus, it is impossible to calculate yield-to-maturity because the maturity date is unknown.

If interest rates drop dramatically between the time the bonds are issued and the mortgage loans are made, the bonds could be called within a year. In extreme cases, this could result in a cash shortfall because insufficient time is available for interest earned on the revenue fund to compound in order to pay the costs of issuing the bonds. On the other hand, prepayments of mortgages might be slower than expected, extending the average life of the supersinker beyond 10 years.

Supersinkers should not be purchased for appreciation because subsequent buyers will be reluctant to pay much of a premium. They will fear a call at par, which can occur at any time. Because of the unknown call date, supersinkers should be registered so you can be contacted if there is a call. What a disappointment to present your coupons at the bank only to find that they have been called and have not paid interest for the last six months.

I. Private Insurance

Four large insurance companies provide the majority of insurance on municipal bond issues. They are MBIA (Municipal Bond Investors Assurance Corporation), AMBAC (American Municipal Bond Assurance Corporation), FGIC (Financial Guarantee Insurance Company), and BIG (Bond Investors Guaranty). HIBI (Health Industry Bond Insurance), an affiliate of the insurer industrial Indemnity suspended the insurance of new bonds after September 30, 1985. Standard & Poor's downgraded the quality rating of bond issuers insured by HIBI, resulting in an automatic downgrading of the 300 issues insured by HIBI, which were valued at $6 billion.

The issuers of municipal bonds seek insurance if they believe that it will lower the interest they must pay to sell their bonds. Insurance automatically improves the rating from Standard & Poor's, which assigns bonds insured by the above companies a AAA rating. Moody's Investors Service now gives an Aaa rating to all companies but AMBAC and a new company called Capital Guaranty Insurance Co., formed in 1986. For a further discussion of insurance see Part II, Chapter VII.

J. Bond Bank Backing

A municipal bond bank is an arrangement for pooling small issues of a state's municipalities and districts. By pooling, a bond bank can offer larger issues that attract more bidders and reduce the costs of marketing and underwriting. For the buyer, it reduces the risk of holding debt of small, and often unrelated issues. See Part II, Chapter VII.

K. Letter-of-Credit (LOC)

A LOC is a commitment by a bank to pay principal and interest if an issuer is unable to meet bond obligations. It is frequently used as a means of increasing the creditworthiness of a short-term borrowing such as commercial paper, industrial development bonds, and housing bond issues.

Some LOCs only cover the put feature of a bond, thereby giving the issuer financial coverage in the event that more bonds are tendered for redemption than the issuer can accommodate. Other LOCs secure bonds for only a portion of the life of the issue. In the event it is only for a portion of the bond's life, the rating of the issue could fall unless other provisions have been made to supplement the bond's security.

In assessing the value of the LOC, the commercial rating companies evaluate the security of the bank. Banks do not have to maintain separate reserves to cover their LOCs, unlike private insurance companies which are subject to strict reserve requirements. In the past, there was no limit to the number or amount of LOCs which could be issued, except for limitations relating to a specific borrower. The Federal Reserve Board and The Bank of England agreed to require capital reserves for LOCs issued by commercial banks. Investment banks and other foreign banks are not subject to similar capital requirements.

In late 1983, the credit ratings of a number of the largest U.S. commercial banks were downgraded. Accordingly, bonds secured by LOCs from those banks were also downgraded.

L. Moral Obligation Security

Revenue bonds that are strongly supported by the legislature of the state that issues them sometimes contain a "moral obligation" clause. The moral obligation implies that the state will support the bonds in the event of a cash shortfall although the state is not legally liable to do so. If the bond issue is in good favor with the legislature, the legislature will authorize replenishment of the reserve fund if necessary. Aside from the moral obligation, there is the hard financial fact that the state or its agency will incur higher legal costs the next time it borrows if its agencies default. New York, New Jersey, and Pennsylvania agency bonds secured by moral obligations have been bailed out by these states. In these cases the moral obligation was observed.

M. Book-Entry Bonds

Most municipal bonds sold are represented by a physical certificate that is mailed to the buyer of the bonds upon request. Book-entry only bonds are bonds that have a single underlying physical certificate representing the entire issue. The actual documents for municipal book entry bonds probably reside in New York's Depository Trust Company (DTC), a 13-year-old cooperative body with 137 stockholders, including banks, brokerage firms and federally chartered financial agencies. Investors get statements of account from the brokerage house where the bonds were purchased acknowledging ownership, but they never can receive actual delivery of a physical certificate. Interest payments are mailed every six months as with any registered bond.

Notes

Chapter II

[1]Jane Bryant Quinn, "Catching the Peak," *Newsweek*, (August 6, 1979).

CHAPTER III

A Comparison of Municipal Bond Trusts and Funds

A. Investment Strategy
B. Method of Purchasing Trusts and Funds
C. Management Fees and Sales Charges
D. Determining the Price of a Trust or Fund
E. Redemption of a Trust or Fund—Hidden Costs
F. Reinvesting in a Trust or Fund
G. Quality of Trust or Fund—The Fudge Factor
H. Reading the Prospectus

Municipal bond trusts and municipal bond funds are collections of bonds prepackaged for sale to investors. Purchasing a package is convenient because it makes buying the bonds easier and presumably lessens the need for you to evaluate each bond yourself. Like prepackaged fruits and vegetables, each piece might be as sweet as honey. But sometimes a slightly moldy piece might be buried below the hard shiny fruit you can see through the cellophane. Municipal bond packages come in two styles, unit investment trusts (which we will call trusts) and open-ended mutual funds (which we will call funds). They differ in many respects, as described below.

A. Investment Strategy

The difference between a trust and a fund is in investment strategy. A fund *trades* bonds (buying and selling municipal bonds and generally turning over the entire portfolio at least once a year), playing the yield curve in an attempt to maximize its interest income. A trust, by comparison, may only hold the bonds that are selected when it is formed and may not trade bonds. A trust makes interest payments periodically to its investors. As each issue matures and is redeemed, the trust pays the principal to its investors. After most of the bonds mature, the trust terminates. Although the trust cannot buy additional bonds after it is formed, it may sell one or more issues if there appears to be danger of a default.

A fund provides you with the potential for improving your position in a changing market, while a trust provides the stability of a known portfolio. One irony of the conservative trusts is that they can buy higher-yielding and lower-rated bonds for their portfolios because they do not have to worry about resale. For example, hospital bonds are infrequently traded and high-yielding, making them ideal for trusts. A 1982 report appearing in the *Journal of Portfolio Stock Management,* which compared funds to trusts, concluded that the "active management of a municipal bond portfolio is likely to be inferior to a buy-and-hold strategy."[1]

B. Method of Purchasing Trusts and Funds

Funds and trusts are sold pursuant to a prospectus, which outlines the customer services rendered, the management and operating charges, the potential risks to shareholders, minimum investment amounts, and other pertinent information. Funds and trusts provide portfolio diversification, bookkeeping services, safekeeping for securities, and regular distribution of income.

Trust units or fund shares may be purchased directly from a company selling them or indirectly through a broker, a municipal bond house or possibly a bank. Many large brokerage firms, such as Merrill Lynch, put together and sell their own trust units or funds. Whether they are purchased directly from the issuer or indirectly through a broker, the sales charge is the same. Sellers sell trust units or fund shares issued by a variety of companies.

Neither funds nor trusts can be used as collateral at a bank if you wish to borrow against them. Only the actual bonds may be used for a secured bank loan. (See Part II, Chapter I.)

C. Management Fees and Sales Charges

Certain funds charge a front-end fee called a load. Others are called no-load funds because there is no up front sales charge. However, certain so-called no-load funds charge a back-end fee if funds do not stay invested for a period of years. If the seller's fee is built into the front-end purchase fee of the load funds, there are no additional loads, though they may charge a fee for the distribution of advertising materials.

Trusts generally charge a load of 3% to 6%, which is included in the price the investor pays for the units. Although no-load funds do not charge fees in connection with the purchase of shares, the sponsors of no-load funds earn management fees for managing the funds' trading activities and some charge for advertising costs. By contrast, the trusts charge only a minimal management fee, reflecting their low-cost, buy-and-hold strategy. Thus, over the long term, it costs less to own trust units than to own shares of a fund. Funds charge annual management fees, which average about 0.8%, while the annual management fee of trusts is 0.15%. Thus, a one-time sales fee of 4.5% for a trust unit would equal five or six years of the continuing management fees for fund shares.

D. Determining the Price of a Trust or Fund

A Trust unit is initially sold at a fixed price, which reflects the net-asset value of the bonds held by the trust plus the load. The net-asset value is determined by dividing (a) the value of the bonds held by the trust plus any cash and other assets, such as interest accrued but not received, minus all liabilities, by (b) the total number of trust units to be sold.

$$\text{Price of trust unit} = \frac{\text{value of bonds and other assets} - \text{liabilities}}{\text{total number of units to be sold}}$$

The yield of the trust is calculated as a current return (see Part II, Chapter I for a description of current return) without calculating possible capital gains or losses or trying to estimate the yield-to-maturity.

In like manner, shares of a fund are based on a dollar amount reflecting the net-asset value of the bonds in the fund. By comparison, money market funds only invest in short-term paper, and the price of their shares remains at $1 per each share.

E. Redemption of a Trust or Fund—Hidden Costs

If you wish to redeem (sell) your trust units, the sponsor of the trust will generally buy them at a price that is fixed weekly. The value of a trust unit is based on the current offering price of the bonds in the portfolio less a certain percent, often 3% to 4% or possibly more. Though there is no sales charge as such, the sponsor hopes to make money on the spread (the 3% to 4%) when it resells the trust units to other investors. Because of the spread, a trust's yield will be lower than its quoted yield if you sell the units prior to maturity.

There is an additional reason why a trust's yield might be lower than the quoted yield. When the trust units were purchased, the yield quoted included the sales charge, which was spread over the entire life of the trust. For example, assume you purchased a trust with a 30-year life and a 4% sales charge. Assume further that you sell your units after four years. In this case, the effective sales charge is allocated over four years rather than 30 years. As a result, the effective sales charge rises more than seven fold, from .0013 (4% ÷ 30) per year to 1% (4% ÷ 4) per year, and reduces the yield of the trust unit accordingly. Thus, although trust units are generally as salable as shares of a fund, the load on the trust may substantially reduce the overall yield as compared to a no-load fund.

The redemption of fund shares is simple. You can request payment by calling or writing to the sponsor. The shares are redeemed at the fund's net asset value, which is calculated daily by the fund. The net-asset value is computed in one of two ways by the fund. Some funds use the bid price of the bonds (the price at which a trader offers to buy the bonds). Other funds use the mean between the bid and asked prices of the bonds in the fund's portfolio. The asked price is the price at which a seller offers to sell bonds which he owns.

On any particular day, for any funds, the price to buy or sell fund shares is the same. There is no spread as there is for trust units.

The foregoing analysis indicates that you will get the best price if you sell the shares of a no-load fund that uses the mean of the bid and asked prices to value the fund's portfolio. The Drefyus

Tax Exempt Bond Fund, Inc. uses this method of pricing fund shares. Most of the other funds that we examined used the bid price. You will get the worst price if you sell units of a trust that the sponsor will redeem at 4% below the bid prices of the trust's portfolio. Thus, if you anticipate trading in and out, you should give strong consideration to buying shares of a fund rather than trust units.

F. Reinvesting in a Trust or Fund

Interest earned on your fund shares can be either automatically reinvested in the fund or mailed to you on a regular basis. Interest earned from a trust can usually be reinvested for you by the sponsor for no charge in a no-load fund or sent to you. Trusts with an up-front load levy charges on all newly invested money, whether it is interest earned from the trust or fund or an additional cash investment.

G. Quality of Trust or Fund—The Fudge Factor

In order to maximize the yield of the trust or fund, the sponsor will generally select revenue bonds rather than general obligation bonds because revenue bonds usually yield more than similarly rated G.O.'s. This may become of concern to you because many of the revenue bonds selected for trusts are:

(a) Only rated A by either Standard & Poor's or Moody's but not by both;

(b) Weak A bonds such as Puerto Rico agencies and power authority bonds;

(c) Other bonds generally considered less saleable because they are small or unknown issues, unrated issues, or because there are too many of them for sale in the market.

While the sponsor of trusts and funds state that the bonds are "professionally selected," this only means selected by professionals. Professional selection does not mean selected by experts with a view to getting bonds of the best quality within the stipulated rating. A trust may not even provide diversification. Though there may be 10 bond issues in the portfolio, 80% of the assets may be represented by two issues. If the money is distributed fairly evenly, it may only provide diversification into low-quality bonds that you would not have purchased for yourself.

Some of the professionally selected bonds are in fact the tail ends of issues that remain in the sponsor's inventory because the sponsor was unable to sell the bonds when they were initially offered to the public. A sponsor may also sell other slow-moving bonds in its inventory to a fund or trust. While these bonds may be perfectly acceptable investments for a trust or fund, their purchase may not exactly square with your understanding of "professional selection."

H. Reading the Prospectus

Having made the decision to purchase trust units or shares of a fund, it is important to read each prospectus carefully. Although the prospectuses are usually similar to one another, they can vary. The Security and Exchange Commission does not limit the activities of a fund or trust, as long as the sponsor reveals all pitfalls and plans. The investors will learn of such plans only by reading the prospectus.

In accordance with a 1983 SEC ruling, mutual funds can distribute "simplified prospectuses." These versions are easier to read, but may omit vital information, such as a detailed breakdown of investments by rating or maturity, or historical perspective on fund performance. Also, the simplified prospectuses are not uniform because the funds have some discretion as to what to include. The additional information is available by requesting Part B of the prospectus. You may want to make a mental note to do this at the same time you request the basic prospectus.

Your seller may tell you that the trust prospectus is available only after you buy a trust or fund. Trusts do tend to sell out very quickly, and it may be that the trust will be sold by the time you receive the prospectus. In that event, ask the seller to send you a prospectus of a trust in the same series as the one under consideration. That way you will be better prepared to purchase the upcoming trust in the series because the prospectuses are usually similar.

One of the most important principles stated in this book as a guide for investors is NEVER GO LONG-TERM (never buy a bond, a trust unit, or fund shares where the maturity of the underlying bonds is more than 13 years away). The reason for this advice is fear of inflation, which results in high interest rates. If interest rates go up, the price of your bonds goes down. If the maturity dates of your bonds are relatively short, your downside risk is minimized because you can hold your bonds to maturity and they will be redeemed for full face value.

If you are interested in information on either trusts or funds, continue to read the detailed evaluations of these vehicles in the next two chapters. If not, move directly on to Chapter VI.

Notes

Chapter III

[1] Duane Stock, "Does active management of municipal bond portfolios pay?," *The Journal of Portfolio Management*, (Winter 1982), pp. 51–55.

CHAPTER IV

Evaluation of a Trust

A. The Costs of Owning a Trust Unit
B. Calculations of the Yield on a Trust Unit
C. Special Types of Trusts
   1. Trusts of One State
   2. Deep Discount Trusts
   3. Trust Issues Backed By Letters of Credit
   4. Floating-Rate Trusts
   5. Insured Trusts
D. General Comparison of Owning Trust Units and Individual Municipal Bonds
   1. Liquidity
   2. Minimum Investment
   3. Diversification and Professional Selection
   4. Custodianship and Recordkeeping
   5. Monthly Payment of Income
   6. Reinvestment of Income
E. Sampling of Issuers of Unit Investment Trusts

Unit investment trusts are called trusts in this chapter. Because they are not managed, trusts end when most bonds in the portfolio have matured. The first municipal bond trust was formed in 1962 by John Nuveen and Ira Haupt. Since that time, the trust market has burgeoned into a $25 billion-a-year business. The sponsors of the trusts sell the trust units to the public.

A trust is a legal entity formed under state law that purchases and holds a portfolio of individual municipal bonds for the sole benefit of investors, who are beneficiaries of the trust. All income of the trust, after expenses, must be distributed at least annually to the investors. Most trusts allow you to receive a monthly or quarterly return. A trust cannot buy additional bonds after its formation, but it may sell a particular issue if it seems to be in the investors' interest to do so. If more than a predetermined percentage of the trust's portfolio is sold or called, the sponsor may terminate the trust, sell all remaining issues and liquidate.

A. The Costs of Owning a Trust Unit

In brief, the costs of owning a trust unit include a generally higher price than you might pay if you purchased the bonds individually because a sales charge and various other fees are included.

The price at which trust units are sold to you is called the public offering price. The price depends on two things. The first is the offering price, which is defined as the price at which the bonds could be purchased directly by the public. Since prices in the bond market are negotiable, an individual purchaser of a bond could conceivably do better than the price set for the bonds included in the trust. The second part of the price is a sales charge, or load, which varies from one trust to another. This one-time charge can vary from 3% to 6% of the offering price. The amount of the sales charge is stated in the prospectus.

The calculation of the public offering price for a given trust unit is:

$$\frac{\text{Public Offering}}{\text{Price Per Unit}} = \frac{\text{Offering Price of Bonds + Sales Charge}}{\text{Number of Units offered for Sale}}$$

Another cost borne by the investors are fees for trustees, sponsors, and evaluators, which are usually not more than $1.50 annually per unit of $1,000 face value. In addition, there are various other fees and charges that are paid by the trust and borne by the investors in certain unusual circumstances.

A common misconception is that a trust unit can be sold back to the sponsor at an investor's original cost. It is true that a sponsor will generally repurchase trust units, although the sponsor is generally not *legally* required to do so. However, the purchase price that the sponsor will pay for the unit is the net-asset value of the bonds in the trust's portfolio minus a "spread." The spread might be as much as 3% to 4%, or $30 to $40 per $1,000 unit. The spread might also be greater. Though not so designated, this is in effect a back-end load. In addition, as stated in Part II, Chapter III, the net-asset value usually reflects the bid price of a trust's portfolio.

Another cost is not as evident. It is tied to the payment schedule of interest. A trust pays interest monthly, quarterly, or semiannually, so you can anticipate income in tidy lump-sum payments. However, interest payments received by the trust may be held in a noninterest bearing account until they are distributed to unitholders. This is equivalent to receiving a check for $1,000 and putting it in a drawer for a couple of months before depositing it. Although it does not benefit you, the bank is able to profit from the large sums held in noninterest bearing accounts.

B. Calculations of the Yield on a Trust Unit

The yield on a trust unit is expressed as a current return. As described in Part II, Chapter I, the current return may be quite different from the yield-to-maturity calculation. The current return is computed by dividing the net annual return (the amount of municipal interest receivable each year) by the public offering price. The various fees outlined above under the section on costs are taken into account in computing the net annual return.

The current return does not fully take into account the discount or premium feature of the individual bonds in the trust. The current return also does not take into account the fact that there may be call features that could reduce the trust's net annual return over its life. For example, if all bonds in the trust were purchased at par, then the current return would be the same as the yield-to-maturity. If, however, the individual bonds purchased by the trust were below or above par, the current return computation would not be the same as its yield-to-maturity. No trust prospectus gives an approximation of yield-to-maturity.

The conclusion that the current return on a trust is not comparable with the yield-to-maturity on an individual bond is of great importance because yield-to-maturity is the way that municipal bonds are priced. Thus, you cannot rely on the current return without further investigation in comparing the return on a trust to the return on an individual bond.

A number of reputable municipal bond sellers have independently told us that trusts are priced to yield less than the equivalent bonds. There are two mark-ups. First, the bondhouse sells the bonds to the trust and makes a profit. Then the trust adds on a sales charge and sells them to the public.

Our conclusion is that there is a significant advantage with respect to yield if you purchase the actual bonds rather than trust units because you can tell exactly what the yield-to-maturity is on the individual bonds, and the quality and maturity of the bonds can be tailored to your needs.

C. Special Types of Trusts

In order to make the trust units more attractive, they have been tailored in different styles mimicking the features available in individual bonds. There are trusts that hold bonds issued by only one state, deep discount trusts, triple-A trusts backed by insurance companies or letters of credit issued by banks, and floating-rate trusts. These various kinds of bond packages suffer the limitations of individual bonds with the same characteristics.

1. Trusts of One State

Trusts that are restricted to owning issues from one state appeal to investors who live in that state because interest generally is not subject to state or local income taxes of the issuing state. States with high income tax rates for which unit investment trusts have been created include California, Massachusetts, Michigan, Minnesota, New Jersey, New York, Ohio, and Pennsylvania.

One of the major selling points of trusts is that they offer diversity by enabling you to share in a large portfolio of bonds. While one-state portfolios may contain a wide variety of bonds, bankruptcy or near insolvency on the part of the state itself could jeopardize the ability of some of the other issuers to meet their debt obligations. The prospectus clearly spells out this potential risk by describing the fiscal history of the state and its subdivisions, and the ratings of the bonds to be included in the portfolio.

2. Deep Discount Trusts

A deep discount trust purchases bonds in the secondary market that are selling well below par or zero-coupon bonds that are original-issue discount bonds and which do not pay any current interest. If you think interest rates will drop, and have no need for current income, this type of trust is exceptionally desirable. The advantage of zero-coupon bonds is that all interest income is reinvested at its yield-to-maturity and there is one payment of capital and interest at maturity. However, the trust should not be structured so that interest bearing bonds are all called before the zero-coupon bonds come due. If the zero-coupon bond remains outstanding after all interest bearing bonds have come due, there will be no stream of income to pay the trust expenses. As a result, the trust will be prematurely terminated, probably causing a loss to the investors.

3. Trust Issues Backed by Letters of Credit

If bonds in a trust are backed by letters of credit, such bonds are backed by the guarantee of specific banks or corporations. If the bond issuer cannot meet interest or principal payments, or if it commits an act that results in the loss of the bond's tax exempt status, the issuers of the letters of credit are required to make payments of principal and interest. These letters of credit or guarantees, however, are only as good as the bank or corporation that issues them. If the bank suffers losses due to poor economic conditions, which result in an inability of borrowers to meet their obligations, then the letters of credit are worthless. Thus, the greater the financial strength of banks or corporations backing the bonds, the more secure the entire portfolio.

4. Floating-Rate Trusts

A floating-rate trust invests only in securities that have floating rates. The rates are often adjusted according to the prime rate, the rate charged by a bank to its best customers for short-term loans. If interest rates drop, holders of floating-rate trust units have lost by failing to lock in high yields when the opportunity was presented. However, even if interest rates rise, after the trust is purchased, you will not necessarily benefit all that much because issuers may call their bonds if they can do so or there may be a cap on how high the interest rate can be adjusted upward.

5. Insured Trusts

If you like the belt-and-suspenders approach to investing, you might consider an insured municipal bond trust for added protection. Insured trusts are rated AAA by Standard & Poor's because the bonds in the trust are either insured until they mature, or for as long as the trust holds them. If the bond issuer has difficulty paying the principal or interest payments, the insurance company will make the payments if it can. Among the drawbacks to these kind of trusts is a reduction in your yield by about 20 to 50 basis points because of the cost of the insurance. Another point is that to be eligible for insurance, a bond must be of good quality anyway, so it is not likely to default. A purpose of purchasing a trust is to provide diversity to protect against the one issue which may default. An insured trust will provide additional protection to a portfolio already shielded from default through diversification of ratings and locations.

D. General Comparison of Owning Trust Units and Individual Municipal Bonds

There are six potential advantages of purchasing units of a trust rather than the actual municipal bonds. However, these advantages, discussed below, apply only to investors with limited funds to invest and who have little interest in learning enough about individual bonds to buy them directly. These advantages are as follows:

1. Liquidity

Liquidity is the ease of being able to sell your trust unit. The first step in selling a trust unit is to call your seller to determine the over-the-counter price for your units. Compare that price with the redemption price offered by the sponsor of the trust.

It should first be understood that the sponsor usually does not legally obligate itself to purchase your trust units. The sponsor merely states in the trust prospectus that it intends to make a market and repurchase the units from investors who wish to sell. Thus, if you really need to sell because of adverse market conditions, your units may be unsalable. If the sponsor will not buy them, it is unlikely that anyone else will, except at a huge discount. By contrast, if you hold an actual municipal bond, the number of potential buyers is larger.

Even when the sponsor will purchase your trust units, the amount you will receive may be substantially less (or more) than your purchase price. This is because the net-asset value of a trust unit may have declined or increased because interest rates have changed. As already mentioned, the sponsor will purchase the unit at a discount from its net-asset value. The discount may be 3% to 4% or possibly more.

Thus, the purported advantage of liquidity may present no substantial advantage over selling a well-regarded bond.

2. Minimum Investment

The minimum investment for a trust unit is usually only $1,000. This is a real advantage because it is unusual to be able to purchase bonds in face amounts of less than $5,000. However, there are many deep discount bonds that you can buy for a lot less than $5,000. For example, in February 1982, a $5,000 face value AAA 2% coupon bond due in 6 years sold for $3,293.

3. Diversification and Professional Selection

The purported advantage of diversification for the investor who has limited cash to invest in municipals is sometimes misleading. First, diversification is not as necessary for bonds as it is for stocks. For example, if you invest all your funds in U.S. Treasury bonds you would have no need for diversification if you are merely concerned with risk because Treasury bonds are risk-free. Similarly, if you have under $50,000 to invest, you could invest in only AAA rated municipal bonds and feel very secure even though your holdings are not diversified. In fact, it is advantageous to be able to select the bonds you wish to own.

By contrast, unless they are insured or specifically set up to be AAA, many trusts invest a substantial amount of their portfolios in weak A bonds or bonds rated A by only one rating service, in order to maximize the return on the portfolio. Thus, the trusts may frequently hold bonds that you may not wish to own, such as weak revenue bonds. A substantial amount of Washington Public Power

Supply Systems (WPPSS) bonds were purchased and held by trusts. Some of a trust's bonds may also be callable or slow selling bonds, or bonds without bond resolutions or trust indentures for which no secondary market exists. It does not seem sensible to buy many weaker bonds rather than one strong one in the name of diversification. Although there are now some trusts that are rated AAA, their yields are generally lower than you could get by buying individual AAA bonds yourself, and most of these AAA trusts are long-term trusts, which we strongly recommend against. So much for diversification and professional selection.

4. Custodianship and Recordkeeping

Trusts will do the coupon clipping and recordkeeping for you. However, most substantial brokers and some banks will do the same at minimal cost. Examples are Merrill Lynch's Cash Management Account, Citibank's Focus Account, and Paine Webber's Resource Management Account.

5. Monthly Payment of Income

This is an advantage if you need it, but not a reason to buy a trust. We also noted earlier that one cost here is that interest payments may be kept in a noninterest bearing bank account prior to distribution.

6. Reinvestment of Income

A trust will reinvest your income for you in another trust. However, you will have to pay the load on your new investment and (unlike the funds), you will have to wait until you have accumulated enough money to buy additional units.

Our final points, which you should consider in comparing an investment in a trust to buying individual bonds, are:

First, one advantage of an individual bond is that you can choose the year you wish it to come due. Thus, you can take into account financial planning such as college tuition or purchase of a house. If you decide that your circumstances have changed, a bond of a well-known issuer can be expected to sell at a better price than the trust.

Second, most trusts hold only long-term bonds. These trusts have been frequently marketed to unsophisticated investors who only look at the current yield in evaluating investments. Since long-term bonds yield more than shorter-term bonds, a long-term trust will have a higher current return. However, be aware that because of the threat of inflation, which results in rising interest rates and falling bond prices, long-term bonds result in a substantially higher degree of risk. If you are risk adverse, it is more desirable to receive an 8% yield-to-maturity on a 7½ year bond than to get a 9% current return on a 22½ year trust. This is a major factor to prevent you from losing money because of interest-rate fluctuations.

If you do go long-term to achieve a higher return on your investments, you should understand that you are engaging somewhat in an interest-rate play that may result in gains or losses on your investment. The potential gains and losses arising from long-term bonds held individually or in unit trusts are significantly larger than those arising from intermediate or short-term bonds. Many investors over the last 10 years have lost large sums of money because they went long-term and interest rates went up.

Our analysis indicates that you should only consider buying a trust unit if you have less than $50,000 to invest and have little inclination to get involved with selecting your own investments. This book is detailed enough to give you the sophistication you need to buy the individual bonds, which are superior to buying trust units.

E. Sampling of Issuers of Unit Investment Trusts

Bear, Stearns & Co.
55 Water Street
New York, New York 10041

Dean Witter Reynolds, Inc.
130 Liberty Street
New York, New York 10006

E. F. Hutton & Co., Inc.
One Battery Park Plaza
New York, N.Y. 10004

Fidelity Distributors Corp.
82 Devonshire Street
Boston, MA 02108

John Nuveen & Co., Inc.
209 S. LaSalle Street
Chicago, IL. 60604

Kemper Financial Services, Inc.
120 S. LaSalle St.
Chicago, IL. 60603

Lebenthal & Co., Inc.
25 Broadway
New York, New York 10004

Merrill Lynch, Pierce, Fenner
  & Smith, Inc.
1 Liberty Plaza
New York, N.Y. 10080

Paine Webber Inc.
1221 Avenue of the Americas
New York, NY 10017

Prudential-Bache Securities, Inc.
100 Gold Street
New York, NY 10038

Rotan Mosle, Inc.
1500 South Tower
Pennzoil Place
Houston, TX 7702

Shearson Lehman Brothers Inc.
American Express Tower
World Financial Center
New York, NY 10285

Van Kampen Merritt, Inc.
2 Penn Center Plaza
Philadelphia, PA 19102

CHAPTER V

Evaluation of a Fund

A. The Nature of a Fund
B. The Costs
    1. Sales Charge on Purchase of Fund Shares
    2. Management Fees and Expenses
    3. 12b-1 Plans
    4. Possible Capital Gains Trap
C. Quality of Bond Portfolios
D. Maturity of Bond Funds
    1. Long-Term Bond Funds
    2. Intermediate-Term Bond Funds
    3. Money Market Municipal Bond Funds
E. Special Features and Services of Funds
    1. Professionally Managed Portfolios
    2. Automatic Withdrawal Plans
    3. Free Check Privileges
    4. Monthly Interest Income Payments and Automatic Reinvestment
    5. Sweep Account
    6. Record Keeping and Recording
    7. Ease of Redemption
    8. Exchange Privileges Among a Family of Funds
F. Analysis of Bond Fund Yields
G. Conclusions and Recommendations
H. A Sampling of Issuers of Intermediate Funds

A. The Nature of a Fund

A municipal fund is an open-ended mutual fund that generally invests exclusively in a portfolio of municipal bonds. The purpose of the fund is to generate tax-exempt interest and trade the portfolio to obtain trading gains from shifts in the municipal bond market. The legal form of a fund is generally a corporation (although a few are Massachusetts Business Trusts). A special provision of the Internal Revenue Code provides a tax exemption to funds that hold municipal bonds. The funds pass the municipal income on to their shareholders, who pay no federal tax on such income. In addition, the funds pass trading gains and losses and other taxable income to shareholders, who must report such items on their personal tax returns.

The portfolio of a fund is valued daily by pricing services at either the bid price of the bonds or at the mean between the bid and asked price of the bonds, depending upon the fund. See Section E of Part II, Chapter III.

Unlike stocks, there are few bonds that will provide substantial capital appreciation when compared to other similarly rated bonds. Bonds tend to move in unison, in response to actual and anticipated interest rate changes. Variations in price result from oversupply or undersupply, buyer preferences, and other market factors including credit risk.

B. The Costs

1. Sales Charge on Purchase of Fund Shares

Shares of a fund are purchased directly from the company managing the fund, unless the fund is a load fund, in which case shares may also be purchased through brokers. Load funds require you to pay a sales charge, which is expressed as a percentage of the purchase price, at the time you buy shares of the fund. A no-load fund is more attractive than a load fund because a no-load fund enables you to buy and sell shares without incurring sales charges. The success of the no-load funds has lead to the development of back-end-loaded funds. In such a fund, there is no load to purchase the fund, but there is a substantial 5% load if you sell within the first year. The load gradually diminishes to zero at the end of five years.

There is no indication that load funds outperform similar no-load funds. The minimum investment in a no-load fund is generally higher than in a load fund. The initial investment in a no-load fund generally ranges from $1,000 to $2,500. However, load funds often enable you to buy a share for as little as $100, with subsequent investments of $25.

If you buy or sell the fund through a broker, instead of directly from the fund, then the broker is entitled to a fee even if the fund is no-load. The brokers are paid a commission by the load funds if they sell their products. You pay the broker directly if you purchase a no-load fund through them.

The potential cost to you of a load is magnified if the fund's shares are sold within a short period of time. If a fund is yielding 6.3% a year for example, and you paid a sales charge of 4.17%, your effective rate of return would be 2.13% (6.3%–4.17%) if you sold your shares after 12 months, assuming that the shares have not changed in value. If you plan on holding the fund for a longer period, then the effective cost of purchasing a load fund is distributed over the time the shares are held.

2. Management Fees and Expenses

Do not conclude that buying shares in a no-load funds means that you incur no costs. There is no free lunch! The funds all charge fees for management and operating costs, which generally total 1% annually, in addition to any sales charge you might pay to purchase shares. On a $10,000 investment, this means you would incur fees of approximately $100 annually. It is wise to review a fund's charges before you buy shares in it because the fees vary from one fund to another.

3. 12b-1 Plans

Initially the Securities and Exchange Commission approved the 12b-1 Plan to enable no-load funds to recoup the costs of advertising, and thereby compete more effectively with the load funds. However, it was viewed by all funds as an additional and somewhat hidden source of income. As a result, the 12b-1 fee can range from .04% to 2% depending upon the fund. Some funds have not instituted 12b-1 plans.

4. Possible Capital Gains Trap

Your timing in purchasing shares of the fund may result in an unexpected tax cost. The funds must distribute annually all of its income to its shareholders, including its capital gains, to keep its tax-exempt status. The distribution of capital gains usually occurs shortly after the fund's fiscal year has ended. While you might think that receipt of the capital gain distribution would be a benefit, it is actually a detriment if you had recently purchased the shares. The value of the fund's shares will decline by precisely the amount of the capital gain distribution. So far you are even because you'll get cash equivalent to the value your shares have lost. The detriment arises from the fact that you must pay tax on the capital gain. Let's look at an example. Assume you own one share of a fund that cost $100 when you bought the share on January 1, 1984. The fund realized a capital gain of $10 per share on that date. On February 1, 1984, you receive a $10 capital gain distribution. Here are the consequences: On February 1, 1984, you will receive $10, and the price of a fund share will decline from $100 to $90. In addition, you would have to report the $10 as a capital gain on your 1984 tax return.

C. Quality of Bond Portfolios

Bond funds are frequently purchased by investors because they provide diversified portfolios. To buy a diversified portfolio for yourself, you would need at least $50,000. The general funds invest heavily in utility revenue bonds to maximize their yields. The balance of the portfolio is invested in other revenue issues, a few general obligation bonds, and project notes. You may not be satisfied that such a portfolio gives the kind of diversification you desire. The prospectus will tell you what is currently in the fund's portfolio. Read it with care. If you would not buy such bonds yourself, why buy a fund that makes such investments?

Bond funds also vary in their mix of the ratings of bonds. Vanguard, T. Rowe Price, or Scudder funds indicate that they will invest 95% of their assets in the highest grades rated by either Moody's (Aaa, Aa, A) or Standard and Poor's (AAA, AA, A). Other funds might invest only 80% of their portfolios in the same grades. At the other end of the scale are the so-called high-yield funds, which will invest in any quality mix deemed appropriate to achieve a high yield. Such funds should be called high-risk funds as well as high-yield.

The theory behind high-yield funds is that historically defaults have been few, and permanent defaults even fewer. (See Part II, Chapter VIII). Thus, as long as there is diversity of bond holdings, even a default on one or more issues should not unduly damage the fund. Meanwhile, the fund is maximizing its income by buying low-rated and out-of-favor bonds. All of this is perfectly acceptable as long as you understand the nature of the fund and the risks involved. The trade refers to the kind of bonds included in this portfolio as junk bonds and to the funds as junk-bond funds.

The kinds of bonds selected by high-yield funds include:
- *Lower-rated bonds*. The fund might purchase low-rated bonds and bonds that are rated by only one rating agency, indicating a possible weakness of the bonds.
- *Unrated Bonds*. Although bonds are unrated, they may still

be acceptable investments. Bonds may be unrated not because they are unsatisfactory but because the issuer did not request and pay for a rating. However, there is always concern that the issuer did not seek a rating because the best it could get would have been a low one. An alternative explanation could be that the issue was small and privately placed so a rating was not necessary.

- *Put bonds*. This is a very conservative investment allowing the fund to divest itself of low-yielding bonds by selling them back to the issuer at a predetermined price if interest rates are rising.

High-yielding funds also utilize a variety of hedging tactics. Webster's Dictionary defines hedging as: "Attempting to lessen or avoid loss due to price fluctuations by making counter balancing investments." The objective is to lessen the risk, giving up the hope for potential profit in order to avoid potential losses.

Instead of trading the actual bonds, bond futures contracts might be purchased as a hedge against interest-rates changes or as a trading technique to realize gain. However, there is a limit stated in the prospectus on the amount of money which may be invested in futures contracts. Futures contracts are used to buy and sell commodities that will be delivered at a future specified date.

The funds have traditionally invested in Treasury bond futures though some fund managers may also invest in the new municipal bond futures contracts. As reported in *Credit Markets* the contracts are based upon an index of 50 recently issued term bonds that are designed to produce a reliable indicator in long-term municipal bond issues.

The purpose of the futures market is to enable players in the municipal market to hedge their positions. For example, an underwriter holding long-term municipal bonds could gain protection from adverse swings in interest rates by selling municipal futures. Theoretically, if interest rates rose, the value of the bonds would decline, but the value of the futures contracts would increase, thus minimizing the loss. Funds may also purchase put options and write call options on futures contracts in order to hedge the interest rate risk if this activity is declared in the prospectus. The fund hedges its portfolio against the risk of rising interest rates. This is not a perfect hedge. The increase in the futures contracts may not completely offset the decline in value of the bonds in the portfolio, or the fund manager may have taken a position and lost money.

A fund may also enter into repurchase agreements, called repos. Repos are agreements to sell securities for a fixed period with an agreement to repurchase them at a fixed price. They are usually outstanding only a day or two. These vehicles are used for very short-term investments and entail risk because interest rates are not predictable, and the fund may loose money on the transaction.

The fund might also invest in demand notes or privately arranged loans and participations. A demand note is one which is payable on request. If it is for a substantial amount, the fund might be required to sell bonds at inauspicious times to meet its obligation or it may provide temporary funds at a lower interest rate than currently available. Privately arranged loans and participations provide the fund with money from individuals instead of institutions. Whether the arrangements are beneficial for the fund is dependent upon the nature of the agreements reached.

A particular fund may select from among the possibilities mentioned or may use all of them in varying degrees. Success depends upon a certain amount of skill and a lot of luck in judging the movement of interest rates.

D. Maturity of Bond Funds

In the previous section, it was noted that bond funds could be classified on the basis of risk. Thus, the funds could be categorized as insured, or a high-quality, low-risk portfolio; a high-yield, higher-risk portfolio; or a diversified portfolio.

Funds may also be categorized on the basis of the maturity of the portfolio: long-term bond funds, intermediate-term bond funds, money market bond funds or creative combinations of various maturities.

1. Long-Term Bond Funds

Long-term bond funds hold bonds with an average maturity of about 25 years. They generally have the highest current yield of the three categories of funds because long-term bonds generally yield more than intermediate- and short-term bonds. Long-term bond funds are also the most volatile; i.e., the price of long-term bond funds vary by a larger margin than that of intermediate- or short-term bond funds as a result of the same movement of interest rates. The bulk of tax-exempt bond funds are long-term funds.

The long-term bond funds are the easiest to market because they generally have the highest current yields. Since most purchasers of bond funds are unsophisticated in their appreciation of the problems of long-term bonds, the fund's sponsor merely markets them on the basis of current yield.

If it were possible to choose an ideal time for investing in a long-term fund, it would be when you think interest rates will fall. The value of the shares would increase as rates decline. The worst time to participate in a long-term fund is when interest rates are rising. Unless there are a substantial number of new investors flooding the fund with new money to purchase the new, higher-yielding bonds, the price of the shares of long-term bond funds will decline substantially when interest rates are rising.

2. Intermediate-Term Bond Funds

Intermediate-term bond funds (funds that hold bonds with average maturities of between 2 and 10 years) are a fairly recent phenomenon. With the increasing individual participation in the municipal bond market, many people have come to understand the risks of long-term bonds—if interest rates increase, the value of long-term bonds will decrease substantially. These investors sought less volatility and more preservation of capital. Their objectives could be more easily achieved by an investment in an intermediate-term bond fund. For example, during the period from June 30, 1980, to June 10, 1982, a time of rising interest rates and falling bond prices, the intermediate-term bond funds performed much better than long-term funds. Thus, a typical intermediate-term fund such as Fidelity Limited Term Municipals outperformed the Dreyfus Tax Exempt Bond Fund (a long-term fund) for the three-year period ending June 30, 1982, by 13.8%.

The theory behind the intermediate-term funds is that by going out two to 10 years, you can earn a higher return than on the tax-exempt money market funds (3½% to 4½% yield in 1986), without taking the severe risk of a long-term fund. As of September 1986, the yield difference between a one-year and a 20-year AAA-rated general obligation bond was 265 basis points, while the difference between a one-year and a five-year bond was 115 basis points. Thus, by extending your maturity from one to five years you could make up almost half of the extra yield you would get on a 20-year bond with only a small increase in risk.

In September 1986, the current yields on bond funds were as follows:

Tax-Free Money Market Fund (less than 1 year life) = 3.98%
Tax-Free Intermediate-Term Fund (10-year life) = 7.23%
Tax-Free Long-Term Fund (21.4-year life) = 7.65%

3. Money Market Municipal Bond Fund

The money market municipal bond funds are also a fairly recent addition to the world of funds. They perform the same function as a liquid assets fund such as the Dreyfus Liquid Asset Fund, which holds CDs of banks, commercial paper, and other short-term obligations. The only principal difference between the money market municipal bond funds and other money market funds is that the former generate income that is free of federal income tax (although they are not free of state income tax). All money market funds maintain their price at $1 per share and have no market gains or losses for the investor to worry about. The problem with the money market municipal bond funds is that they generally have a low yield, 4% in August 1986.

The money market municipal bond funds are very useful vehicles in the following four situations:

(a) They are useful as a source of liquid assets because check-writing privileges are available on a number of them.

(b) They are sensible investments if, on an after-tax basis in your tax bracket, they yield more than taxable money market funds.

(c) They may be used as a vehicle to accumulate funds for a later investment in actual bonds (when the $5,000 minimum has been accumulated.)

(d) They may be a good investment when interest rates are low and you are waiting for rates to rise. They are good investments in this situation because they maintain their face value and there is little or no risk involved. Moreover, in a time of rising interest rates, the yield on such funds might float upward. However, historically they have not gone as high as taxable money market funds.

E. Special Features and Services of Funds

The funds provide special services that are not available if you hold the individual bonds. These services involve the ease of investing and receiving income. They include a professionally managed portfolio; automatic withdrawal plan; free checking privileges; monthly receipt of interest income payments or automatic reinvestment; sweep accounts; record keeping and recording; ease of redemption; and exchange privileges among a family of funds.

1. Professionally Managed Portfolios

Bonds are selected by the fund's managers and are sold and bought according to the movement of the market. Some funds report an annual 46% turnover of the portfolio, while others have a 200% annual turnover. Such high turnover does not necessarily result in high performance despite the appearance of active management. However, it does result in substantial costs, which are charged to the fund.

Past performance is also not an indicator of how well a fund will perform in the future. The market strategy of yesterday might not be suitable for today.

To review fund performance, a bird's eye view is easily available in the August issue of *Forbes* each year. Information provided includes the date the fund started, dividend and capital gains return, total assets, maximum sales charge, and annual expenses per $100 of investment.

2. Automatic Withdrawal Plans

You can receive monthly or quarterly payments of a specified amount from the fund. The appropriate number of your shares would be redeemed to pay for this. Some funds provide this service for free; others charge $5 per withdrawal. The actual cost of this service and the others specified below are borne by the fund rather than by the managers.

3. Free Check Privileges

Some funds allow you to write checks on your account for free. However, the minimum amount of each check can be as high as $500. This is an important benefit because it permits you to earn tax-free interest on your checking account. Some funds will return the canceled checks, but others will only return checks that you specifically request.

4. Monthly Interest Income Payments and Automatic Reinvestment

Interest is computed daily and may be paid to you monthly by check. Alternatively, you can elect to have the interest reinvested instead of receiving payment. With long-term funds especially, the compounding of interest reinvested in the fund is a valuable service producing a compounded overall return. In addition, it reduces the need for immediate action on income earned in the fund.

5. Sweep Account

If this feature is selected, specific banks or brokers will automatically purchase shares of a fund when the balance in your bank or financial account reaches a certain level. If your account falls below a certain level, a specified dollar amount of your fund shares will be redeemed and the proceeds contributed to your bank or other account.

6. Record Keeping and Recording

The funds issue monthly statements about their progress. At the end of the year, the fund reports to you all income divided as follows: taxable, tax-exempt, and capital gain. Form 1099 is used to report income to shareholders and a copy of this form is filed with the Internal Revenue Service in January.

The funds maintain records on all bonds. The bonds are held by a custodian, which is usually a bank. An independent accountant

Evaluation of a Fund

periodically counts the bonds and performs an audit to verify the fund's accounts. The manager of the fund is responsible for overseeing the clipping of coupons on unregistered bonds and the orderly entry of interest from registered bonds.

7. Ease of Redemption

An important feature of a fund is the ability to obtain your money quickly. Some funds are very slow in processing requests, so you should ask how quickly requests for redemptions are usually honored.

Shares can usually be redeemed by telephone, wire, or letter. Processing can take from one to seven days. If shares are bought and redeemed within a week, it may take 15 days before a check is issued. The longer period is to make sure your initial check has cleared, and to discourage active trading of funds.

You should be aware that if the bond market is in chaos because of a major default or for some other reason, and the fund is having difficulty selling bonds to redeem all shares tendered, some funds specifically reserve the right to suspend redemptions or to distribute bonds from the fund's portfolio to you instead of cash. This has never happened, but it is included in some prospectuses as a protective measure.

8. Exchange Privileges Among a Family of Funds

In many funds you may transfer cash from one fund to another within a family of funds. Fund families usually include a short-term money market fund and a long-term fund, in addition to stock funds and various taxable and tax-free funds.

Many families do not permit active trading among the different funds to take advantage of changing interest rates. However, the exchange privilege would permit you to swap one fund for another for tax purposes and realize a loss on your tax return in appropriate cases. They can discourage frequent swapping by maintaining the right to suspend the privilege or limiting the number or frequency of swaps.

F. Analysis of Bond Fund Yields

There are two aspects in the evaluation of the yield of a bond fund:

The first is current return. Specifically, this is the amount of money earned annually by the fund per share divided by the price per share. We will refer to this percentage as the return from income. This return is equivalent to the income you would receive if you collected the coupon payments on a municipal bond. Such income is exempt from federal tax but not generally from state income tax unless the fund only holds bonds issued by your state of residence.

The second aspect is the realized and unrealized trading gains and losses of the fund. Realized gains and losses means the fund has actually sold a particular bond at more or less than it paid for it. Unrealized gains or losses result from the movement of interest rates, which is reflected in a bond's market price; however, since the bond has not been sold, the gain or loss is unrealized. This increase or decrease in a fund's market price per share, expressed as a percentage per year, is referred to here as the return from capital. The total return is the sum of the return from income and the return from capital. The realized gains and losses are subject to federal and state income taxes. The unrealized gains and losses are not reportable for tax purposes.

If you call a municipal bond fund, the logical question to ask is: "What is the fund yielding?" The person representing the fund will tell you the fund's current return, which is the estimated income of the fund divided by its current price, i.e. the return from income. For example, if the fund is selling at $10 a share, and it is estimated that $1 of income will be produced annually by the portfolio of bonds, the current yield of the fund will be 10%. However, the current return gives you only half the answer. In order to evaluate the total return of the fund, you must also take into account realized and unrealized gains and losses for the year, i.e. the return from capital. This is unknowable. Therefore, you cannot evaluate what total return you will receive on your investment in either a long-term fund or an intermediate-term fund. However, the yield on a money market municipal fund, which is indicated as the current yield, is the actual overall yield because the short-term securities are managed to maintain a net asset value of $1.00. Since long-term bond funds are more volatile than intermediate-term bond funds, the total return on the long-term funds will be harder to estimate.

Generally, long-term funds have current yields that are between one and two percentage points higher than intermediate-term funds. For the year ended August 30, 1986, intermediate-term funds paid out about 7.6% in current income, while long-term funds paid out about 8.2%. The long-term funds generally earn and pay out higher returns from income to reflect the greater risk of a substantial decline in the price of long-term bonds.

For each of the years 1980 to 1982, when interest rates were increasing and bond prices were falling, the long-term funds performed worse overall than the intermediate-term funds. This is an expected result because when interest rates are increasing and bond prices are falling, long-term bond prices are more volatile and thus decline more than intermediate-term bond prices. The reverse is also true. When interest rates are declining and bond prices are increasing, long-term bond prices will increase more than intermediate-term bond prices. Thus, in the year ended June 30, 1986, intermediate-term funds appreciated by about 13%, while long-term funds increased by about 15%.

An important observation is that for the years 1980 to 1982, years of rising interest rates, the total return for the intermediate-term funds was better than the total return for the long-term funds. However, as expected, in 1983 the total return on the long-term funds greatly exceeded the total return on the intermediate-term funds. Overall, for the years 1980 to 1983, the intermediate-term funds generally were a superior investment. Not only did they outperform the long-term funds, but the investors in the intermediate-term funds had less potential risk of a price decline.

Neither the long-term funds nor the intermediate-term funds in general performed well over the four-year period 1980 to 1983. Almost all of the high current returns from income were wiped out by the decline in the fund's price per share, even taking into account the big recovery in share prices for 1983!

G. Conclusions and Recommendations

In view of the foregoing, our recommendations regarding investments in municipal bond funds are as follows:

1. Long-Term Funds

An investment in a long-term bond fund should be viewed as an interest rate play. You are betting that interest rates will decline or remain the same. The current income earned from a long-term fund may be more than completely offset by a decline in the market value of the shares. This occurred in the years ended June 30, 1980, 1981, and 1982, when municipal bond yields were at an all time high. The funds had to divest their lower yielding bonds in a market of rising interest rates in order to increase the current return of the portfolio.

2. Intermediate-Term Funds

Intermediate-term funds are more stable than long-term funds and thus give a more predictable return. However, even the intermediate-term funds had most of their return from income eliminated because of the decline in price of the fund shares for the years ended June 30, 1980, 1981, and 1982.

In comparing intermediate-term funds to actually holding individually purchased intermediate-term bonds, the bonds present a much better investment. Although if you were to sell your bonds in the face of rising interest rates you would have a loss on the principal, if you held your bonds to maturity you would receive every dollar of principal back. In comparison, an intermediate-term bond fund keeps trading its bonds. As a consequence, there is no guarantee that the fund will regain principal lost in earlier years.

For example, if you were to buy a five-year bond at 100 in year one and in year two the bond declined to a price of 75 because of rising interest rates, you would still get back all 100 if you held the bond to year five. By comparison, if you held an intermediate-term bond fund for five years, there is no guarantee that the fund would recoup its losses in the later years.

The yield on the actual intermediate-term bonds is also higher than the yield on intermediate-term bond funds because there are no management fees or operating expenses when you hold the actual bonds yourself. Funds that turn over their portfolio every year incur substantial trading expenses without necessarily increasing the overall return to you.

3. Money-Market Funds

Money market municipal bond funds make sense in certain limited situations. First, they are a good place to park temporarily uninvested funds. Second, they are a good place to put your money if you think interest rates are going to rise because you will not lose any principal and the yield on your fund will tend to float upward. However, these funds are not good investments for the long run because the yields are usually quite low.

4. Overall Summary

In conclusion, other than the money market municipal funds and possibly the short-intermediate funds in certain circumstances, the funds are not a good investment. They are a worse investment vehicle than either owning the individual bonds or owning a municipal bond trust. The major advantages of the funds are the ease with which you can trade in and out, and the good price that you will generally receive on a sale of your shares. If you intend to do a lot of in-and-out trading of municipal bonds, no-load funds should be seriously considered because you will not have to pay a fee when you buy or sell no-load fund shares.

H. A Sampling of Issuers of Intermediate Funds

The following sponsors sell money market and long-term funds. Those funds with an asterisk before their name also sell intermediate funds. We have defined an intermediate-term fund as one that has a maturity of three to 10 years. Babson calls its intermediate-term fund short-term, Vanguard, Calvert, Fidelity and Merrill Lynch call intermediate-term funds limited-term, or limited maturity.

Babson Tax Free Income Fund
3 Crown Center
2440 Pershing Road
Kansas City, Missouri 64108
(800)821–5591/(816)471–5200

*Calvert Tax Free Reserves
1700 Pennsylvania Avenue
Washington, D.C. 20006
(800)368–2748/(202)951–4820

Dreyfus Corp.
600 Madison Avenue
New York, New York 10022
(800)223–5525/(212)715–6000

*Fidelity Mgt. Group
82 Devonshire Street
Boston, Mass. 02108
(800)554–6666/(617)523–1919

IDS (Investors Diversified
  Services)
Box 369, IDS Tower
Minneapolis, Mn. 55440
(800)IDS-IDEA/(800)437–4332

Lexington Management
  Corporation
Box 1515, 580 Sylvan Avenue
Englewood Cliffs, N.J. 07632
(800)526–0056/(800)932–0838(N.J.)

*Merrill Lynch, Pierce, Fenner
  & Smith, Inc.
165 Broadway
New York, New York 10080
(212)637–7455

Midwest Advisory Services
522 Dixie Terminal Bldg.
Cincinnati, Ohio 45202
(800)543–0407/(513)579–0414

T. Rowe Price Associates,
  Inc.
100 E. Pratt Street
Baltimore, Md. 21202
(800)638–5660

Scudder, Stevens & Clark,
  Investment Counsel
175 Federal Street
Boston, Mass. 02110
(800)225–2470/(617)426–8300
(MASS only)

*Vanguard Group
Drummer's Lane
Valley Forge, Pa. 19482
(800)523-7025/(800)362-0530
(PA only)

Notes

Chapter V

[1]David Zigas, "Regulations Begin to Scrutinize Municipal Futures Proposal After Mostly Positive Comments," *Credit Markets,* Vol. 1, No. 8, (April 20, 1984), p.1.

CHAPTER VI

Evaluation and Credit Analysis Of General Obligation and Revenue Bonds

A. General Obligation Bonds
    1. Description of General Obligation Bonds
    2. Evaluating General Obligation Bonds
B. Revenue Bonds
    1. Description of Revenue Bonds
    2. Strengths and Weaknesses of Revenue Bonds
    3. Types of Revenue Bonds
        a. Housing Bonds
        b. Hospital Bonds
        c. Water and Sewer Bonds
        d. Electric Utility Public Power Bonds
        e. Student Loan Bonds
        f. College and University Bonds
        g. Industrial Development Bonds
        h. Pollution Control Bonds
        i. Tax Allocation Bonds

A. General Obligation Bonds

1. Description of General Obligation Bonds

Having decided to invest in municipal bonds, the logical first choice to consider is a general obligation bond, generally called a G.O. These bonds are backed by the full faith and credit and all the financial resources of the issuing state, county, or municipality, unless specifically limited by law. Thus, real estate taxes and other taxes theoretically could be levied without limitation in order to pay bond interest and principal.

In 1970, G.O. bonds accounted for 75% of all municipal bonds issued, but only 40% in 1982. The reason for this decline is found in the tax-revolt laws that have been passed recently, such as California's Proposition 13. These laws limit spending, demand balanced budgets, and prevent the raising of taxes. However, there are still many G.O.'s being issued today, and previously issued G.O.'s are also available to you.

The 1986 tax bill will further reduce the issuance of G.O. and revenue bonds. Formerly, a bond was considered tax-exempt if 25% or less of the proceeds benefited a private entity. The new law would limit private use to 10% of the proceeds, thereby restricting the uses to which borrowed money could be applied.

2. Evaluating General Obligation Bonds

The strength of a G.O. bond depends upon the financial health and economic potential of the taxing power of the state or municipality that issued it. Analysts evaluating a G.O. bond seek to determine the financial strength of the issuer by exploring its economic and administrative nature. Their analysis seeks to determine trends in employment; the growth of population, wealth, and local industry; and the vulnerability of public employees' pension funds.

G.O. bonds are not of equal quality because municipalities are not equally well managed or financially endowed. Limitations on taxation in certain municipalities place their promises of full faith and credit at lesser value than others. States have the most diversified revenue sources, including personal income taxes, corporate and business taxes, property taxes, sales taxes, user fees, death and gift taxes, severance taxes, and federal grants-in-aid. Importantly, state legislators have the ability to broaden the tax base by writing new laws. Local governments, including counties, municipalities, and school districts, rely mainly on property taxes unless the state government granted a broadened tax base, which might include sales and income taxes.

Inflation has swelled municipal coffers through increases in tax revenues. These taxes include individual and corporate taxes, sales and gross receipt taxes, and motor vehicle taxes. The higher income has resulted in improved credit ratings. State and federal grants supplement property taxes, and in poor municipalities with eroded property bases, the aid monies have become the primary revenue source.

Issuers use various techniques to improve the credit ratings of their G.O. bonds, all of which are taken into consideration by the rating agencies. For example, Wisconsin has waived its right to immunity from suits from bondholders to show good faith. Other G.O. bonds have double protection in that they are secured by both the credit of the issuer and also by the credit of a particular agency. For example, Illinois issued G.O. Transportation Series A bonds, which are secured and paid from the gasoline taxes of the state's transportation fund and also secured by the resources of the state. These are called double-barreled bonds because they have two sources of security. These and other concessions by a state are reflected in the ratings given to the bonds.

Specific factors that tend to reduce the attractiveness of a G.O. issue and create uncertainty regarding the creditworthiness of a long-term bond include:

a. Limitations placed on the tax rate that can be levied on real

Evaluation of General Obligation and Revenue Bonds

estate, such as California's Proposition 13 and Massachusett's Proposition 2½, which substantially reduced the amount of real estate taxes that these states may collect. Because real estate taxes are a major source of revenue for most issuers, these restrictions reduce a state's creditworthiness.

b. Fluctuations in funds provided by states and the federal government can have destabilizing effects on municipal budgets. The total of grants, subsidies, matching grants, cost-sharing programs, and revenue-sharing programs is not guaranteed over the entire life of 20-, 30-, or 40-year bonds issued by a municipality. Federal programs often provide only start-up costs or a portion of capital costs.

c. Funds from revenue authorities used to supplement general funds have been reduced. Declining profitability of revenue authorities, such as electric utilities, and increased protection for revenue bond holders have also reduced the flow of income into general funds.

d. Dependence on a single industry or crop increases the vulnerability of a tax base. If the industry becomes depressed or the crop fails, it becomes more difficult for the municipality to pay its debts. Michigan is a prime example of a state that suffered from the decline of heavy industry.

e. The strength of local banks is significant. If the local bank fails, the municipality could be unable to obtain money to meet its obligations. Many defaults occurred during the Depression because local banks failed due to the general economic malaise.

f. The characters of municipal officials play a role in the desirability of the bonds. Most officials perform their duties without attracting criticism. However, in instances where dishonesty is an issue, it is wise to evaluate the bonds of a municipality carefully. While it does not mean the municipality will default, a scandal will temporarily depress the market.

g. The debt trend is an indicator of trouble. If a municipality's debt has been increasing in relation to its tax base for a number of years, it may be an indication that the future financial stability of the municipality is shaky. Indications of possible problems include increases in the amount of debt, the requirement of paying off sizable issues in one year, and increases in the amount of the annual interest payment.

B. Revenue Bonds

1. Description of Revenue Bonds

Revenue bonds are supported by the revenue generated by a particular bond issuer. Revenue bonds are issued in support of housing, hospitals, water and sewer projects, electric utilities, student loans, and college and university development. Prior to the Tax Reform Act of 1986, some private corporate projects, including industrial development and pollution control projects, were financed with tax-exempt revenue bonds. The municipality under whose auspices revenue bonds were issued generally had no legal responsibility for them. Unlike G.O. bonds, a public referendum is not required for the approval of Revenue Bonds. The principal and interest payments are paid by the issuer in large part from fees paid by the users of the project being financed. User fees have a variety of names, but they can be grouped into two major categories: fees for usage and lease-back fees.

Fees for usage support water, sewer, and electric revenue bonds. Highway and bridges raise funds through tolls and concessions. A toll is a fee for usage and a concession is a fee for access. For example, a restaurant might pay an access fee for permission to open along a highway. Docks and airports charge fees to shipping companies and airlines for the use of space. Housing bonds are supported by mortgages, a fee for use of money, by rents, and by payments for use of living space. Student loan bonds are paid by interest on the loan, again a fee for use of money. College and university bonds are funded by fees paid by students, rents from university housing, entertainment charges to the general public, and contract fees for special research. Utility bond user fees are secured by one of three different bonds or contracts. Customers sign contracts that are either *take or pay,* in which the purchaser agrees to pay only for power made available; *take or pay, hell or high water* in which the purchasers must pay even if no power is received; or *take and pay*, in which the purchaser pays only for the supply that is used. Though *take or pay, hell or high water* contracts may appear to be very secure, they are still being tested in the courts. In the State of Washington they were overturned on the basis that many of the participants did not have legal authority

Evaluation of General Obligation and Revenue Bonds

to enter into the contracts. However, the legality of those contracts has been upheld in Massachusetts in the case of the Massachusetts Municipal Wholesale Electric Co. See Part II, Chapter XV.

Lease-back arrangements occur when a facility is built for a hospital, school, or industrial development project. The municipality or its agency issue bonds to build the facility, which is then leased to the issuer. The rent paid is sufficient to pay off the bonds. When the bonds have been paid off, the corporation is usually granted the right to purchase the facility for a nominal sum. The lease-back arrangement is frequently used for hospitals and industrial development bonds.

2. Strengths and Weaknesses of Revenue Bonds

Revenue bonds present attractive investment possibilities for you. However, there are certain factors about which you should be aware because they increase the amount of risk. These are as follows:

a. Start-up situation funding tends to be riskier than funding for improvements on existing structures. Most instances of default have occurred when the users who were going to pay for the services never materialized, or where cost overruns for new systems resulted in the projects being canceled.

b. Cost overruns on construction projects, such as nuclear power plants, which are to be funded by rate increases may meet consumer resistance. Industrial users of the services may relocate if they can.

c. Individual consumers may resist rate increases resulting from construction that primarily helps industrial users of services, but results in raising the residents' costs or vice versa.

d. Issues backed by a single line of credit, even if it is strong, are considered more at risk than bonds with diversified debtors based upon large geographic support and a number of users. A group of hospitals or a number of municipalities floating bonds, for example, is viewed as more secure than one strong hospital or municipality. The theory is that a weak link in a chain can be mended.

e. Revenue bonds are classified as having a first or second lien on revenues. First-lien bonds must be paid before the second-lien bonds, making the former a more desirable investment.

f. Guarantees do not constitute a 100% assurance that bonds will be honored in the event of default. Despite its confidence-building name, a guarantee can be fraught with loopholes. You must inquire specifically about what is being guaranteed and think about what the guarantee does not cover. It is comparable to your own insurance policies, which often cover everything, *but* the one thing you need them for.

g. An open-ended covenant for bonds, where an unlimited number of bonds can be issued and the number of participants for a particular line of credit is unlimited, is viewed as more risky than one that limits expansion (closed-ended covenant). It is considered better to buy a known quantity than an open-ended variable one.

h. Any limit on profit or income of the bond issuer, such as tax ceilings or limits on hospital profits, indicates greater risk and should be accompanied by a higher yield.

i. Finally, the most important point. It must be clear that the issuer can generate enough revenue to pay the bonds' interest and principal as it comes due. Vague statements should be taken as a warning sign that there might be a problem in the future. You can specifically ask the seller of the bonds what the debt-service ratio is. Debt service is the amount required to pay the interest on the debt. To be minimally adequate, available revenues must suffice to pay debt requirements at least 1 ½ times, to allow for fluctuations in revenues. Thus, if the total highest debt service is $100,000 per year, the amount of money available to repay the debt service should be $150,000 per year. The higher-rated bonds will provide more coverage than that over the life of the bond, offering you better protection against unforeseen circumstances.

3. Types of Revenue Bonds

Having outlined the general risks for revenue bonds, it will be useful to examine the strengths and weaknesses of each kind of revenue bond.

All municipal bonds which were issued prior to August 8, 1986, will continue to be tax exempt despite the provisions of the Tax Reform Act of 1986, which restricts or eliminates the issuance of certain municipal bonds thereafter. Although certain revenue bonds issued after August 8, 1986, will be tax exempt under the regular federal income tax, they may be subject to the alternative minimum tax. See Part II, Chapter XIII.

a. Housing Bonds

The federal and local governments have issued bonds to support housing construction as a result of the shrinkage of rental properties and the increase in the number of new households created each year. A major consideration in evaluating housing bonds is whether they are insured. Federally insured housing bonds are rated AA or AAA if they are fully covered. Uninsured housing bonds are generally in the A or BBB category. Examples of insured housing bonds are those that are FHA insured, Veterans Administration (VA) guaranteed, or privately insured mortgages.

Moral obligation housing bonds, debt for which a state has made a moral commitment to support, are generally rated one category below that state's G.O. debt. A moral obligation commitment evidences the state's intention to appropriate money for restoring the debt service or capital reserve to its minimum requirement. There is substantial uncertainly about a state's actual responsibility for those bonds because they do not require voter approval and circumvent debt limits. However, state governments in various instances have respected their moral obligations when the issuing agency was unable to satisfy its financial obligations. The Urban Development Corporation case in New York is one example. In April 1968, the New York State Urban Development Corporation was established by the state legislature primarily to construct subsidized housing and other projects in urban renewal areas. On February 25, 1974, only seven years later, the UDC defaulted on $100 million of bond anticipation notes. Unable to refinance its debt, the UDC was faced with a potential default on $7.1 billion of outstanding bonds. UDC bondholder notes had received the moral obligation pledge, and New York State did make good on the defaulted notes. Making the payments indicated that the state was ready and able to accept this obligation though these bonds lacked the voter approval of general obligation bonds. Other states have exhibited a similar willingness to support moral obligation issues.

There are four kinds of municipal housing revenue bonds. Each has a different purpose and special security provisions. All are managed through state and local housing finance agencies. Bonds are sold by the agencies to finance the following programs:

(1) State housing agencies float bonds for builders of multiunit apartment buildings for the elderly. Some of these have federal

insurance and are very creditworthy. The others are difficult to evaluate.

(2) State housing finance agencies sell bonds to secure funds for the purchase of mostly single-family home mortgages from banking institutions. The bonds are backed by the mortgage revenue and a variety of insurance policies. These bonds are subject to the extraordinary mandatory call provisions described in Part II, Chapter I. This form of financing represented 32% of all long-term municipal bond financings and more than two-thirds of all housing bonds issued in 1980.

(3) Local housing authority bonds, issued by a local housing authority, support the development of multiunit apartment buildings and are secured by a *comprehensive rent subsidy package*. These bonds are sometimes *misrepresented* as if they were insured by the U.S. government. This is not so! The full faith and credit of the Federal Department of Housing & Urban Development (HUD) is only behind the *rent subsidy* and HUD reserves the right to terminate the subsidy if there are extended periods of vacancy or the projects do not meet its specifications.

(4) A state housing or mortgage finance agency can issue bonds to provide loans to lending institutions. The bonds are secured by mortgages or securities that represent 15% of value of the loan. The lending institutions may also secure the loans with irrevocable letters of credit or with certificates of deposit (CD's) from banks. If there is ever a default on a loan, the trustee need only liquidate the portfolio to pay for the bond principal and interest.

The Tax Reform Act of 1986 restricted but did not eliminate the amount of single-family mortgage bonds and multifamily housing bonds that can be issued after August 8, 1986.

b. Hospital Bonds

The market for tax-exempt hospital bonds is a development of the last decade or two. Bonds were issued to build new hospitals, expand existing ones, and finance ongoing operating costs. Hospital bonds are secured by the payments for services rendered. Though sometimes the land and buildings are offered for collateral, this is not of great value because it would be politically unthinkable to foreclose. Once again, public purposes take precedent over bondholders.

Evaluation of General Obligation and Revenue Bonds 119

Due to third-party payments from Medicare, Medicaid, Blue Cross and other insurers, funding for patient care has become more secure, although it cannot be assumed that all insurance plans funding hospital financing are equal. With prospective cutbacks in Medicare and Medicaid payments in 1985, subsequent flows of income will be more vulnerable.

Bond analysts tend to prefer bonds supported by teaching hospitals due to their endowments, advanced technology, and breadth of area served. The analysts prefer hospitals funded by third-party payors, other than Medicare and Medicaid, and hospitals that are remodelling rather than building new facilities. They favor merged chains of hospitals and health maintenance organizations (HMO's), which are also large organizations providing a broad range of services.

Hospital revenue bonds are usually in the A classes (A, A+ or A–) although a small percentage of hospital bonds are rated AA. Hospital bonds are viewed as less secure than similarly rated G.O. bonds or water and sewer revenue bonds. The market for hospital bonds has fewer purchasers because the sources of funding are less secure and difficult to predict. Hospital revenue is based on hospital utilization, which is based on patients' and doctors' decisions on which hospital to use. The threat of government controls on health care prices since the mid-1970s has pushed the yield on hospital bonds about 20% higher than general obligation bonds. Any indication of a possible cap on income is a substantial negative factor to be considered.

There have been only two major defaults on hospital bonds. Both of these were start-up projects in areas where the projected population never materialized. (See Part II, Chapter VIII.)

c. Water and Sewer Bonds

Water and sewer bonds are generally thought to be among the safest municipal investments because water and sewer services are absolutely necessary and distribution monopolies are granted to water and sewer companies. However, there is a wide range in the ratings of these bonds.

As with other types of bonds, start-up situations tend to be riskier than bonds floated for the repair of an established system. A new sewer system might be constructed in anticipation of population development that never materializes, or the existing population may prefer to use wells and septic tanks instead of connecting with the new system. In addition, there are the usual problems of cost overruns and construction delays. Certain localities have made it impossible to discontinue service even in the event of nonpayment of utility bills, increasing their default potential.

Problems might also arise if bonds of an existing system are purchased. If it is an antiquated system, more money than initially projected might be required to repair it. Cutbacks in federal grants-in-aid place additional stress on providers grown accustomed to the added federal financial cushion. Though the Clear Water Act of 1970 projected a $90 billion contribution to local waste treatment programs, under President Reagan federal aid has been scaled down to a projected $36 billion. Since October 1, 1984, federal contributions to local sewage construction will also have declined.

Another major consideration is the cost of meeting government pollution-control laws. These mandated installations can substantially raise rates, incurring resistance on the part of residential and industrial consumers. Industries may choose to leave a district rather than pay the additional costs.

Water and sewer bonds tend to sell at slightly higher yields than similarly rated revenue issues because they lack the liquidity of larger and more substantial securities.

The Tax Reform Act of 1986 restricted but did not eliminate the amount of water and sewer bonds that can be issued after August 8, 1986. However, no new limits were placed on government-owned solid waste disposal facilities.

d. Electric Utility Public Power Bonds

Public power bonds were initially floated to subsidize electrification of underdeveloped rural areas of our country. Until 1978, the market for electric revenue bonds was dominated by five well-known and respected entities. Currently, however, there are many diverse issues and types of joint venture projects, complicating the analysts' evaluation of public power bonds.

There are four kinds of utilities: small utilities with their own plants, distribution utilities that purchase power from a generator, large wholesale generators of electricity that sell power to distributors, and combination systems that generate some of their own power.

Massive wholesale utilities generating bulk power tend to be financially stable because they have many customers and distribution systems must pay the wholesalers' charges before they can pay their own debt service because the charges are an operating expense of the wholesaler. Pure distribution systems are less secure. Some municipal systems own their generators, transmission, and distribution systems. These fully owned utility systems have high credit ratings.

Other municipalities join together to issue bonds backed by power supply contracts with each of the participating municipalities. There are approximately 51 agencies established, though not all have issued bonds. The first agency to sell bonds was the ill-fated Washington Public Power Supply System. The supposed strength of the joint-action programs is that if there is a default by one member, the other members will have the ability to absorb the costs. Its power contract is then resold—hopefully. Joint ownership has greatly increased the creditworthiness of bonds in the past because of the recognized names of the issuers; however, the security of the binding take or pay, hell or high water contracts has come under scrutiny. (See Part II, Chapter XV).

The Tax Reform Act of 1986 restricted but did not eliminate the amount of electric utility public power bonds that can be issued after August 8, 1986.

e. Student Loan Bonds

Student loan bonds represent the smallest volume share of revenue bond issues, consisting of 1.8% of all bonds issued in 1982 according to *The Bond Buyer*. They are generally not well received in the investment community due to the negative publicity surrounding the high rates of default on student loans. As a result, they sell at higher yields than comparably rated municipal bonds and have lower resale liquidity. There are three kinds of student loans:

(1) Federal aid is provided to colleges for loans to particularly needy students. There has been a high rate of default among these loans, giving a poor reputation to student loans in general. Municipal bonds do not back this sort of program.

(2) The federal government insures municipal bonds for stu-

dent loans made by private or public agency lenders. These loans are available only in the limited number of states where a state loan guarantee agency does not exist. They are virtually riskless because they are directly insured by the federal government for both interest and principal.

(3) The most common form of security for student loan revenue bonds is in the form of a guarantee by a state guarantee agency, which generally pays 100% of principal and accrued interest in the event of default. These bonds are reinsured by the federal government for less than the full amount. As a result, you must take into account the ability of the guarantee agency to meet its obligations by considering the default rate, the strength of the guarantee reserve fund, and other financial factors. Unless you have the time and energy to evaluate a given offering, these bonds are difficult to judge.

The Tax Reform Act of 1986 restricted but did not eliminate the amount of student loan bonds that can be issued after August 8, 1986.

f. College and University Bonds

The security for these bonds is based upon a variety of income sources. They include government grants and private endowments, revenue from rents from student housing, private and federal research contracts, and entertainment such as sporting events and theater productions. The bonds that receive the highest ratings are those of the larger well-known institutions, which are more professionally administered, better endowed, and more financially secure than the smaller, less influential schools.

g. Industrial Development Bonds

Industrial development bonds (IDB's) and pollution control bonds are really corporate bonds with a tax exemption. Industry qualifies for the tax exemption by purporting to serve some public purpose, for instance, by locating projects in an economically depressed area. Other industrial development bonds have been floated for the following qualifying purposes: ports and docks, sports facilities, manufacturing plants and distribution systems, warehouses, motels, and convention centers.

Industrial development bonds generally pay tax-free interest of at least two percentage points (200 basis points) less than a corporation's interest rate on taxable bonds. In 1979, the coupon on an IDB was 3½ percentage points (350 basis points) less than the taxable interest on corporate bonds.

IDB's tend to have a 25-to-30 year life, which is generally a longer maturity than other bonds. They are also issued as serial bonds. A special feature of most IDB's is the special mandatory call, which usually provides that if the IDB's lose their tax exemption and the bonds become taxable, then the corporation must immediately redeem the bonds at par.

The validity of purpose for which some of the IDB's have been issued has been questioned. For example, McDonald's Corporation opened 52 outlets in Pennsylvania and Ohio in 1979 with IDB financing, according to *Moody's Bond Record*. In many states, the widespread use of IDB's for auto dealerships, golf courses, fast food chains, racquet ball clubs, shopping centers, office and medical buildings, country clubs, and others has led to a discussion of the propriety of tax exemptions for such purposes. Those who support the use of public funds through tax exemption point to the stimulus new businesses give to a region. Congress, however, in the Tax Equity and Fiscal Responsibility Act of 1982 (TEFRA) and the Tax Reform Act of 1984 has restricted the issuance of IDB's. For example the small-issue exemption ($1 million or less) for bonds issued after December 31, 1982, has been eliminated if their use was for automobile sales or service, or for recreation and/or entertainment. More importantly, TEFRA required that IDB issues be approved by an elected official or legislator following a public hearing before issuance. The object is to limit IDB use to projects endorsed by the community. The Tax Reform Act of 1986 ends or restricts many IDBs. In this Act, IDBs are defined as such if 10% or more of the proceeds are used by private entities.

h. Pollution Control Bonds

The Clean Air Act of 1970 and the Water and Pollution Control legislation of 1972 mandated that governments and businesses install pollution control devices to improve the quality of the air and water. To finance those improvements, pollution control bonds were sold. Like the IDB's, the ratings of these bonds are based on the creditworthiness of the issuing companies. All pollution control bonds issued after the effective dates in the Tax Reform Act of 1986 are subject to tax.

i. Tax Allocation Bonds

As a result of limitations placed on state and local governments to raise taxes, tax allocation bonds were devised as a means of allocating the costs of development to the areas directly being assisted. In many states, tax allocation bonds are supported with back-up security of the issuing municipality's general obligation tax pledge. In those instances, the rating given the bonds is based upon the ultimate security of that pledge. Where the pledge is lacking, the bonds must be evaluated on the ability of improvements to generate additional property taxes, which are then pledged to pay for debt service on the tax allocation bonds.

Many states issue tax allocation bonds, including California, Iowa, Minnesota and Oregon. California has had the longest history of issuing such bonds. They have become widely used since the passing of Proposition 13.

No tax allocation bonds are rated higher than A because the redevelopment agencies that issue them have no ability to set tax rates or to control tax reform legislation that may affect the revenue stream securing the bonds. In California, the passing of Proposition 13 rolled back tax rates to 1% of full market value and assessed values to 1976 levels, substantially reducing the incremental property tax revenues supporting the tax allocation bonds. Areas with substantial manufacturing or retail land use paid less taxes as a result of a change in California's property tax law exempting business investory from taxation.

Other considerations include whether the bonds are senior lien bonds with first call on the tax increments or if there are other claims on the revenues with priority. Are there any other disbursements from the incremental taxes that would reduce the flow of funds, such as California's state law requiring 20% to be set aside for low- and moderate-income housing? Are there escrow accounts established to help insure a flow of funds for bond payment? Are the businesses in the redevelopment area financially sound so they can be expected to pay their taxes? Ultimately the question is, can the blighted area under redevelopment thrive with the input of additional funds due to its unique configuration? The value of the bonds rests on the ability of the area to thrive.

notes

[1] The most comprehensive easily available source on this subject is by Robert Lamb and Stephen P. Rappaport, *Municipal Bonds: The Comprehensive Review of Tax Exempt Securities & Public Finance*. New York: McGraw Hill Book Company, 1980.

CHAPTER VII

The Rating Agencies and Methods Used to Improve Ratings

A. The Rating Agencies—General Information
   1. Beginning of the Rating Agencies
   2. Methods Used to Establish Ratings
   3. Duplicating the Ratings
   4. A Guide to the Ratings
   5. Comparison of the Rating Systems
   6. Unrated Bonds
   7. Limitations of the Ratings
B. Methods Used by Issuers to Improve their Ratings
   1. Methods Employed by States
      a. Providing Organizational Support—Pooling Borrowing Needs
      b. State Guarantees of Municipal Bond Issues
   2. Federal Guarantees for Municipal Bonds
   3. Private Bond Insurance
      a. Insurance Companies
      b. Insurance of Municipal Bonds by Banks: Letters of Credit

A. The Rating Agencies—General Information

1. Beginning of the Rating Agencies

Moody's Investors Service began rating corporate bonds in 1909 and municipal bonds in 1919. It dominated the rating field until 1950 when Standard & Poor's entered the arena. In the beginning, both companies sold financial manuals containing ratings to investors and dealers, and they did not charge the issuers. There was an unfounded fear that charging the issuers would put the rating companies out of business.

In 1968, Standard & Poor's requested payment from issuers for its service. Moody's followed suit in May of 1970. The two largest agencies generally agree on ratings; variance between their ratings is usually no more than one grade. For example, an issue might get a Baa rating from Moody's and an A rating from Standard & Poor's.

2. Methods Used to Establish Ratings

After a rating agency agrees to rate an issuer, information is requested including all pertinent material, legal documents, the prospectus, and financial reports. Legal opinions from the bond counsel are reviewed. If the issuer has been rated before, the files are updated. After the analysts and rating committee agree upon a rating, the issuer is notified and the ratings are listed in *The Bond Buyer* and other periodicals. Questionnaires are sent requesting updated information from the issuer on an annual basis, and credit reviews are generally conducted every two years. Ratings may be withdrawn by the rating agencies if sufficient current information to monitor credit standing is not available.

The objective of the rating agencies is to keep all information in computer banks, inputting updated information. The computers compute significant ratios and flag major changes for the analysts' attention assisting them in deciding if a new credit review is advisable.

Issuers are supposed to keep the rating agencies apprised of changes, and their underwriters make presentations to the agencies on their behalf. There is also a review process whereby an issuer can request an opportunity to present changes in its economic circumstances. Since the rating categories are broad, there must be a significant shift in the credit position of the issuer to warrant change.

One way to move swiftly into a top rating category is to play a game called "rent-a-rating."[1] The game is won when an issuer of low-grade paper buys credit enhancement from a commercial guarantor that guarantees timely payment of principal and interest. The rating agencies place greater weight on the quality of the guarantor than on the underlying rating of the issuer. This is partly the result of the flood of municipal bonds that came to market in 1985 and the value the rating agencies decided to place upon the insurance. In 1985, over half of the 4,519 rated municipal issues that came to market had credit enhancements. The marketplace places different values on the offerings depending upon their evaluation of the underlying ratings of the issuer.

3. Duplicating the Ratings

There have been many efforts to reproduce the ratings that are given to bond issues. Analysis includes consideration of major debt, revenue, wealth, and size. Based primarily upon these factors, ratings were predicted accurately only 50% to 70% of the time, mainly because ratings include the subjective evaluation of the analysts. The ratings are part judgment and part factual analysis.

4. A Guide to the Ratings[2]

The ratings have certain limitations that should be kept in mind. First, no two bonds will be of exactly the same quality even if they have the same rating. The ratings cannot reflect fine shadings of risk. Second, ratings do not indicate the future market performance of bonds. Investors must consider factors such as changes in interest rates and economic trends that were not considered in the evaluation of the investment quality of a particular issue. Market performance for type of issue, particular maturity, or geographic locality may also affect price. These limitations tend to be overlooked in the process of purchasing a bond, but they cannot be emphasized too strongly.

It should be noted that Moody's rates short-term notes and Standard & Poor's does not, though they both rate commercial paper. Short-term notes represented $21 billion in new financing in 1980 and have expanded since then because of the development of municipal bond money market funds. Standard & Poor's reason for not rating short-term notes is that these notes have weaknesses that are not predictable. Bond anticipation notes, for example, are repaid only if the debtor can issue bonds to repay the notes. The issuance of new bonds can be a problem in a tight credit market. The large defaults of New York City and the New York Urban Development Corporation were both in short term notes that were unrated by Standard & Poor's.

An investment grade is a designation given by a national rating service if it includes a bond in one of its top categories. These include the ratings of AAA to BBB by Standard & Poor's, and Aaa to Baa by Moody's. Investment grade includes obligations which are eligible for investment by various institutions, such as banks, insurance companies, and savings and loan associations. Triple-A bonds are considered "solid as a rock" for the long-term. The future as perceived through the bond analysts' crystal ball clouds as the ratings decline. Triple-B ratings are considered adequate security, though the issuer is more subject to the vagaries of misfortune. Single- and double-B rated bonds are considered speculative by both Moody's and Standard & Poor's, while C ratings flash danger of default signs. Standard & Poor's D rating indicates the bond is in default. Standard & Poor's and Moody's both have provisional (PR) or conditional (CON) ratings assigned to a project that is under construction and does not have the anticipated cash flow. An NR or non-rating by Standard & Poor's indicates that there is insufficient information on which to base a rating or that the rating company does not rate that particular kind of bond.

Within a particular category, Standard & Poor's uses the plus (+) or minus (−) to show relative standing within the major municipal rating categories. Moody's uses numbers to indicate strength in a particular category.

Reproduced below is an abbreviated version of Standard & Poor's Municipal Bond Ratings. Though Moody's Investor's Service uses different terminology, the description of the ratings are quite similar.

Key to Standard & Poor's Municipal Ratings:

AAA . . . The highest rating. Capacity to pay interest and repay principal is extremely strong.

AA . . . Very strong capacity to pay interest and repay principal; differs from the highest-rated issues only to a small degree.

A . . . Strong capacity to pay interest and repay principal, although they are somewhat more susceptible to the adverse effects of changes in circumstances and economic conditions than bonds in higher-rated categories.

BBB . . . Adequate capacity to pay interest and repay principal. Adverse economic conditions or changing circumstances are more likely to lead to a weakened capacity.

BB . . . Lowest degree of speculation: Risk exposure.

B . . . Speculative: Risk exposure.

CCC . . . Speculative: Major risk exposure.

CC . . . Highest degree of speculation: Major risk exposure.

C . . .   No interest is being paid.

D . . .   In default, and payment of interest and/or repayment of principal is in arrears.

Plus (+) or Minus (−) shows relative standing with the major rating categories.

PR . . .   Provisional ratings: Assumes the successful completion of the project being financed and indicates that payment of debt service requirements is largely or entirely dependent upon the successful and timely completion of the project. If the project is not completed, risk of default is unclear.

NR . . .   No rating has been requested, there is insufficient information on which to base a rating, or that Standard & Poor's does not rate a particular type of obligation as a matter of policy.

Short-term notes and commercial paper are rated by Moody's. Factors affecting the liquidity of the borrower or the ability to renew loans are uppermost in importance in short-term borrowing. The designation MIG is used for notes, though occasionally commercial paper receives a similar designation.

You should bear in mind that the security behind a note is not the same as the credit backing of a bond. There is a qualitative difference between the rating of a bond and a note even if they are both rated the best quality in their respective category. A high-quality short-term rating, particularly where support is present, does not necessarily reflect long-term factors. All note issues are unique and are rated on the basis of their individual credit characteristics.

Moody's has a separate rating scale for short-term notes. Short-term notes represented $21 billion in new financings in 1980 and have expanded since then because of the development of municipal money market funds. The funds purchase short-term municipal securities such as construction loan notes, bond anticipation notes, tax-exempt commercial paper and short-term municipal bonds with an average maturity of 150 days or less.

Key to Moody's Short-Term Loan Ratings

MIG 1 . . . Best quality, enjoying strong protection.

MIG 2 . . . Of high quality, with ample margins of protection.

MIG 3 . . . Of favorable quality, with all security elements accounted. Market access for refinancing, in particular, is likely to be less well established.

MIG 4 . . . Of adequate quality, carrying specific risk but having protection; not distinctly speculative.

The MIG rating system included all short-term paper until February 5, 1985, when Moody's assigned a special rating to its short-term variable rate demand obligations (VRDOs). The short-term rating assigned to the demand feature of VRDOs was designated as VMIG (pronounced VEE MIG). The new VMIG symbol distinguishes between variable-rate and traditional short-term paper. The two primary factors indicated by the VRDOs rating are payment upon periodic demand rather than fixed or scheduled maturity dates, and the degree of reliance on external liquidity.

Both Moody's and Standard & Poor's rate commercial paper and unsecured promissory notes issued by large municipal agencies with working capital needs. Municipal notes are payable from anticipated taxes, bond sales or revenue receipts. An issuer will float tax-exempt commercial paper when difficulties are ecounted in issuing longer maturity notes or bonds. Commercial paper is used to obtain working capital while awaiting a propitious time to market long-term bonds, or to take advantage of lower interest rates on short-term borrowing. Maturities for municipal commercial paper usually range from seven to 70 days and are repaid from revenues, refinanced with long-term debt or just rolled over. Commercial paper may be secured with a letter of credit that may irrevocably obligate a bank to pay interest and/or principal, or may limit the bank's obligation to a specific time frame or circumstance.

Key to Moody's Municipal Commercial Paper Rating

Prime 1 (P-1) . . . Superior capacity for repayment.
Prime 2 (P-2) . . . Strong capacity for repayment.
Prime 3 (P-3) . . . Acceptable capacity for repayment.

Commercial paper is short-term unsecured discount obligations and is often issued in lots of $40 million or more. The first issue of tax-exempt commercial paper was the Virginia Electric & Power Company's pollution control offering of December 1972. One of the largest issues to date is the Salt River Project Agricultural Improvement and Power District in Arizona which offered a large $225 million package through Goldman Sachs & Co. Issued in 1981, the initial paper had an average life of 38 days and rates ranging from 3 1/8% to 3 5/8%. Established municipal bond funds and municipal money market funds acquired this commercial paper for their portfolios. Some states, such as Arizona, require enabling legislation before the issuance of commercial paper, while in other states there are no restrictions.

Key to Standard & Poor's Municipal Commercial Paper Ratings

A-1 + ... Overwhelming degree of safety.
A-1   . . . . Very strong degree of safety.
A-2   . . . . Strong degree of safety.
A-3   . . . . Satisfactory degree of safety.
B   . . . . Only adequate degree of safety.
C   . . . . Doubtful degree of safety.
D   . . . . Defaulted.

5. Comparison of the Rating Systems

In a comparative study of Moody's and Standard & Poor's, which cross tabulated ratings on 137 cities,[3] it was found that the two firms' ratings agreed 70% of the time. In the 41 cases in which the ratings differed, Moody's was higher twice and Standard & Poor's was higher 39 times. Standard & Poor's has been viewed for years as more lenient than Moody's.

The agencies emphasize different rating criteria. Standard & Poor's weighs a broad spectrum of socio-economic factors, such as population and economic trends more heavily than the debt-burden ratios which are considered the broadest, most general available measure of the wealth of a community. Debt-burden is the relationship between total debt of all government units and the taxable wealth located within the borrower's boundaries. Though some analysts say that Moody's emphasizes debt burden more than other factors, Edward Kerman, vice-president of Moody's stated that there is no one factor used in analyzing issues that is at all times deemed more important than others at Moody's.

Moody's and Standard & Poor's also differ on their evaluation of certain security features. Moody's looks at the underlying security of the bond issue, giving selective value to additional protective measures. Moody's does not view a pledge of moral obligation or state withholding to pay debt services as criteria for improving a rating. Standard & Poor's, however, places greater value on these mechanisms, which would become operative if an issue defaulted. Sometimes split ratings result when the issuer chooses to pay for an evaluation from both rating agencies.

6. Unrated Bonds

Most of the unrated bonds on the market are issued by small borrowers. Some have ratings withdrawn for lack of information. Others issue new debt without requesting a re-evaluation of the debt-burden that results in a rating withdrawal. Small issues cost more to market because they are not generally known and they lack economies of scale for issuance costs. They are considered less desirable by institutional investors, who like to buy large quantities of an issue to facilitate portfolio management. In addition, small issues are difficult to sell in the secondary market because they are of generally unknown quality. The small issuer might prefer to privately place an issue instead of publicly marketing it.

Another category of unrated borrowers are those who ascertain that the rating they might receive would not reduce the cost of borrowing enough to justify the expense of seeking it. Unlike the small borrower, whose size is a handicap, this type of unrated borrower is a poor credit risk. When the bonds are unrated, there is no easy way for the small investor to distinguish between the creditworthy small issuer and the credit-risk issuer. A bond might also not be accepted for rating because it belongs to a group of securities that are not rated as a matter of policy. For instance, Standard & Poor's does not rate short-term municipal notes, although Moody's does.

7. Limitations of the Ratings

There are two basic limitations of the rating agencies from the perspective of the private investor. First, there is no predictive value in the letter grade indicating whether the bond will improve its rating or decline in creditworthiness over its life, though some indicators of the projected strength of an issuer may be available in the publications of the rating agencies.

Two issuers might have the same rating, although it may be apparent at the time of rating that one is declining, and the other is increasing in strength. This is not a significant issue for bonds that are near maturity because the short-term credit risk from a declining issuer may be no worse than the issue of a town that will eventually be upgraded.

Second, it might appear that the rating agencies are remiss in their evaluations because the ratings do not fortell market declines. However, the position of the agencies is that they make an evaluation at the time of issuance—*at that specific time*—of the issuer's ability to pay interest and principal. Though the bonds are periodically reviewed and adjustments made, the ratings are not meant to be a guide to purchasing, holding, or selling bonds. They reflect a credit judgment, but not the market risk of the bonds. This may be news to you, and not very comforting news at that. The ratings focus on a single risk—an issuer's credit risk. Bond default can occur even if the issuer has sufficient income to meet its obligations. The ability of New York City, UDC, and the others to repay their obligations was always there, but extenuating factors resulted in temporary defaults.

An argument against a rapid downgrading of a bond issue is that it causes harm—both to the issuer and the bondholder. A downgrading makes it difficult for the issuer to borrow. If you feared the possibility of a substantial market decline or default, you might decide to prematurely sell your bonds and thereby realize a loss. You would pay a spread on both the sale of one lot of bonds and the purchase of another, if you were to reinvest in another issue. While this might be appropriate at some point, the rating agencies do not want to take premature action. The lack of timely action by the rating agencies has often been misunderstood and severely criticized. Knowing their philosophy might be helpful in making your investment decisions.

B. Methods Used by Issuers to Improve their Ratings

Small or weak municipalities improve their bond ratings and marketability through state and federal organizational support and guarantees of payment. Another alternative that is increasingly popular is to purchase insurance, or a letter of credit from a bank. Each method of improving ratings will be considered below.

1. Methods Employed by States

a. Providing Organizational Support—Pooling Borrowing Needs

States establish bond banks and state school building authorities to assist small municipal units to borrow at reasonable rates by enabling them to pool their borrowing needs and float one large, guaranteed bond issue.

By pooling, a bond bank can offer larger issues that attract more institutional bidders and reduce the risk of holding debt of small and often unrated issues. The bond bank sells bonds, using the proceeds to purchase the debt issued by the local government units. The bond bank debt is secured by payments made by local government units in addition to one or more of the following: reserve funds; full faith and credit of the municipality; lien on state grants-in-aid; and the state's moral obligation. The states that have adopted bond banks include Vermont (1970), Maine (1972), Alaska (1975), North Dakota (1975), and New Hampshire (1978). Puerto Rico established a Municipal Finance Agency in 1973, which functions like a bond bank.

Generally speaking, state school building authorities raise money for school construction. The new schools are leased to the communities until the bonds are repaid, at which time the local district acquires them. Pennsylvania, Georgia, and Maine use this method extensively. The Virginia Public School Authority operates similarly, but it gains money from the state school construction fund in addition to bond revenues.

b. State Guarantees of Municipal Bond Issues

The word guarantee carries with it the connotation of carrying the full faith and credit of a strong backer for the payment of principal and interest when a weaker debtor fails to meet its obligations. Some states guarantee aid to pay defaulted debt service or local government general obligation bonds. The bondholder would be paid directly from state aid appropriations in the event of default. Several states have enacted this provision, including Indiana, Kentucky, New Jersey, New York, Pennsylvania, South Carolina, and West Virginia. Usually this provision is used in support of bonds issued by school districts. However, guarantees are hedged by conditions. Partial guarantees may include assisting one issuer to obtain financial solvency, but do not assure punctual payment or the avoidance of default. In fact, some guarantees are activated only a substantial period of time after an issuer has failed to resolve its default situation.

Another form of guarantee is to declare a bond issue a moral obligation of the state. Moral obligation is a term used to describe bonds issued by an authority or agency of a state that the state feels a duty to support, though it is not legally bound to do so. The issuer supports bonds carrying the moral obligation label through a back-up fund containing a year's interest and principal drawn from the original bond sale. The issuer promises to maintain that fund for the duration of the time the bond is outstanding. If there is a deficiency in the fund at a stated time, the state is morally—but not legally—bound to restore the reserve to its full stated requirement. The New York State and the New Jersey legislatures have voluntarily paid money into funds when required. In the case of the New York Urban Development Corp (UDC) default in February 1975, the moral obligation of the state only backed the UDC bonds and not the defaulted notes. However, New York State voluntarily came to the rescue. In Connecticut, it is the opinion of counsel, that if the reserve fund backing moral obligation bonds were to be invaded, the reserve would automatically be replenished without special appropriations.

2. Federal Guarantees for Municipal Bonds

The federal government tries to severely restrict the use of federal gurantees to support municipal bonds because federally guaranteed municipals put such municipal bonds in direct competition with federal issues. The most recent maneuver to obtain federal backing was the issuance of municipal bonds secured by home mortgage loans backed by the Federal Savings and Loan Insurance Corporation or the Federal Deposit Insurance Corporation. This form of indirect federal backing was terminated in 1983, but bonds carrying this insurance are still available in the secondary market.

If bonds are federally guaranteed, they will be rated AAA if they cover 100% of principal and interest in the event of default. Some issues that have federal guarantees might be rated only AA or less because the guarantee does not cover all principal and interest or there are contingencies that must be met before the guarantee is activated. For example, the guarantee may pay only 90% of the principal of the mortgage; may only be activated if the property is in good repair; may not apply if the property was destroyed or the builder defaulted; or may only guarantee the underlying mortgage and not the bonds.[4]

The possible weakness of a contingent federal guarantee is demonstrated by the taxable New York State Dormitory Authority Bonds that were guaranteed by the Government National Mortgage Association (known as Ginnie Mae) which have an AAA rating. The protection of Ginnie Mae was secure only *after* the projects were completed. The construction period, being the time of greatest risk, was left uncovered. Thus, bondholders of the New York State Dormitory Authority were horrified when the authority's cash was involved in the bankruptcy proceedings of a small securities firm, Lombard Wall, Inc. The potential inability of the authority to complete construction of its project in effect would have nullified the guarantee. Fortunately, the Dormitory Authority was able to recover most of the $239 million tied up in the bankruptcy.

Hospitals are able to issue municipal bonds with an investment-grade rating even if they would have otherwise been considered high-risk thanks to Federal Housing Administration insurance. The FHA provides default insurance that covers most, but not all, of the costs of a default. Therefore, the stronger the hospital is on its own merits, the better the investment.

Thus, although federal guarantees provide the most secure backing, municipal bonds do not usually carry the full faith and credit of the federal government. Where federal guarantees do exist, they often have conditions that have to be met before the federal government will come to the rescue of the issuer. This has been most recently demonstrated by the Washington Public Power Supply System problems (See Part II, Chapter XV).

3. Private Bond Insurance

An issuer may purchase private bond insurance from an insurance company or a bank in the form of a letter of credit.

a. Insurance Companies

The diversity of issuers and their unknown quality has encouraged the growth of private insurance companies. They add a note of familiarity to the most mysterious bond issues due to their frequent appearance in the market.

Investors' fears of default have led to an upsurge in the number of bond issues that are insured. In 1973, only $1 million of bonds were insured. By 1977, more than $1 billion of bonds were insured; in 1981, almost $3 billion were insured. As the WPPSS default became more of an issue, the demand for insurance mushroomed—in 1984, $20 billion of insured bonds were issued. By 1985, new, insured long-term municipal bonds totaled at least $46 billion, a new record, or almost one-quarter of the $189.6

billion total sold during the year. CREDIT MARKETS, (January 13, 1986), p. 41.

The best known insurance companies are AMBAC (American Municipal Bond Assurance Corporation, and MBIA (Municipal Bond Insurance Association). Newer entries into the bond insurance market include FGIC (Financial Guaranty Insurance Company), and BIG (Bond Investors Guarantee). Bonds insured by all four companies earn a AAA rating from Standard and Poor's. Moody's gives its Aaa rating to all of the foregoing insurance companies except for AMBAC, which is given a Aa rating.

AMBAC invented the business of insuring municipal bonds in 1971. It began issuing individual and bond portfolio insurance in 1974. The insured AMBAC bonds had an AA rating from Standard & Poor's until 1979 when it was upgraded to AAA. AMBAC has been struggling because its former parent, Baldwin-United Corp. (the notorious seller of annuities that went bust in 1983), had not been able to provide sufficient support for the company. Of all the insurers, AMBAC is the only insurer to be hit with default claims, including $75 million in interest and principal over 33 years for defaulted WPPSS 4 and 5 bonds. AMBAC has been given a new lease on life as a result of its acquisition by Citibank, an 80% owner as of July 1, 1985.

MBIA was formed in 1974 and was composed of five insurance companies: Aetna Casualty & Surety, Aetna Insurance Co., the Travelers Indemnity Corporation, Fireman's Fund Insurance Co, and the Continental Insurance Corporation.

MBIA announced plans to reformulate its structure in 1986. Travelers Indemnity Corp. will no longer participate in municipal bond insurance. Instead of insuring bonds and many other products, MBIA will restrict its business solely to bond insurance like the other major insurers.

MBIA has had to share the marketplace with well-capitalized upstarts. Financial Guaranty Insurance Corp. (FGIC) has made impressive inroads into the bond insurance market. In less than 2 years FGIC insured over $11 billion in municipal bonds, virtually monopolizing the housing sector as well as insuring other kinds of issues. Major investors in FGIC include the General Electric Credit Corporation, the General Reinsurance Corporation, the Kemper Group through Luberman Mutual Casualty Company, Merrill Lynch & Co., and Shearson Lehman Brothers Inc.

The latest entrant into the fray of municipal bond insurance is

Rating Agencies and Methods Used to Improve Ratings

Bond Investors Guaranty Insurance Co. (BIG). BIG was formed by Phibro-Salomon Inc., American International Group Inc., Xerox Credit Corp., and Bankers Trust Co. in equal shares. Interestingly, Xerox also owns a 5% share of AMBAC. BIG was given a Aaa rating by Moody's in September 1986, as well as an AAA by S&P and thus should quickly become more prominent.

What are the advantages of purchasing insured bonds? Once an insurance policy is written, it will remain in force until the bond matures. Insurance policies provide protection for 100% of principal and interest with no deductible. If the issuer of an insured bond defaults, the principal and interest payments continue without interruption as a result of payments by the insurer. No claim for payment is necessary on the part of the bondholder.

There are also disadvantages. Such disadvantages are based primarily on an evaluation of the insurance companies' ability to pay. The insurance companies base their ability to pay on a standard defined by George Hempel, a professor of business at Southern Methodist University. Based upon the experience of the Great Depression, it includes a four-year depression with cumulative defaults totalling 16% of the outstanding issues. Jonathan R. Laing,[5] in an article written for *BARRON's*, summarize 'the problems with that standard:' (1) Insurance companies might not recognize the onset of the depression and continue to write policies. (2) Investment income of the insurance companies would decline, hindering their ability to pay. (3) The investment portfolios of insurance companies are loaded with revenue bond issues that are more risky than general obligation bonds, and therefore more subject to permanent losses. (4) A far greater number of bonds today are revenue bonds secured by user fees, instead of property taxes, which secure general obligation bonds. Finally, the insurance responsibilities are distributed among various unrelated insurance companies in order to spread the risk. However, it is an incestuous relationship because the reinsurers are also bond insurers in their own right.

The insurance companies can point to their excellent records. MBIA, FGIC, and BIG can point to no defaults on record, and AMBAC has easily assumed the problems of WPPSS and some minor defaults. From the insurance companies' perspective, they insure bonds that they believe to be riskless. If a default does occur, they expect it to be corrected, and their only obligation is to maintain interest and principal payments until that happens. If a bond issuer ever wishes to come to market again, it has to repay its obligations.

In addition, it is proposed that publicly owned companies that insure and guarantee municipal bonds and other securities be required to make new financial disclosures under an accounting bulletin issued in January 1986 by the staff of the Securities and Exchange Commission. In addition to the SEC proposal, some state insurance officials are considering rules to require specific reserves as backing for their financial guarantees. It adds a measure of comfort to know that there are watchdog agencies that stand ready to protect the investors' interest as bond insurance continues to mushroom.

The emergence of independent reinsurance companies is adding additional financial depth to bond insurers since Mr. Laing voiced his criticisms. In November 1986, Enhance Financial Services, Inc. announced that it had established Enhance Reinsurance Co., a monoline company that will insure municipal bonds. It will be rated AAA by Standard & Poor's and will have a $115 million capitalization, against which it expects to write premiums between $40 million and $60 million the first year.

MBIA and FGIC-insured bonds have traditionally traded closer to the yield of an AA rated bond than one which is rated AAA. Bond issuers that have been insured by AMBAC might also choose to be rated only by Standard & Poor's and thus save the costs of requesting a rating from Moody's, which will be less than Aaa anyway. The market values FGIC and MBIA-insured bonds more than AMBAC-insured bonds which have traded closer to AA—or A ratings. MBIA is viewed as a more substantial insurer as seen in the table below.

Comparative Municipal Bond Yields

	Yield
Uninsured AAA	8.80%
Uninsured AA	10.10%
Insured by MBIA	10.25%
Insured by AMBAC	10.40%
Uninsured A	10.60%

Source: *Fortune* (Jan. 23, 1984), p. 178.

This table reflects in part the different portfolios of AMBAC and MBIA. Certain general obligation bonds and utilities trade with a narrower spread between insured and uninsured than higher-yielding complex revenue municipals. In high-tax states, MBIA and FGIC-insured bonds may trade closer to AAA bonds due to great demand for good quality bonds.

In addition to bonds that come to market already insured, there is a small percentage of bonds that are insured after they have been sold. Here's how it works. Shearson Lehman Brothers buys uninsured bonds, stores them for life in vaults at Citicorp and insures them through the Financial Guaranty Insurance Co. (FGIC). The customer receives a "custodial receipt" instead of the actual bond and is mailed interest payments as with any registered bond.

b. Insurance of Municipal Bonds By Banks: Letters of Credit

Banks can issue letters of credit on municipal bonds. They provide protection to municipal bondholders similar to protection provided by insurance companies. The insurance companies are well known and controlled by New York State's insurance laws. Some of the banks issuing the letters of credit may be unknown to the small investor. The letter of credit is only as good as the banks' credit rating. If a bond defaults, a bank usually retires an issue immediately, whereas the insurance companies will continue to make interest payments and reserve principal payments until maturity; this gives the issuer time to get its affairs in order and, hopefully, resume payments itself. The letters of credit usually run for 10 years, while insurance companies provide protection for the life of an issue.

The use of letters of credits has grown substantially. The banks find letters of credit attractive because it sometimes assists them in obtaining the position of managing underwriting for new issues and also adds substantial income from fees. Recently, the profitability of letters of credit has been reduced because United States banks are now required to set aside reserves to back the letters of credit. Foreign banks with the exception of banks in England are currently not required to do so, thereby enabling them to sell the credit enhancements for less.

notes

Chapter VII

[1] Jack Willoughby, "Uncertain Empires," *Forbes*, (June 16, 1986), p. 134.
[2] All ratings are drawn from publications of Moody's Investors Service and Standard & Poor's Corporation.
[3] T. Gregory Morton, "A Comparative Analysis of Moody's and Standard & Poor's Municipal Bond Ratings," *Review of Business and Economic Research*, (Winter, 1975–1976), pp. 74–81.
[4] Robert Lamb and Stephen P. Rappaport, *Municipal bonds: The Comprehensive Review of the Tax Exempt Securities and Public Finance,* New York: McGraw Hill, (1980), pp. 159–160.
[5] Johnathan R. Laing, "Accident Waiting to Happen? Municipal Bond Insurance is Ballooning—and So Are the Risks," *Barrons*, (December 16, 1985), pp. 84.

CHAPTER VIII

Risks of Investing in Municipal Bonds and How To Avoid Them

A. Risk of Default
    1. Historical Record of Defaults
    2. Defaults and the Ratings
    3. If a Bond Issuer Defaults
    4. How to Minimize the Risk of Default
B. Market Risk of Price Decline
    —How to Minimize Market Risk
C. Liquidity Risk
    —How to Avoid the Liquidity Risk
D. Risk of Theft, Loss, or Damage
    —How to Minimize Theft Risk, Including Lost and Damaged Bonds
E. Early Call Risk
    —How to Minimize the Early Call Risk

Risks! All investments have risks. The rate of interest you receive reflects the amount of risk you are taking. The higher your potential return, the greater the risk you take. Does that mean you should stuff your money in the mattress? No! That is not a solution. Aside from the risk of theft, there is the dreaded risk of inflation, which gnaws away at your dollars every day. One solution is highly rated municipal bonds. Municipal bonds have risks, but compared with most other investments, the risks are small and with care can be reduced to a comfortable level. We will explore the risks of default, inflation, liquidity, theft, and early call and give you some ideas on how to reduce each of them.

A. Risk of Default

Default is the most feared risk of municipal bonds purchasers. Don't be afraid. The looming shadow of a possible default affects only a few issues and most of those on only a temporary basis. Default is the inability of a bond issuer to pay principal and/or interest on time. Some defaults are called technical defaults because of violations of underlying bond covenants. Monetary defaults result from missed payments of principal or interest. A serious default is one in which repayment of principal has to be rescheduled and some principal and interest may never be repaid. A minor default can be corrected within a brief period and may not result in missed interest payments.

Defaults may be separated into two broad categories: (1) the inability to pay resulting from declaration of bankruptcy, the seizure of the borrower's property by some official, inaccurate forecasts of construction/revenue usage and (2) unwillingness to pay due to the repudiation of debt by the issuer. Non-payment of interest or failure to pay principal or other required payments when due, and breaches of financing agreements may be the result of either category. Hilton Head Hospital in Beaufort, South Carolina is an example of the inability to pay. It was built in anticipation of a resort and retirement community that was never built. It has made regular but late payments since it resumed paying interest in 1980. Washington Public Power Supply System (Part II, Chapter XV) is an example of the unwillingness to pay.

1. Historical Record of Defaults

Defaults on municipal bonds have occurred almost continuously since the first bonds were issued, under both good and bad economic conditions. However, the number of defaults grew rapidly and immediately following the four depression periods: 1837–1843, 1873–1879, 1893–1899, and 1929–1937. Defaults occurred in every major kind of governmental unit and in every region of the country.

What is of more importance than the number of defaults is the actual amount of loss of principal and interest. Note that *most defaults were cured!* Table VIII–1 below indicates that during the Great Depression (1929 to 1937), it is estimated that although $2.85 billion was in default (15.4% of all issued debt), by 1937 the debt in default was reduced to only $1.36 billion (excluding repudiations), or 7.3% of debt outstanding in 1929–1937. Significantly, during this period only $100 million was permanently lost (excluding unpaid interest) out of $18.5 billion of bonds outstanding.

Table VIII–2 gives geographic and categorical breakdowns of the recorded defaults from 1839 to 1969.

Revenue bonds played little part in the above figures because the 1929 to 1937 period is the first major default period during which they were outstanding. Even as late as 1937, revenue bonds only amounted to approximately 5% of total municipal bonds. There were only 12 instances of state and local revenue bond defaults from 1929 through 1937. The value of these revenue bonds was about $18.8 million, which was 5.8% of the approxi-

Risks of Investing in Municipal Bonds

mately $325 million of revenue bonds outstanding in 1931. Although the percentage of defaults on revenue bonds was smaller than on general obligation bonds, the actual loss of principal and interest was greater on revenue issues—$6.6 million, which was over one-third of the $18.8 million of revenue bond principal in default. Today revenue bonds are still considered generally more risky than general obligation bonds, though the degree of risk varies with the category of revenue bonds, as discussed in Part II, Chapter VI.

For the period of 1945 to 1965, George H. Hempel, in his book entitled *Postwar Quality of State and Local Debt,* has the following observations:

> A few characteristics of the total number of defaulted situations are discernible. Of the 329 reported default situations, 115, or 35 per cent, were on short-term state and local debts, 92, or 27 percent, were by special districts other than school districts and 47 or 14.3 per cent, were on revenue bonds. The time distribution of the default situation for which the date of default was available revealed that there was at least one default in every year studied after World War II, no noticeable cyclical pattern in recorded defaults due to the relatively mild postwar recessions, and an increasing trend in the absolute number of reported defaults in the postwar period.
>
> The dollar amount of state and local debt in default provides a clearer answer about the extent of the debt payment difficulties in the postwar period. The principal actually in default and the principal upon which interest is in default at the time of the difficulty totals approximately $325 million for all state and local units which have defaulted from 1945–65. This total is slightly over .3 percent of the total state and local debt outstanding at the end of the 1965 fiscal year. Approximately $294 million, or 91 percent, of the estimated total amount of principal in default is the responsibility of 27 municipal units involved in major default situations.* All but six of these major default situations were on revenue bonds.[3]

---

*The term major default situations is used to describe well-documented default situations that are clearly neither temporary nor technical and that involve at least $200 thousand of principal in default or principal upon which interest is in default.

TABLE VIII-1

Comparison of the Extent of Defaults by State and Local Units in Major Default Periods
(dollar figures in thousands)

Period	Average State and Local Debt Outstanding	Total Indebtedness of Defaulting State and Local Units	Per Cent of Debt Outstanding	Past Due Interest and Principal[a]	Per Cent of Debt Outstanding	Loss of Principal and Interest[b]	Per Cent of Debt Outstanding
1837–43	$245,000	$125,000	51.0	n.a.	—	$ 15,000	6.1
1873–79	1,000,000	245,000	24.5	n.a.	—	150,000	15.0
1893–99	1,300,000	130,000	10.0	n.a.	—	25,000	1.9
1929–37	18,500,000	2,850,000[c]	15.4	320,000[c]	1.7	100,000	.5

Source: Based on data from George H. Hempel, "The Postwar Quality of Municipal Bonds," unpublished dissertation, University of Michigan, 1964, pp. 84–161.

[a] Does not include interest on unpaid interest.

[b] Does not include interest on unpaid interest, interest due after a debt was repudiated or interest lost due to refunding at a lower interest cost.

[c] Overdue interest plus debt upon which interests is in default was $1,355,000 or 7.3 per cent of debt outstanding in 1929–37. This figure is not available for the earlier default periods.

n.a. = not available.

TABLE VIII-2
Recorded Defaults, By Type of Local Government Unit and Geographical Region 1839–1969

	1839 -49	1850 -59	1860 -69	1870 -79	1880 -89	1890 -99	1900 -09	1910 -19	1920 -29	1930 -39	1940 -49	1950 -59	1960 -69	Total Defaults	Number of Local Governments In 1967[a]
By Type of Unit:															
Counties and parishes		7	15	57	30	94	43	7	15	417	6	12	24	727	3,049
Incorp. munics.	4	4	13	50	30	93	51	17	39	1434	31	31	114	1911	18,048
Unincorp. munics.		4	9	46	31	50	33	5	10	88	7	4	26	313	17,105
School districts				4	5	9	11		14	1241	5	23	60	1372	21,782
Other districts				2	1	12	11	7	107	1590	30	42	70	1872	21,264
By Geographical Region:															
New England States[b]										7				18	3,045
Middle Atlantic States[c]	1	5	6	19	11	13	13	4	4	251	9	4	4	350	10,437
Southern States[d]	1		1	32	29	36	25	9	51	1863	16	33	10	2172	9,478
Midwestern States[e]	2	9	28	84	46	89	68	6	18	1152	18	34	76	1630	37,359
Southwestern States[f]			1	19	7	79	27	5	24	707	25	36	76	1042	9,588
Mountain States[g]				2		17	2	8	17	270	6	4	112	329	4,289
Pacific States[h]		1	1	2	3	22	14	3	70	520	5	1	3	654	7,052
Totals	4	15	37	159	97	258	149	36	185	4470	79	112	294	6195	81,248

[a]The number of local government units has changed rapidly. For example, in 1932 there were 127,108 school districts, 8,580 other districts, and 175,369 States and local government units.
[b]Connecticut, Maine, Massachusettes, New Hampshire, Rhode Island, and Vermont.
[c]Delaware, District of Columbia, Maryland, New Jersey, New York, and Pennsylvania.
[d]Alabama, Arkansas, Florida, Georgia, Kentucky, Louisiana, Mississippi, North Carolina, Tennessee, Virginia and West Virginia.
[e]Illinois, Indiana, Iowa, Michigan, Minnesota, Missouri, Nebraska, Ohio, North Dakota, South Dakota, and Wisconsin.
[f]Arizona, Kansas, New Mexico, Oklahoma, and Texas.
[g]Colorado, Idaho, Montana, Nevada, Utah, and Wyoming.
[h]Alaska, California, Hawaii, Oregon, and Washington.

Sources: Default Information in *The Daily Bond Buyer, The Commercial and Financial Chronicle,* and *The Investment Bankers' Associations Bulletin;* default lists from Federal Deposit Insurance Corporation, Life Insurance Commission, and U.S. Courts, and Albert M Hillhouse. *Defaulted Municipal Bonds* (Chicago, Municipal Financial Officers Association, 1935) Number of local government units from: U.S. Department of Commerce, Bureau of Census, *Census of Governments, 1967. Vol 1* "Governmental Organization," (Gov't Printing Office, 1969)

City Financial Emergencies: The Intergovernmental Dimension Washington, Advisory Commission on Intergovernmental Relations, 1973.

In 1932, during the heart of the Depression, only 1.7% of all municipal bonds were in default, compared with 3.5% of railroad bonds, 5.4% of public utility bonds, 7.2% of industrial bonds, and 19.4% of foreign bonds.[4] The length of time for a default to be corrected during the Great Depression was about six years.

Defaults included the notes of the New York State Urban Development Corporation (1975), the general obligation notes of New York City (1975), and the bonds of Cleveland (1978). The UDC defaulted on February 20, 1975, on a $100 million note issue.[5] This default was cured by May 1975 with a $140 million revolving credit put together by 11 New York Clearing House banks.

Two hospital revenue bond issues with a Standard & Poor's BBB rating also defaulted in the mid-1970's. One was Midlands Community Hospital in Nebraska, the other was Hilton Head Hospital in South Carolina. Both hospitals are taking steps to rectify the defaults. Hilton Head Hospital went into default in 1976. The last coupon to be paid on a timely basis was paid on July 1, 1977, until past due interest payments resumed on September 1980. Since then, regular but late payments have continued. The hospital has been catching up on past due debt service payments on an accelerated basis. Hilton Head Hospital was built in anticipation of a resort and retirement community that did not materialize within the forecast period. Midlands Community Hospital was similarly constructed based on unrealized projected use. It never defaulted on interest, only principal payments. In January 1983, it retired $320,000 face value of its bonds, its first principal payment in 10 years. There is still an outstanding debt of $19.7 million.

A more recent issue that teetered on the brink of default is the San Jose Unified School District in California, one of that state's largest school districts. It had a $12 million deficit in its budget, and was required by an arbitrator to immediately pay its employees nearly $3 million in back pay and interest.[6] It was rated Aa by Moody's until its rating was suspended. On June 30, 1983, the district voluntarily filed for bankruptcy under Chapter 9 of the Federal Bankruptcy Code. Under Chapter 9 a state or municipality gets protection from its creditors while it restructures its debt. Chapter 9 also grants protection against interference with the operators of state or local government.

The causes of bankruptcies are often intertwined with the determination of a municipality's residents to cut back on expenditures and thereby keep their tax rates down. Proposition 13, passed in California in 1978, substantially reduced local property taxes and forced local governments to rely on the state legislature for revenue. Taxes could not be raised to cover the difference because the state had placed a ceiling on the per pupil allotment, with any funds above that amount remanded to the state for distribution to poorer districts. The San Jose Unified School District was also affected by a declining student population resulting from the high cost of San Jose housing, which placed the homes beyond the reach of young couples. A militant teachers' union pressed for wage increases and was granted them by a federal mediator. The school trustees agreed with the mediator, hoping the state legislature would cover the difference. When it was evident that no extra money was forthcoming from the state and that the union would not renegotiate its contract, the school trustees were left with no alternative but to seek protection under the bankruptcy law.[7]

The outcome of this bankruptcy should gratify any bondholder. There is a requirement of Section I of the California Constitution, commonly known as Proposition 13, that nothing in Proposition 13 should impair the ability of local governments to meet their obligations made before 1978. As a result, the bondholders' rights were not impaired, and they were paid according to schedule. The judge ruled that the major cause of the indebtedness, the high-priced labor contracts signed by the school, could be repudiated and wages rolled back to 1981–1982 levels. A Moody's rating of Baa1 was instated on April 9, 1985.

2. Defaults and the Ratings

The defaults since 1971, when both major rating agencies were in existence, indicate that the agencies have been slow to change their evaluations of creditworthiness in response to deteriorating conditions among big clients. This is partly because the same condition can exist for years without appreciably worsening or impairing payment, until some chain of events tips the balance and causes a default. The ratings only relate to an evaluation of the issuer at the time the rating is done; they do not indicate the future financial performance of the issuer nor the market performance of the bond. Defaults which are caused by non-monetary events such as adverse litigation or *force majeure* will not be indicated in ratings.

A review of some of the issues that defaulted and their ratings in the 1970's is instructive. New York City bonds were suspended by Standard & Poor's and were rated A by Moody's shortly before their default in 1975. The rating dropped quickly once it became clear default was around the corner. Following the default, the City reorganized its debt, and new long-term bonds were issued by the Municipal Assistance Corporation, a New York State agency formed after the default, which sold bonds secured by New York City's sales tax revenues to raise money for the city. By 1983 the City was boasting a revenue surplus and its bonds were upgraded to an investment-grade rating of Baa. Critics of New York City's investment grade rating will point to the serious deterioration of the City's infrastructure (bridges, sewers, subways, etc.) as an indication of future financial difficulties. The ratings reflect current and anticipated performance, and the agencies reserve the right to downgrade should the situation worsen in the future. In fact, ratings are adjusted downward far more often than upward. Cleveland, Ohio, defaulted on about $15 million in notes in 1978. Cleveland's bonds held an A rating for 11 years up to mid-1978. In that year Moody's revised its rating downward four times, and Standard & Poor's suspended its rating altogether.[8] The city eventually restructured the debt, stretching repayment from one year to 14 years. However, the new debt carried a higher interest rate.

The Washington Public Supply System (WPPSS) is the largest municipal unit ever to default. The giant WPPSS has $8.3 *billion* of bonds outstanding. All WPPSS bonds are now unrated, though bonds issued for plants 1, 2 and 3 are still paying interest. Bonds issued for plants 4 and 5 are in default.

WPPSS terminated plants 4 and 5 in 1982, after which suits were filed by ratepayers (residents of Washington) claiming the utilities that belong to WPPSS did not have legal authority to sign contracts promising to pay for the plants. The Washington State Supreme Court upheld the ratepayers' position, to the shock of the financial world. As of this moment there is no financial solution in the offing. For an analysis of this case and the lessons to be learned from it, see Part II Chapter XV.

Risks of Investing in Municipal Bonds

3. If a Bond Issuer Defaults

Municipal bonds are considered one of the safest investments available. Defaults are few, and bankruptcies are fewer. In the event of a default, the rights of the bondholders are set forth in the issuers' bond resolution, which are reviewed by bond counsel. The lawyers hired to write opinions on the bonds, state that the securities are tax-exempt and that the issuer is qualified to sell them.

All bond resolutions, and thus the rights of the bondholders, are tempered by the political, social, and economic tenor of the times. The bondholders may receive less than they are due, but never more. If the bondholders receive a court judgement entitling them to payment, they still have to wait for the municipality to muster the funds. Unlike a private bankruptcy, the municipality's assets cannot be sold, since a seizure of property could disrupt public services. However, creditors of bankrupt municipal industrial development bonds can seize the buildings, land, and equipment of the private enterprise for whose benefit the bonds were sold if it facilitates payment of debt and those assets were pledged as bond security.

If there is a default, the individual does not have to confront the municipality alone. The bond trustee, usually a bank, is empowered to defend the rights of the bondholders and to see that the issuer honors its obligations. Unfortunately the trustee bank usually has local ties making many remedies objectionable. Trustees are sometimes loathe to give up strong local banking relationships in favor of some distant high income individuals. Alternatively, the bondholders can form a committee supported by at least 50% of the bondholders to direct the action of the trustee.

Bondholders can sue not only the defaulting municipality, but also underwriters, bond lawyers, engineers, and others who were involved in selling the issue. In the event of default, one available remedy is the acceleration of maturities. This means that once bankruptcy is declared, all the bonds become immediately due and payable. This remedy has relevance only in instances where money can be realized from sale of property. Otherwise it works to the detriment of bondholders by eliminating future interest payments. Any reserve funds, construction funds, or other collateral is secured on behalf of the bondholders. If the issuer is unable to redeem the bonds, the result is likely to be a restructuring of the issuer's debt or the establishment of an oversight authority such as New York's Municipal Assistance Corporation, a financial control board.

The issuer is usually anxious to resolve the default because its continuation denies the municipality access to the credit markets. Why should investors trust a borrower that does not meet its obligations? Long periods of default provide negative publicity resulting in increased borrowing costs for years to come.

In the event of a declaration of bankruptcy by a municipality, all bondholders' rights and remedies blur because of the untested nature of the bankruptcy law passed in 1979. That law makes it easier for municipalities to seek protection from creditors. The new rules give more discretionary power to the federal bankruptcy judges in resolving such situations.

New York City's fiscal crisis in 1975 illustrated that the social and political needs of the populace takes precedence over the supposedly iron-clad legal protection of bondholders. Workers must be paid and city services must continue to function in the face of financial crisis. Although the New York City general obligation bonds stated that the full faith and credit of the City supported its debt and that the bondholders had first claim on the City's assets and revenues, this was not true in practice. In reality, the social and political needs of the City took precedence over the bondholders' legal protection. It was concluded by City officials that the City's employees must be paid on time and all services must continue, even in the face of a financial crisis, in order to avert a worse disaster.

New financing techniques and the lack of voter-approved security structures, which are untested in the courts, leave the outcome of future court cases unknown.[8] Uncertainty is presented by moral obligation bonds, commercial bank-backed letters of credit, put bonds, tax-exempt commercial paper, lease-rental bonds and bonds supported by take-or-pay contracts where the issuers may charge for services whether or not they fulfill their contracts.

4. How to Minimize the Risk of Default

We have developed the following guidelines to minimize default situations by avoiding bonds that may default.

(a) Beware of revenue bonds that were sold without voter approval and to which a vocal sector of the public will be opposed.

For example, the antinuclear power movement coupled with declining fuel prices has undermined the ability of electric utility plants to complete their nuclear power projects. Repudiation of debt has historically occured only when the residents feel that the debt was clearly not in the public interest.

(b) Unless you are willing to perform your own financial analysis, buy highly rated or insured bonds. Though even highly rated bonds may suffer a technical default, there is a favorable likelihood of the prompt correction of the default, as in the case of the San Jose school district.

(c) Be prepared to hold the bonds until the default is resolved, unless you consider the situation hopeless. More has been lost by selling out at distressed prices than by holding the bonds until the resolution of the problem.

(d) Critically evaluate newly conceived bond products even if they provide higher yields than plain-vanilla bonds.

(e) Avoid issuers with inordinately large amounts of debt outstanding coupled with a higher-than-average return for the particular grade of bond. These factors often indicate more risk than is acceptable. This scenario preceded both the New York City and Washington Public Power Supply defaults.

(f) Never buy bonds issued to fund a large, new building project if this project comprises the bulk of an issuer's assets unless you feel comfortable with the track record of the issuer and can receive assurance of the validity of the underlying contracts.

(g) Consider purchasing portfolio insurance from Wisconsin based Industrial Indemnity Corporation or other insurers. If you are anxious about your portfolio and would prefer holding insured bonds, an alternative to swapping your bonds is to buy portfolio insurance. If your portfolio is $500,000 face value or more, at least 75% of your portfolio is rated Baa/BBB or better and no single issue constitutes more than 40% of the insured portfolio, it may be insurable. The premium you pay for insurance is effective as of the original policy date and does not change if a bond's ratings are lowered or even if there is a default. In case of a default, the payments by the insurer on behalf of the defaulted issuer are tax exempt, just as the original interest payments would have been.

Peace of mind does not come cheap. The cost of protecting principal and interest payments ranges from 4 to 35 basis points. The costs can be somewhat recouped if you purchase higher-yielding, lower-rated bonds than you normally would. If the cost of insurance protection is less than the spread between the higher-rated and lower-rated bonds, you have some additional income without the accompanying risk of default. However, low-rated bonds that have real risk will probably be uninsurable.

B. Market Risk of Price Decline

A primary risk in owning municipal bonds is the risk of a price decline. There is also a corresponding chance for price appreciation. The risk of price decline is not a factor if you are prepared to hold a bond to maturity. It is a factor if you are considering the purchase of shares in a municipal bond fund, or if you are anticipating the sale of a bond prior to maturity.

There are five factors that may affect the market price of a bond in the secondary market:

1. The principal cause of a price decline is generally a rise in interest rates. For example, if a bond was issued at par with an interest coupon of 8%, and interest rates on similar bonds rise to 9%, the bond would be sold at a discount from par in order to make the effective rate of interest for the new buyer equal 9%. The discount narrows as the bonds approach maturity.

2. The downgrading of a bond will result in a price decline due to the added credit risk. This means that the likelihood that the debtor will be unable to meet its obligations is increased so the bond is less valuable.

3. Bad publicity may result in a price decline—even if the economic condition of the bond issuer has not changed dramatically—because of reduced demand for the issue.

4. The oversupply of a particular issuer's bonds may result in a lower market price because institutional investors often limit their holdings of bonds from particular issuers or areas. As the market becomes saturated, the price of the bonds may drop.

5. Too limited supply of a particular issue may adversely affect a bond's price because the issue may not be attractive to institutional investors who purchase large blocks of bonds. It is difficult to sell an unknown bond to individual investors because they may be

Risks of Investing in Municipal Bonds

wary of an issuer with which they are not familiar. Bond houses will be less willing to purchase the bonds of a small issuer because they will have difficulty selling the securities.

How to Minimize Market Risk

Two important general principles relating to municipal market risks are as follows:

1. The shorter the life of a municipal bond, the less affected it will be by the market fluctuations in interest rates. Accordingly, the volatility of market price changes in municipal bonds increases as the life of the bond increases, due to the fact that the municipal market has historically maintained a positive yield curve.

2. Bonds with longer maturities usually have higher yields than bonds with shorter maturities, but the risk of price declines is also greater. Money funds, for example, are able to maintain a quote of a dollar per share because even if interest rates rise, the entire portfolio comes due at par within one year.

If you buy a three-year bond, its price would probably not change substantially over its life. However, a bond with a maturity of 20 years or longer faces the unpredictability of the future and the resulting possibility of wide price swings. A 10-year bond, which is considered intermediate-term, pays an average of 1/2% to 1% less than a 20- or 30-year bond. However, the 10-year bond has less price risk if it must be sold before maturity.

Our strong recommendation is: NEVER BUY A BOND WITH MORE THAN A 13-YEAR MATURITY. Remember, if you buy a 12-year bond, at the end of six years you will have a six-year bond, and a six-year bond generally will not sell at a substantial discount from your purchase price. If you invest in a long-term bond, you are speculating on interest rates. If this is what your plan is, fine. However, don't buy a long-term bond merely to increase your yield by 3/4 of a percentage point.

An additional risk of long-term bonds is the risk of repudiation or default by the issuer. Such risk might materialize in hard times if the debt outlives the purpose for which the funds were raised. For example, if the issue financed a construction project that has become obsolete, the public might view the continuing debt with increasing disfavor. If you fear obsolescence before the bond is redeemed, buy bonds with lives of 13 years or less.

Do not seek the lowest price and the highest interest rate if the bond under consideration is substantially out of line with similar issues. It may be that large investors have knowledge of a looming problem about which you are not aware. If a bond is selling at 40 basis points above similarly rated bonds with the same maturity, this might be a danger sign rather than a great buying opportunity. For example, many small investors bought high-coupon New York City and Washington State Power Supply issues just before they defaulted because the yields were so attractive. At the same time, large institutions were unloading their holdings of these issues. The large supply of these bonds on the market was the reason why the yields increased.

Another warning sign is a widening spread between the dealers' bid and asked prices. The normal spread is two to three points (200 to 300 basis points). If the spread is higher than three points it means dealers are concerned about the issue and demand a premium for holding such bonds in their inventory. However, the spreads of all bonds will widen in times of market turbulence. Spreads on some actively traded bonds are published in *The Wall Street Journal* and *The New York Times*.

C. Liquidity Risk

The liquidity risk is the risk that you will not be able to sell your bonds at the prevailing market price at the time you wish to dispose of them. Certain kinds of bonds are more vulnerable than others to the liquidity risk. Bonds that are poorly rated, unrated, or not of investment grade have poor liquidity because dealers would have trouble reselling them. Bonds may lose their liquidity if the issuer is located in the vicinity of another issuer in jeopardy of default. For example, new issues emanating from Washington State were tainted for a time by the teetering condition of the Washington Public Power Supply System and the state for a time had to pay a premium because of proximity.

How to Avoid the Liquidity Risk

1. Buy A- or better-rated bonds of large, well-known issuers. General obligation bonds of states are the most sought after issues.

2. If purchasing small lots, buy them in anticipation of holding them to maturity. Diversify your portfolio as to maturity dates, for example, three-year, six-year, and 12-year bonds. Buy bonds with your particular needs for money in mind.

If you know that you may have to resell bonds prior to maturity, you should purchase bonds in units of $25,000 if possible. Lots of $25,000 are more desirable than smaller odd lots, because bonds in $25,000 lots are the easiest to sell to brokers and will bring higher prices. If you have a large portfolio, it might be a good idea to have some odd-lot issues, to maximize your yield-to-maturity and some lots of $25,000 in case you need to sell early.

D. Risk of Theft, Loss, or Damage

Registered bonds are replaceable if they are stolen, lost, or damaged. Loss or destruction of unregistered, or coupon bonds is something like losing cash from your wallet. Unlike registered bonds, coupon bonds are marketable, though a reputable buyer would ask for proof of ownership before purchasing them.

How to Minimize the Theft Risk, Including Lost and Damaged Bonds

Put your bonds in a vault. Since thefts of vaults do occur, though not frequently, an added measure of security is vault insurance. In addition, a copy of the face of the bond or a record of all names, CUSIP and registration numbers and a copy of your confirmation should be kept in a separate place in the event of damage or loss.

Another protective measure is to place your bonds in a cash-management type account with a brokerage firm or a bank trustee. A trustee charges an annual fee, a brokerage house does not. Having a cash-management type account also facilitates new purchases and sales through the brokerage house. However, those accounts are not without problems. One difficulty is that it might take a long time (three to six weeks) to receive your bonds once you request them. You need to have your bonds in hand before you sell them because delivery is supposed to be made five business days after sale. Also, bonds held for free in a brokerage house are held in street name (in the name of the brokerage house), and therefore not immediately obtainable in the event of a financial disaster. Another risk is that your heirs might not find your account upon your death.

E. Early Call Risk

Some bonds are callable, at the issuer's option, on certain dates. Other bonds have mandatory call features, which arise if certain events occur. An early call is a risk because your proceeds from the redemption may have to be reinvested at a lower interest rate. Thus, the original calculation of yield-to-maturity may be incorrect because the interest earned on the investment is not compounding at the same high rate of interest. For example, if you purchased a 10-year bond at par yielding 13%, and it was called after two years because interest rates dropped to 9%, you would have to reinvest your principal at the lower rate. In another situation, if you purchased a bond at a high premium price and the bond is redeemed at par, you would have suffered a loss of capital. For example, if you purchased a bond at a price of 138 ($1,380) and it was called after one year at 103 ($1,030), you would have immediately lost $350, plus the higher yield-to-maturity you would have received over the life of the bond.

A call date, if one is present in a particular bond, is set at issuance. All bonds in an issue may be called on a particular date, or only some bonds may be called by lottery. Issuers publicize bond redemptions in trade or financial newspapers and occasionally in local papers, but they are easy to miss. (Some bond sellers provide a free notification of redemption service for good customers.) If the bond is registered, the issuer notifies the bondholder directly. However, if a coupon bond has been redeemed you might not discover this until you present a coupon for redemption and it is rejected.

It is best to keep a record of call dates and interest payment dates of coupon bonds and check with the bond salesman or the issuer before the call date so you are not caught unaware. This problem will not exist with respect to the purchase of bonds issued after July 1, 1983, because all new issues must be registered. It should also not exist if your bonds are held by a bank or brokerage firm because such custodian should be aware of calls and take appropriate action.

Beware of a mandatory call or sinking fund provisions that are not listed on your confirmation. Mandatory call provisions are inherent in single-family housing bond issues and may affect multi-family housing as well. Mandatory call provisions require that bonds be called if a certain amount of capital from mortgage payments is accumulated or if the proceeds from the sale of bonds have not been used for the original purposes. Sinking funds retire a certain percentage of bonds in selected years. Frequently you will not be told about these provisions unless you ask.

How To Minimize the Early Call Risk

a. Buy low-coupon bonds selling at a discount if you don't need current high-coupon income and if a discount bond has a similar yield-to-call after the tax on capital gains as a par or premium bond. The discount bonds are unlikely to be called by the issuer since the coupon interest paid is below prevailing market rates.

b. Ask the sellers for call dates, including mandatory call and sinking fund provisions, on all bonds purchased.

c. Calculate the yield-to-call as well as the yield-to-maturity to determine if a particular bond is a good investment. Take into account that you may have to reinvest your funds at the call date.

d. Consider selling bonds with high coupons before the call date to realize a gain. Calculate your profit after deducting the tax on capital gains from the profits you made on the principal and the costs of selling the high-coupon bond and buying another one. Of course your premium above par will be small if the call date is relatively close and the buyers of bonds fear there will be a call.

notes

Chapter VIII

[1] George H. Hempel, *Postwar Quality of State and Local Debt*, (Washington: National Bureau of Economic Research, 1971), p. 32.

[2] Advisory Commission on Intergovernmental Relations, *City Financial Emergencies: the Intergovernmental Dimension* (Washington, 1973), p. 10.

[3] Hempel, *supra.*, p. 27.

[4] Sylvan Feldstein, 'Introduction' in James E. Spiotto Chairman, *Current Municipal Defaults & Bankruptcy*, New York: Practicing Law Institute, 1983. p. 9.

[5] Thomas F. Mitchell, "Disclosure and the Municipal Bond Industry," *The Municipal Bond Handbook*, Vol. I, Frank J. Fabozzi, Sylvan G. Feldstein, Irving M. Pollack and Frank G. Zarb, Editors, Homewood, Illinois: Dow Jones Irwin, 1983, p. 628.

[6] "Coast School District Declares Insolvency," New York Times (May 22, 1983).

[7] Robert Lindsey, "San Jose Schools Declare Insolvency in Wake of Tax Revolt," *New York Times*, (May 30, 1983).

[8] Joseph Asher, "The lessons of Cleveland," *ABA Banking Journal*, (February 1980), p. 48.

[9] Sylvan Feldstein, "The Changing Nature of the Municipal Bond Industry," *The Municipal Bond Handbook*, Vol. I, *Supra.*, p. 4.

CHAPTER IX

The Proper and Improper Uses of Municipal Bonds

A. Proper Uses of Municipal Bonds
 1. Financial Security—Savings for Retirement and Emergencies
 2. Supplement Current Income
 3. Current Support of a Needy Relative or Dependent
 4. Future Needs of Children
 5. Trust for High Tax Bracket Beneficiary
 6. Confidentiality
 7. Corporate Uses of Municipals
 8. Tax Swaps to Create Tax Losses
B. Improper Uses of Municipal Bonds
 1. Qualified Plans
 2. Low-Bracket Taxpayers

Now that you have an understanding of the mechanics of municipal bonds, we will explore ways that you can use your new knowledge. As you might expect, municipal bonds are not appropriate in all investment situations. This chapter will discuss some investment situations in which municipal bonds are appropriate, and times when you would do better to put your money into something else.

When your primary objective is to obtain the highest possible predictable after-tax income on your investment, rather than capital appreciation, municipal bonds are what you are looking for. Municipal bonds have moved into the forefront of investment planning as a result of their high after-tax yields, the plunge in the value of collectibles including stamps, coins, diamonds, and antiques; the decline in value of gold and silver; and changes in tax rules that prevent you from offsetting tax-shelter losses against your salary and portfolio income. The specific situations in which municipals should be particularly considered are discussed below.

A. Proper Uses of Municipal Bonds

1. Financial Security—Savings for Retirement and Emergencies

Everybody needs a financial cushion to provide for retirement and for bad times. Sickness, disability, and loss of job are spectors haunting everyone. Today, when the pace of change is accelerating, careers do not always proceed in predictable ways. Industries and jobs frequently become obsolete, and white collar workers, including middle managers, are facing unprecedented job loss and forced early retirement. White collar workers in the insurance industry, steel industry, automobile industry, and the oil and gas industry are losing their jobs due to streamlining required to reduce management costs.

It is prudent for you to face up to these uncertain economic circumstances by embarking on a savings program. Municipal bonds provide an ideal vehicle for such saving because of their high after-tax yields and safety.

Moreover, in an emergency, you can place your municipal bonds in a margin account, such as the Merill Lynch Cash Management Account, and borrow against them. If you have $20,000 worth of A-rated municipal bonds in a Merrill Lynch Cash Management Account, you can borrow 70% of their value, or $14,000, at the broker loan rate (7% in August, 1986).* In this way, if you need cash you can avail yourself of a large pool of liquid funds without having to sell your bonds. Interest on the above loan would be $980 a year ($14,000 × 7%). However, if the bonds yielded 6½%, the interest income earned on them would be $1,300 a year (6½% × $20,000), large enough to repay the expense of the borrowing. Alternatively, highly rated municipals are quite liquid so they can easily be sold to a dealer or brokerage firm.

If you plan to retire at a certain age and will be in a lower tax bracket after you do, you can buy municipal bonds that will come due at that time and then reinvest the proceeds in higher-yielding taxable bonds. However, if your tax bracket will still be above 28% after retirement because you have a large pension, annuity, or other sources of income, it may be worthwhile to keep municipal bonds.

Municipal bonds are considerably more liquid than investments such as real estate, collectibles, or tax shelters. Moreover, short-term bonds and usually intermediate-term bonds, hold their value well compared to stocks and many other investments.

---

* As discussed in Part II, Chapter XIII, the interest deduction on such borrowing will be disallowed if it is determined that the debt was incurred to purchase or carry municipal bonds. Internal Revenue Code Section 265(2).

2. Supplement Current Income

Instead of spending $20,000 on a new car or similar large purchase, you should consider using the money to buy municipal bonds. In September 1986 you could receive a 6½% return on an intermediate term bond, or $1,300 each year on a $20,000 investment, for the term of the bond; you could use this $1,300 to buy something special or take a short vacation *every year* and still have the $20,000 principal. As discussed above, in an emergency the $20,000 of bonds can be margined and you could borrow $14,000 on the security of your bonds. Although this is not quite having your cake and eating it too, it is keeping your cake and continuing to nibble. If you wish to spend the coupon income each year, a high-coupon bond might be appropriate. However, if you can afford to save some of the interest, then you might buy $25,000 of low-coupon bonds with the $20,000 cash.

3. Current Support of a Needy Relative or Dependent

Under the tax rules in effect prior to the enactment of the Tax Reform Acts of 1984 and 1986, a needy relative or dependent could be supplied with funds on a pre-tax basis in two ways. First, a 10-year trust (also called a Clifford Trust) could have been created for the benefit of the relative or dependent. The Tax Reform Act of 1986 eliminated this income-shifting technique.

Second, prior to the 1984 Tax Reform Act, an interest-free loan could have been made to the relative or dependent and such person would then have invested such funds in taxable investments. The Tax Reform Act of 1984 eliminated all of the tax benefits of this device. Thus, the only way to support a needy relative or dependent tax-free is by purchasing municipal bonds.

If municipal bonds are used to support a dependent, you would take the tax-free income generated by the bonds and pay the amount required to the relative. By using municipal bonds you have complete control of the investment funds, you may be able to claim a dependency exemption[1] and you may be able to deduct certain medical expenses paid for your dependent[2] if you provide more than half of the dependent's support. If you give less than $10,000 (or $20,000 if you are married), there would be no adverse gift-or-estate-tax consequences.

4. Future Needs of Children

Sending your children to college, or helping them get started in a business or a profession when they graduate requires a lot of money. As stated above, prior to the Tax Reform Act of 1976 you might have accumulated the funds by means of a 10 year or Clifford trust. However, the 1986 Tax Reform Act generally eliminates the benefit of parental income shifting to children under age 14 by taxing any investment income attributable to property received from the parents and any other investment income in excess of $1,000 at the parents' top marginal tax rate. Municipal bonds may be used for this purpose for the same reasons that they make sense for supporting a needy relative. They offer the simplest and least expensive method of providing support with pre-tax dollars. Municipal bonds are particularly flexible in providing funds for higher education because you can buy bonds that come due when a child is ready for college.

5. Trust for High Tax Bracket Beneficiary

If a trust is established for a high tax bracket beneficiary, municipal bonds should be considered as a potential investment because under trust tax rules, tax-exempt income earned by a trust and distributed to a beneficiary is tax-exempt in the hands of the beneficiary.

6. Confidentiality

If you buy an unregistered municipal bond with coupons attached, a certain degree of confidentiality may be achieved. Complete confidentiality is not available because the firms that sell municipal bonds to investors must keep records of transactions and banks often request your social security number when cashing coupons. Moreover, many reputable firms will not accept cash in payment of the bonds.

The Proper and Improper Uses of Municipal Bonds 173

The IRS has announced that for the first time, on the individual federal income tax return in 1987, there will be a line requesting you to report the amount of your municipal bond interest. Failure to answer that question correctly will potentially subject you to charges of fraud. There is no statute of limitations on fraud charges and the sentence may be a jail term.

7. Corporate Uses of Municipals

If you control a regular corporation, rather than what the Internal Revenue Service calls a Subchapter S corporation, and the corporation has excess funds, an investment in municipal bonds may be an appropriate investment if the corporation is in a high income tax bracket. As a general rule, however, there is no reason for an individual to contribute his municipal bonds to a regular corporation.

Subject to the Tax Reform Act of 1986 rules, municipal bond interest will be received tax-free by a corporation. The Tax Reform Act of 1986 provides a stiff new alternative minimum tax at the rate of 20% on corporations. One new item of tax preference is one-half of the amount by which the corporation's financial statement income exceeds its regular taxable income increased by all other preferences. For this purpose, municipal bond income increases the corporation's financial statement income and thus might result in the corporation being subject to the alternative minimum tax. In addition, municipal bond interest on certain private-purpose bonds is a tax preference item for purposes of the alternative minimum tax.

8. Tax-Swaps to Create Tax Losses

This subject is discussed in Part II, Chapter XIII.

B. Improper Uses of Municipal Bonds

There are two investment situations in which municipal bonds are generally not indicated as an investment vehicle.

1. Qualified Plans

A qualified plan such as an IRA, Keogh, or other pension or profit sharing plan should generally not invest in municipal bonds because the income earned by these entities are not subject to tax in any case. Moreover, an investor or beneficiary of a qualified plan will pay the same tax on a distribution whether the money came from tax-exempt or taxable investments. However, during August of 1986, some pension fund managers invested in municipal bonds because the yield on long-term municipal bonds was higher than on Treasury bonds. In this situation, these managers believed that municipal bonds had a better chance of capital appreciation than did Treasury bonds.

2. Low-Bracket Taxpayers

Low-bracket taxpayers, individuals whose top marginal tax bracket is below 28%, should not invest in municipal bonds because they can usually do better with taxable securities.

notes

Chapter IX

[1] Internal Revenue Code Sections 151, 152.
[2] Internal Revenue Code Section 213(a)

CHAPTER X

How and From Whom to Buy Municipals

A. The Sellers
    1. How they Earn their Money
    2. How to Select a Seller
B. Sources of Information on Municipal Bonds
C. Purchasing the Bonds
    1. The Primary (New Issue) Market
    2. The Secondary Market
    3. The Confirmation and Payment
    4. Guidelines for Talking with the Sellers

A. The Sellers

1. How They Earn Their Money

Institutions which sell bonds to the public, such as banks, general brokerage houses, and those specializing in municipal bonds, earn their money by taking a market risk, betting that they can sell their inventory of bonds for more than they paid for them. If interest rates rise substantially while an institution has a large inventory of bonds, it may lose a lot of money. The losses are magnified if the seller borrows funds to increase the size of its bond holdings. Such borrowing is called leverage. A leveraged position increases an institution's exposure to market changes. If the institution does not sell enough of its securities, it may have to liquidate part of its portfolio at a loss to repay the loans.

Some brokerage firms are called full-service firms because they offer a variety of services and handle all kinds of transactions. Other firms specialize in municipal bonds. Both kinds of firms have specialists including traders and analysts who are particularly knowledgeable about municipal bonds. These specialists act as resource centers if you have a question that the seller, the person handling the customer accounts, cannot answer.

The sellers will locate bonds with particular characteristics if they do not have them in inventory. They can find a bond with a specific maturity, coupon, risk, or issuer, if they know you are looking for something special. Other services provided by sellers include information about bond ratings, computations, advice on market conditions, and information on special issues.

Perhaps you are thinking of contacting a discount broker. Discounters charge less for stock transactions than do full service houses. However, it does not appear that a discount broker can provide you with either a lower price for municipal bonds or with the necessary advice and service. Discounters do not hold an inventory of bonds from which you can purchase. They purchase the specific bond you request, whether or not it is selling at a desirable price. If you had done enough shopping to determine a bond was a good value, you could buy it directly from the owner without using the discounter. It is unlikely that a discounter could provide you with a better price.

If you are a good customer of a particular seller, there might be some price flexibility. If you ask for a reduced price it is discussed with the office manager and a decision is made. Big purchasers are sometimes able to negotiate a discount.

For people with substantial portfolios, some banks and brokerage houses will agree to manage your money, buying and selling your bonds according to their judgment. For this service they charge an annual fee plus transaction costs. They say that they keep their portfolio management departments separate from their bond trading departments, which sell bonds. Our organization, The Scarsdale Investment Group, Ltd., shops the market for the bonds of best quality and most attractive price for the client. Since we hold no bonds, we have no conflict of interest over what to purchase.

2. How to Select a Seller

Instead of choosing a particular institution that markets bonds, it is better to select a particular seller who is recommended by a friend or relative. The seller should try to keep you happy so your entire family will continue to work through the firm.

It is important that the seller have some interest and familiarity with municipal bonds. Most sellers have area specialties including stocks, options, commodities, etc. and might be inclined to switch you from municipal bond investing to their own areas of interest. Be aware that a seller makes a living from selling stocks, bonds, and other investments, and he may not make as much money from selling municipal bonds as from selling other investments. For a retail investor such as you, the spread the bond house earns can range from an unusual low of one quarter of one percent ($12.50

per $5,000 par value) on large blocks of actively traded bonds to a high of four or five percent ($200 or $250 per $5,000 of face value) for odd-lot sales.

Some experienced sellers will not have the time or patience to deal with a small or inexperienced customer. If that is your impression, find another seller who is willing to work with you in the hopes of building his customer base. You should feel comfortable with your seller, and he should find the information that you need.

Although you may have one particular seller with whom you like to deal, it is wise to compare prices with those offered by other sellers. Through comparison shopping, your seller will know you are knowledgeable and give you competitive prices.

A seller is a bond merchant, but he is held to a higher standard than most merchants by the Federal Securities Act of 1933. When being presented as a securities broker and/or dealer, a seller implies that he is acting according to a professional standard. Sometimes mistakes are made. For example, bond prices may vary slightly from what you expected or yields might be off because of "rounding." Your confirmation slip should reflect what you have agreed to purchase. If there is a discrepancy, call your seller and ask for a clarification and if necessary a corrected confirmation before you pay the bill.

B. Sources of Information on Municipal Bonds

Unlike stocks, which can be followed daily in the newspapers, most municipal bond prices are not listed anywhere. This is because there are thousands of issuers whose bonds represent only a fraction of the total market, and most of those bonds are infrequently traded. *The New York Times* and *The Wall Street Journal* list a few issues that are widely sold and frequently traded, as seen in the sample below:

Tax-Exempt Authority Bonds

Bonds	Bid	Ask	Chng
Alabama GO 8⅜s 2001	90	92	- ½
Battery Prk 6⅜s 2014	61	65	......
Chelan Co 5s 2013	58½	61½	......
Clark Co.Apt10½s 2007	96½	98½	- ½
Col SPE 3⅞s 2003	67	70	- ½
Del R PA 6½s 2011	65	68	- ½
Dgs Co PUD 4s 2018	42	44	......
Georgia MEA 8s 2015	79½	83½	......
Interm't Pwr 7½s 2018	70	74	......
Interm't Pwr10½s2018	94½	96½	......
Intermt Pwr 14s 2021	117	120	......
Jacksonville ER 2013	89½	92½	......
LA. Off. Ter. 6½s 2008	65	68	......
→ M.A.C. N.Y. 7½s 92	89½	92½	- ½
M.A.C. N.Y. 7½s 95	87	90	- ½
M.A.C. N.Y. 8s 86	99	103	......
M.A.C. N.Y. 8s 91	97½	100½	- ½
M.A.C. N.Y. 9.70s 2008	97½	100½	- ½
M.A.C. N.Y. 9¾s 92	101½	104½	......
M.A.C. N.Y. 10¼s 93	109	112	......
Mass Port 6s 2011	65	68	......
Mass G.O. 6½s 2000	72½	75½	......
Mass Whl 6⅞s2015	54	57	......
Mass Whl 13⅜s2017	103½	106½	......
MetroTrsAth 9¼s2015	90	95	-1
Mich Pwr 10⅝s 2018	101	103	......
Neb PPD 7.10s 2017	70	73	......
NJ Tpke 4¾s 2006	59	62	- ½
NJ Tpke 5.70s 2013	66	68	......
NJ Tpke 6s 2014	66	68	......
NY MtgAy 9½s 2013	96	98	......

Bonds	Bid	Ask	Chng
NYS Power 5½s 2010	62	66	......
NYS Power 6⅝s 2010	69½	72½	......
NYS Power 9½s 2001	102½	105	......
NYS Power 9⅞s 2020	97	100	......
NYS Thruwy 3.10s 94	69	72	......
NYS U D C 6s 2013	58	62	......
NYS U D C 7s 2014	68	70	......
NC E MPA 11¼s 2018	101½	105½	......
Okla Tpke 4.70s 2006	67	70	......
Port N.Y. 4¾s 2003	57½	61½	......
Port N.Y. 6s 2006	67	70	......
Port N.Y. 7s 2011	74½	78½	......
Port N.Y. 10½s 2008	103	106	......
Salt River 9¼s 2020	93	96	......
So. Car. P.S. 10¼ 2020	99	102	......
Tx Mun PA. 9½s 2012	90	93	......
Valdez 5½s 2007	61½	64½	......
Valdez 6s 2007	62½	65½	......
Wash PS 6s 2015F	12	15	......
Wash PS 7¾s 2018F	12½	15½	......
Wash PS 9⅞s 2012F	12½	15½	......
Wash PS 12½s 2010F	14½	17½	......
Wash PS 6s 2012	44½	48½	......
Wash PS 7¾s 2017	50½	54½	......
Wash PS 9¼s 2011	60½	64½	......
Wash PS 13⅞s 2018	85	88	......
Wash PS 14¾s 2012	95	98	......
Wash PS 15s 2017	90½	93½	- ½

F-Traded Flat
*Source other than N.A.S.D. †Ex coupon.

How do you crack the code? Read down the list and pick one you like. As an example, try M.A.C., N.Y., the bonds of the Municipal Assistance Corporation.

Bonds	*Bid*	*Ask*	*Chng*
M.A.C. N.Y. 7½s 92	89½	92½	–½

First you see the issuer's name and the bond's description. In this example, the M.A.C. bond has a coupon rate of 7½% and matures in 1992. The bond houses were generally offering to sell this bond at 92½ and offering to purchase such bond at 89½.

Traditionally, bond people drop the last zero on a price quotation. This is because bonds used to be sold in multiples of $100 instead of $1000. For this bond, 89 means $890 and the ½ means ½ of $10, or $5. While buyers were willing to pay $895, the sellers were asking 92½, or $925, a difference of $30, a three-point spread. The –½ shows that today this bond closed at a price $5 less than the previous day. When translated into yield-to-maturity, the bid was at 9.40% and the ask was 8.83%, a difference of 57 basis points.

Brokers and dealers are another source of information. The staffs at the municipal bond brokerage houses will send lists of bonds offered for sale. A list usually includes security description, yield-to-maturity (but not yield-to-call), and price. Some lists also contain yield after the tax on capital gains, a very important number when buying discount bonds. Brokerage houses may also publish data on new issues or explanations about security provisions that affect an entire class of bonds.

The most important source of information is, however, your individual seller. When a call is made to the seller, you might ask "What do you have in your inventory that is triple-A and no more than 10 years out?" The seller looks in his inventory and replies. You may ask, "What is the security on that bond? What is the yield-to-maturity and the yield-to-call? Is there call protection and a premium if the bond is called?" The seller will answer all your questions. If he does not know the answer, he should call his firm's trader to find the answer.

If you are seeking a particular kind of bond that an institution does not have in inventory, the seller might check the wire services to see if it is being offered in the market. The sellers have access to *The Bond Buyer's* Munifacts teletype system and the Blue List, which is the most widely distributed set of dealer offering sheets, circulated daily to the sellers by Standard & Poor's. Current offerings from this service are also listed by the Blue List Ticker, which is a minute-to-minute computerized version of the Blue List. Dealers also employ the Kenny Wire run by J. J. Kenny & Co., and the C-Wire Service run by Chapdelaine & Co. (N.Y.).

C. Purchasing the Bonds

1. The Primary (New-Issue) Market

New-issue prices are established by a syndicate, a group of investment bankers who buy, or underwrite, a new bond issue from the municipal authority (the issuer) and offer it for resale to the general public. During the initial sale of the bonds (approximately 30 days) all the participants in the underwriting syndicate must sell the bonds for the same price. The offering prices cannot be changed without the consent of most of the members of the syndicate. When the syndicate is dissolved and the municipality receives its money for the bonds, any unsold bonds are priced according to the wishes of the dealers.

Tombstone—Exhibit A

In the opinion of Bond Counsel, under existing statutes, regulations, rulings and court decisions, interest on the Series A Bonds is exempt from all present Federal income taxation, and the Series A Bonds and the interest thereon are exempt from all present taxes imposed by the State of Florida except taxes imposed by Chapter 220, Florida Statutes, on interest, income or profits on debt obligations owned by corporations as defined in said Chapter 220.

Legal Opinion

NEW ISSUES

RATINGS:
Standard & Poor's: AAA
(Insured by Industrial Indemnity Company under Health Industry Bond Insurance ("HIBI") Program)

Rating

$36,040,930.00	$15,848,609.20
City of Pensacola	Santa Rosa County
Health Facilities Authority	Health Facilities Authority
Health Facilities Revenue Bonds	Health Facilities Revenue Bonds
(Baptist Hospital, Inc.)	(Baptist Hospital, Inc.)
Series A	Series A

Name of Issue

Dated: November 1, 1983   Due: November 1, as shown below

Amount	Maturity	Interest Rate	Amount	Maturity	Interest Rate	Amount	Maturity	Interest Rate
$185,000	1984	5.50%	$745,000	1988	7.50%	$1,020,000	1992	8.75%
210,000	1985	6.00	800,000	1989	8.00	1,110,000	1993	9.00
405,000	1986	6.50	865,000	1990	8.25	1,205,000	1994	9.25
695,000	1987	7.00	945,000	1991	8.50	1,325,000	1995	9.40

Serial Bonds

$40,715,000   10⅛% Term Bonds due November 1, 2014

Price of all Bonds: 100%
(Accrued Interest to be added)

Term Bonds

$1,664,539.20 Compound Interest Bonds
(Interest Compounded Semi-annually and Payable at Maturity)

Zero Coupon Bonds

The Compound Interest Bonds are dated their date of delivery.

Maturity Value	Maturity	Yield	Present Value	Price (% of Maturity Value)
$1,440,000	1996	10.00%	$409,622.40	28.446%
1,440,000	1997	10.10	366,667.20	25.463
1,440,000	1998	10.20	327,585.20	22.749
1,440,000	1999	10.25	294,336.00	20.440
1,440,000	2000	10.25	266,328.00	18.495

The Series A Bonds will be limited obligations of each Authority and not general obligations of the State of Florida, its Authorities, City of Pensacola, Santa Rosa County or any other political subdivision of the State of Florida. Neither the credit nor the taxing power of the State of Florida, City of Pensacola, Santa Rosa County or any other political subdivision of the State of Florida is pledged to the payment of the principal of, redemption premium, if any, or interest on the Series A Bonds. The Authorities have no taxing power.

The Series A Bonds will be issued and secured under the provisions of the Bond Indenture of each Authority and will constitute a separate issue of each Authority. The Series A Bonds are payable solely from revenues to be derived by each Authority from loan payments under their respective Loan Agreement with

Limitations of Responsibility for Repayment

BAPTIST HOSPITAL, INC.
(Pensacola, Florida)

Baptist Hospital, Inc. is a Florida not-for-profit corporation providing health care services to the residents of the City of Pensacola and the region encompassing northwest Florida and south Alabama. The corporation currently owns and operates Baptist Hospital, an acute care hospital with 520 licensed beds, located in Pensacola, Florida, and leases the 52-bed Jay Hospital in Jay, Florida and the 50-bed Valley Springs Community Hospital in DeFuniak Springs, Florida. Baptist Hospital, Inc. is a member of the Voluntary Hospitals of America, Inc., a cooperative consisting of 61 health care institutions in 32 states. The Series A Bonds should not be construed, in any way, to be a liability of the Voluntary Hospitals of America, Inc.

Description of Issuer

Payment of principal of and interest on the Series A Bonds is insured by Industrial Indemnity Company, a Crum & Foster insurance company.

Insurance

The Series A Bonds are offered when, as and if issued and received by the Underwriters subject to prior sale, to withdrawal or modification of the offer without notice, and to receipt of the unqualified approving opinion of Bryan, Wood, Ivey, Mitchell & Petty, New York, New York, Bond Counsel. No Series A Bonds of either issue will be sold unless all Series A Bonds of both issues are sold at the same time. Certain legal matters will be passed upon for City of Pensacola Health Facilities Authority by its Counsel, Clark, Partington, Hart, Hart & Johnson, Pensacola, Florida, for Santa Rosa County Health Facilities Authority by Thomas G. Morton, Jr., Esquire, County Attorney for Santa Rosa County, Florida, for Baptist Hospital, Inc. by its Counsel, Beggs & Lane, Pensacola, Florida, and for the Underwriters by their Counsel, Wolf, Block, Schorr and Solis-Cohen, Philadelphia, Pennsylvania. The Series A Bonds were delivered in New York, New York, on December 13, 1983. Bonds of particular maturities may or may not be available from the undersigned or others at the above prices on or after the date of this announcement.

Bond Counsel

Kidder, Peabody & Co.
Incorporated

Lead Underwriter

Bear, Stearns & Co.	A. G. Becker Paribas Incorporated	Blyth Eastman Paine Webber Incorporated	Alex. Brown & Sons
Donaldson, Lufkin & Jenrette Securities Corporation	Drexel Burnham Lambert Incorporated		A. G. Edwards & Sons, Inc.
The First Boston Corporation	Goldman, Sachs & Co.		William R. Hough & Co.
E. F. Hutton & Company Inc.	Lehman Brothers Kuhn Loeb Incorporated		Matthews & Wright, Inc.
Merrill Lynch Capital Markets	John Nuveen & Co. Incorporated	Oppenheimer & Co., Inc.	Prudential-Bache Securities
L. F. Rothschild, Unterberg, Towbin	Salomon Brothers Inc		Shearson/American Express Inc.
Smith Barney, Harris Upham & Co. Incorporated			Thomson McKinnon Securities Inc.
Dean Witter Reynolds Inc.			Ziegler Securities, Inc.

Underwriting Syndicate

January 9, 1984

Exhibit B

Legal Opinion

In the opinion of Bond Counsel, interest on the Bonds will be exempt under existing law from Federal income taxes and from New York State and New York City personal income taxes.

NEW ISSUE

Name of Issuer

$400,000,000

The City of New York

General Obligation Bonds

Fiscal 1985 Series B

Dated: November 15, 1984 **Due: November 15, as shown below**

Interest will be payable semi annually, beginning May 15, 1985, and on each November 15 and May 15 thereafter. The Bonds will be issued as registered bonds in the denomination of $5,000 or an integral multiple thereof. Principal of the Bonds and redemption premium, if any, will be payable at the office of the City's Fiscal Agent, Manufacturers Hanover Trust Company, New York, New York, or a successor Fiscal Agent. Interest on the Bonds will be payable by check mailed to the addresses of the registered owners of the Bonds. The Bonds will be subject to redemption prior to maturity as described in the Official Statement.

Serial Bonds

Maturity	Amount	Interest Rate	Price	Maturity	Amount	Interest Rate	Price
1985	$14,820,000	6 %	100%	1998	$ 8,800,000	10¾%	100%
1986	14,820,000	7	100	1999	8,800,000	10¾	100
1987	14,820,000	7¾	100	2000	8,800,000	10⅞	100
1988	22,220,000	8¼	100	2001	8,800,000	10⅞	100
1989	22,220,000	8¾	100	2002	13,100,000	10⅞	99½
1990	8,800,000	9¼	100	2003	13,200,000	10⅞	99½
1991	8,800,000	9½	100	2004	13,200,000	10⅞	99½
1992	8,800,000	9⅝	100	2005	13,200,000	11	100
1993	8,800,000	9¾	100	2006	13,200,000	11	100
1994	8,800,000	10	100	2007	13,200,000	11	100
1995	8,800,000	10¼	100	2008	13,200,000	11	100
1996	8,800,000	10½	100	2009	13,200,000	11	100
1997	8,800,000	10⅝	100				

Term Bonds

$100,000,000 10⅞% Term Bonds due November 15, 2014 Priced to Yield 11%

(Accrued interest to be added)

Bond Counsel

The Bonds are offered subject to prior sale, when, as and if issued by the City and accepted by the Underwriters, subject to the approval of the legality of the Bonds by Rogers & Wells, New York, New York, Bond Counsel to the City, and subject to certain other conditions. Certain legal matters in connection with the preparation of the Official Statement will be passed upon for the City by Lord, Day & Lord, New York, New York. Certain legal matters will be passed upon for the Underwriters by Brown, Wood, Ivey, Mitchell & Petty, New York, New York. It is expected that the Bonds will be available for delivery in New York, New York, as provided in the Official Statement, on or about November 20, 1984. Bonds may or may not be available from the undersigned or others at the above prices on and after the date of this announcement. The offering is made by the Official Statement, copies of which may be obtained in jurisdictions in which this announcement is circulated from such of the undersigned or other brokers or dealers as may lawfully offer the Bonds in each jurisdiction.

Underwriting Syndicate

Merrill Lynch Capital Markets · Goldman, Sachs & Co.

Morgan Guaranty Trust Company of New York · Chase Manhattan Capital Markets Corporation · Citicorp Capital Markets Group Citibank, N.A.

Bear, Stearns & Co. · Chemical Bank · Dillon, Read & Co. Inc.

Ehrlich-Bober & Co., Inc. · E. F. Hutton & Company Inc. · PaineWebber Incorporated

Prudential-Bache Securities · L. F. Rothschild, Unterberg, Towbin · Salomon Brothers Inc

Shearson Lehman/American Express Inc. · Smith Barney, Harris Upham & Co. Incorporated

Bank of America NT & SA · Bank of Boston The First National Bank of Boston · Bankers Trust Company · The Bank of New York · Alex. Brown & Sons Incorporated · Continental Bank Continental Illinois National Bank and Trust Company of Chicago

Donaldson, Lufkin & Jenrette Securities Corporation · Drexel Burnham Lambert Incorporated · A. G. Edwards & Sons, Inc. · European American Bank and Trust Company

First Chicago The First National Bank of Chicago · First Interstate Bank of California · Fleet National Bank · Glickenhaus & Co. · Harris Trust and Savings Bank

Irving Trust Company · Kidder, Peabody & Co. Incorporated · Lebenthal & Co., Inc. · Manufacturers Hanover Trust Company · Marine Midland Bank, N.A.

Matthews & Wright, Inc. · Morgan Stanley & Co. Incorporated · National Westminster Bank (USA) · The Northern Trust Company · John Nuveen & Co. Incorporated

The Philadelphia National Bank · Roosevelt & Cross Incorporated · Security Pacific National Bank · Shawmut Bank of Boston, N.A.

Southeast Bank, N.A. Miami · Thomson McKinnon Securities Inc. · Wertheim & Co., Inc. · Dean Witter Reynolds Inc.

Adams, McEntee & Company · Advest, Inc. · Allen & Company Incorporated · Barr Brothers & Co., Inc. · Boettcher & Company, Inc.

Langdon P. Cook & Co. Incorporated · Dain Bosworth Incorporated · Douglas & Co. Municipals, Inc. · First Albany Corporation · First Southwest Company

First Tennessee Bank N.A. Memphis · First Wisconsin National Bank · Gruntal & Co., Incorporated · Halpert, Oberst and Company

Hanifen, Imhoff Inc. · Chester Harris & Co., Inc. · Herzfeld & Stern Inc. · Hutchinson, Shockey, Erley & Co. · Josephthal & Co. Incorporated

J. J. Lowrey & Co. · McDonald & Company Securities, Inc. · McLaughlin, Piven, Vogel Inc. · Moore & Schley Municipals, Inc.

Moseley, Hallgarten, Estabrook & Weeden Inc. · The Ohio Company · Oppenheimer & Co., Inc. · Printon Kane & Co.

Samuel A. Ramirez & Co., Inc. · Rauscher Pierce Refsnes, Co. · Refco Municipal Securities Inc. · Rodman & Renshaw, Inc.

Donald Sheldon & Co., Inc. · Herbert J. Sims & Co., Inc. · Stephens Inc. · Swiss American Securities Inc. · Ziegler Securities, Inc.

American Securities Corporation · Baird Patrick & Co., Inc. · Baker, Watts & Co. · Banco Popular de Puerto Rico

George K. Baum & Company · Bevill, Bresler & Schulman Incorporated · Blunt Ellis & Loewi Incorporated · J. C. Bradford & Co.

Brislin & Woram · Clayton Brown & Associates, Inc. · Burgess & Leith Incorporated · Butcher & Singer Inc.

Cain Brothers, Shattuck & Company · Carolan & Co., Inc. · The Cherokee Securities Company

The Connecticut Bank and Trust Company Hartford · Conners & Co., Inc. · Coogan, Gilbert & Co. · R. W. Corby & Company Incorporated · Cowen & Co.

Craigie Incorporated · Cralin & Co., Inc. · Cranston Securities Company · Cronin & Marcotte, Inc.

Cumberland Securities Company, Inc. · Daniels & Bell, Inc. · Doft & Co., Inc. · Dolphin & Bradbury · A. Webster Dougherty & Co. Incorporated

Dougherty, Dawkins, Strand & Yost Incorporated · F. H. Downs, Hannon Division of Bussell & Co. · Emanuel Municipal Securities Ltd. · Ernst & Company

Faherty, Aliaga & Co. Incorporated · Fahnestock & Co. · Ferris & Company Incorporated · The Fidelity Bank Philadelphia · First Charlotte Corporation

First Huntington Securities Corp. · First of Michigan Corporation · The Frazer Lanier Company Incorporated · Gabriele, Hueglin & Cashman, Inc.

Gibraltar Securities Co. · William R. Hough & Co. · Howard, Weil, Labouisse, Friedrichs Incorporated · Interstate Securities Corporation

Janney Montgomery Scott Inc. · Jefferies, Wagenseller & Company (A Division of Jefferies & Company, Inc.) · Ladenburg, Thalmann & Co. Inc. · Laidlaw Ansbacher Inc.

The Leedy Corporation · Legg Mason Wood Walker Incorporated · M. G. Lewis & Company, Inc. · Liss, Tenner & Goldberg, Inc. · Mabon, Nugent & Co.

Mann, Urfer & Co., Inc. · Meuse, Rinker & Chapman, Inc. · Mid-State Securities Corp. · Miller & Schroeder Municipals, Inc.

E. A. Moos & Co. Incorporated · Morgan, Keegan & Company, Inc. · Newman & Associates, Inc. · R. W. Peters, Rickel & Co., Inc.

Philips, Appel & Walden, Inc. · D. A. Pincus & Co., Inc. · Piper, Jaffray & Hopwood Incorporated · Wm. E. Pollock & Co., Inc.

Powell & Satterfield, Inc. · Prescott, Ball & Turben, Inc. · Pryor, Govan, Counts & Co., Inc. · Purcell, Graham & Co., Inc.

Arch W. Roberts & Co. · Rogers & Lamb · Rooney, Pace Inc. · Russell, Rea & Zappala, Inc. · Ryan, Beck & Co. · Seasongood & Mayer

Shatkin Lee Securities · Stanley Co. · Stifel, Nicolaus & Company Incorporated · Stoever, Glass & Co., Inc. · Stone & Youngberg

Tollner & Bean, Inc. · Tripp & Co., Inc. · Tucker, Anthony & R. L. Day, Inc. · Underwood, Neuhaus & Co. Incorporated

Union Planters National Bank of Memphis · Van Kampen Merritt Inc. · Michael A. Weisser, Inc. · Wheat, First Securities, Inc.

R. D. White & Company · A. H. Williams & Co. Incorporated · Williams Securities Group, Inc. · A. W. Zucker & Co.

November 13, 1984

An advertisement, called a tombstone, is published in newspapers describing the new offering of the issue and issuer. Exhibits A and B are reproductions of official statements for a revenue bond issue and a general obligation issue, respectively. Available through the seller is a prospectus, which is an official offering statement. Called a "red herring" among bond people, it is a detailed description of the worst possible scenarios that could affect your investment.

An underwriter for a particular issue has more price flexibility for that issue than a dealer who did not participate in the underwriting syndicate, due to the take-down concession. The take-down concession is the discount from the list price allowed to a member of an underwriting syndicate on any bond sold. Thus, initially a member of the underwriting syndicate is able to buy the bonds from an underwriting pool and sell them at the set price and make a better profit. However, if the bonds do not sell, each participant must absorb an agreed-upon share. Because the underwriters acquired the bonds for less initially, they can more flexibly reduce the price to the investor (after the syndication period) if there is a reason to do so.

New bonds are sold on a "when-issued" basis. You must pay for them when they are issued. If they are not issued, the agreement is not binding and you will have to find other bonds to purchase. New bonds can take months before they are finally issued, especially if they have a high coupon. It may also be weeks before your seller will know if the issue has been canceled. If so, you must look for another bond to purchase.

2. The Secondary Market

You can buy municipal bonds either as new issues or in the secondary market. Once municipal bonds are part of the secondary market, each bond house sets its own price for them. If you wish to compare prices, it might not be possible to discover the exact same bond at another bond house unless an issue is just out of syndicate or is extremely large. Consideration then must be given to bonds with similar ratings and forms of security to see if they are priced about the same. Based upon all you have read and know, you must make a judgment if the offered bond is a good value.

3. The Confirmation and Payment

The Municipal Bond Securities Rulemaking Board, an independent, regulatory organization under federal supervision, has established uniform practices for dealers, dealer banks, and brokers of municipal securities. The conclusion of a transaction must follow the prescribed rules of this organization. Such rules include the following:

a. Confirmation slips must be sent within one business day to a purchaser.

b. Payment must be made on the fifth business day after the trade (unless otherwise arranged).

c. Payment for new bonds purchased on a when-and-if basis must be completed no sooner than the fifth business day after the final confirmation, the final date to be arranged. Though sellers take orders for new bond issues, the issue may be delayed or canceled if there is insufficient demand or circumstances change.

d. The confirmation can take different forms, but it must include the same standard information. One confirmation slip is reproduced below:

The features of the confirmation that should attract your attention include:

1—Capacity Code, which indicates whether your transaction

SALES		A	B	TRANS. NO.	TR	CAP*	SETT	TRADE DATE	SETTLEMENT DATE
1	5	1	1		1	2	0	1/31/84	2/08/84	2/08/84

ENTIFICATION NO. CONTRA PARTY/CUSTOMER — SPECIAL DELIVERY INSTRUCTIONS

300540 1
To insure proper credit please return confirmation with check for the net amount of this trade to

WE	QUANTITY	CUSIP	SECURITY DESCRIPTION
Sld	10000.	946541EQ8	Waynesboro, Georgia Public Housing Authority

INTEREST ACCRUED
FROM: 11/1 TO: 2/8 3.875%
Moody's: Aaa
Due 5/01/91

PRICE	PRINCIPAL	INTEREST	*SPECIAL CHARGES	NET AMOUNT
73.176	7317.60	104.41		7,422.01
9.000% YIELD				

*capacity code

was directly with the firm whose name is listed on the confirmation, or whether they were acting as intermediaries.

2—Trade date—the date you bought the bond.

3—Settlement date—the date by which you must pay for the bond.

4—Delivery instructions—the place the bonds are to be sent after you pay for them.

5—Quantity—the face value amount of bonds you purchased.

6—CUSIP number—the bond fingerprint used to identify the bonds in all transactions.

7—Security description—the exact title of the bond including the name, the interest rate, the maturity date, the date it was first issued, and the first call date. If a bond is registered, this information will also be included as part of the description.

8—The yield-to-maturity or basis (9.000%).

9—Price—the dollars you agreed to pay per $100, in this case 73.176.

10—To obtain the principal amount, the quantity ($10,000) is multiplied by the price of the bond expressed as a decimal (.73176); $10,000 × .73176 = $7317.60.

11—The interest refers to the accrued interest that you must pay to the seller ($104.41).

12—Net amount equals the sum of the principal amount and the accrued interest. This is the amount of the check you send to your seller.

13—Call features are listed at the bottom of the confirmation and as part of item (8). If the bond is not callable, nothing will appear in the box. If the seller makes a representation, such as the bond has no mandatory call or it is a put bond, you can specifically request that information appear on your confirmation if it makes you feel more comfortable.

4. Guidelines for Talking with the Sellers

Be aware that a seller sells bonds both from the inventory of his own institution and from the bonds advertised on the various wire services. The seller may be able to give you a better deal if you buy from his inventory. Some institutions charge a fee if they go to the wire and shop for a bond on your behalf. Compare the bonds offered from both sources to see which deal is more favorable. Sellers often offer bonds at prices more closely related to what the bonds cost them than to prevailing market rates; thus, bonds from a seller's inventory may be comparatively inexpensive in some cases.

Know what a seller's offer means. Have a piece of paper and pencil ready to jot down the following information: the coupon, the name of the bond, yield-to-maturity, yield-to-call, rating, bond security, call protection, and price.

Be clear what your own needs are, and how long you can keep your money tied up in bonds. Are there going to be expenses in the short term, or is it possible to lengthen the maturity for a higher yield? How do you evaluate the inflation risk?

Ask the seller if there is any leeway in the price of the bonds if you buy an odd lot. Be aware of the prices at which comparative issues are selling so that you have a basis of comparison. If you are just shopping, the seller may have little patience because bond prices change from day to day and sometimes from hour to hour. If you are a serious customer, the seller will spend time with you. The seller can sometimes reduce the price by taking less money for himself, but obviously, there must be sufficient incentive.

Understand that if you are in the market for 10 bonds, and a seller has just what you are looking for in a 25 bond lot, you will probably be out of luck. In the retail municipal bond market, an odd lot is anything less than $25,000 (25 bonds). For institutional purchases, anything less than $100,000 in face value is considered an odd lot. Some bonds are sold AON—all or nothing, where the seller will sell the bonds only if all the bonds in that particular lot are purchased. Other bonds are sold in multiples of or in lots of 5, 25, 50, 100, or 200 bonds of $1,000 each.

Find out how much time you have before the bond you are considering will be offered to another buyer. The offering price on particular bonds might be "out firm" for two minutes or two hours. That means that for the time period stated you have the right to purchase the bonds at the agreed-upon price. The time period is based on how much customer interest there is in those bonds. To spread the risk, some institutions hold bonds in joint accounts, so that many sellers are selling bonds from a collective pool. Individual sellers cannot hold bonds when other sellers have customers. The seller is permitted to call the customer to remind him that the agreed upon time period is about to lapse. If you are a good customer, the seller will try to be accommodating.

Here are a few things you should avoid when buying or selling municipal bonds. First, don't tell your seller that you wish to invest a specified sum of money without proper consideration of the yield on your purchase. For example, if you say you have $12,000 to invest, the seller might sell you $15,000 face value of bonds selling at the discounted price of 80 ($800 per $1,000 bond). Though the total dollar price will equal $12,000, the yield might be 8% rather than 9%, the current going rate for that particular bond. Remember that bonds are usually sold on the basis of yield-to-maturity, not by price. A bond is attractive when the yield-to-maturity after the tax on capital gains compares favorably to other bonds in the same category.

Second, don't tell the seller to sell your bonds "at the market." Stocks are sometimes sold in this fashion. The seller is asked to sell the stock at the prevailing price at the time of sale. However, municipals are sold into the inventory of the bond house, at a price that is profitable to them. Comparing price offerings for your bonds will be the only way you can negotiate the best deal for yourself. There could be as much as a six-point spread between your worst and best offers.

Finally, if a seller suggests you sell a bond to reap a capital gain, calculate the cost of selling the bond and the additional cost of purchasing a new one. Paper profits may be dissipated after the transaction costs and taxes are included.

CHAPTER XI

Selling Strategies and Techniques

A. Reasons for Selling Municipal Bonds
   1. Taking Gains
   2. Raising Cash for Personal Reasons or Investment
   3. Weeding Out Bonds of Declining Quality
   4. Portfolio Consolidation
   5. Bond Swaps
      a. Kinds of Swaps
         - Tax Swap
         - Reduction of Maturity Swap
         - Improve Rating Swap
      b. Cost and Timing of Bond Swap
B. Selection of Bonds for Sale to Raise Cash
C. Procedure for Selling a Bond

A. Reasons for Selling Municipal Bonds

This chapter will consider five principal reasons for selling one or more of your municipal bonds before they mature.

Briefly stated, the reasons are (1) to take gains in anticipation of a market decline, (2) to raise cash for personal reasons and for other investment opportunities, (3) to weed out bonds of deteriorating quality, (4) to consolidate your portfolio, and (5) to swap or exchange one bond for another for tax purposes in order to increase the yield or rating of your bonds or to reduce the maturity of your holdings.

1. Taking Gains

A bona fide reason for a bond sale is to get out before interest rates rise and prices decline. However, interest rates cannot be predicted with any degree of certainty or regularity.

You may also consider selling a bond that you hold if it is selling at a premium. For example, if you sell your bond at 125, you would have an immediate gain of $250 for each $1000 of face amount if you bought the bond at par. But you would not keep all of that $250. You must pay a tax on your capital gain to the government and pay an additional spread to the broker if you purchase another bond with the money from the sale. Consider selling a callable premium bond that is selling substantially above par. Taking the gain in this case may be prudent because the higher return would be lost if the bond were called.

2. Raising Cash for Personal Reasons or Investment

If you think you will need cash in the near future, it is wise to buy short-term bonds that will come due before the money is needed. In this way, you will avoid the cost of selling your bonds to a broker.

If you are met with an unforseen event that requires cash, an alternative to sale might be to use the bonds as collateral for a loan. You could place your bonds in a cash management type account at a brokerage house or pledge them with a bank for a personal loan. This procedure is sensible if you have a short-term need for cash and wish to keep your bonds. Care must be taken in this regard. If the bonds drop substantially in value, the loan could be called or additional collateral required. Another problem is that your interest deduction on the loan may be disallowed. (See Part II, Chapter XIII on Taxes.)

3. Weeding Out Bonds of Declining Quality

Another reason for selling a bond is if you anticipate that the bond will be downgraded by the rating agencies or that bad news will affect the issuer. An evaluation of your holdings should be undertaken on a regular basis to weed out bonds that have declined in quality and thus have become riskier to hold. This advice applies to even a portfolio built with a buy-and-hold strategy in mind. However, if a default or a downgrading is imminent (meaning you found out about a problem too late), you should not be hasty and sell into a depressed market because permanent defaults are rare.

4. Portfolio Consolidation

If you review your portfolio and discover that you have purchased a variety of small issues, resist the impulse to sell the small issues and reinvest in a single, larger issue. Though it is neater and easier to manage fewer bond issues, the cost of consolidation will probably outweigh the ease of management. You will not receive favorable bids for odd lots because there is no institutional demand for them and they are more difficult to sell. The dealer's spread will therefore be sizable. You should have benefited from buying small issues initially. As our friend has said, he goes to the bank every month to clip his coupons anyway, so a few more or less does not matter. If the bonds are registered, the difficult work is checking off the receipt of the check in the mail every six months. This is work?

5. Bond Swaps

A bond swap is an exchange of one bond held by an investor for a different bond with similar but not identical characteristics such as yield-to-maturity, maturity length, rating, coupon, and issuer.

a. Kinds of Swaps

There are three principal kinds of swaps for municipal bonds: tax swaps, reduction of maturities swaps, and improve rating swaps.

Tax Swap—Tax swaps are the most common municipal bond swaps. In a tax swap, you exchange a bond in which you have an unrealized loss for another bond with similar characteristics. The objective is to recognize a loss for income tax purposes, without substantially changing your economic position.

In order to pass a possible Internal Revenue Service challenge that your swap is a wash sale (i.e., the bonds are substantially identical and the loss should be disallowed), the bonds should differ in two out of the three following characteristics: issuer, coupon, and maturity, with maturity differing by at least three years.

An example of an excellent swap, though unusual in its circumstances, is to swap defaulted bonds for other defaulted bonds. After WPPSS No. 4. and No. 5 power plants defaulted in the summer of 1983, investors had the choice of selling their bonds for 13 cents or so on the dollar, or holding on in anticipation of a rescue operation by the Federal Government. For example, an investor holding $10,000 face value WPPSS No. 4-5 bonds with a coupon of 12½%, maturing in 2010, and selling at a price of 14 could swap them for $10,000 face value WPPSS No. 4-5 bonds with a coupon of 7¾%, maturing in 2018 and selling at $11. If the first bonds were originally purchased at $10,000, there would be a total loss of $8,600. By contrast, if the bonds were not swapped, no current loss could be taken for tax purposes, even though the bonds were in default, because the bonds could not be shown to be worthless. The cost of the transaction at a firm specializing in this kind of swap would be 1 point or 1½ points—either $100 or $150 per $10,000 of bonds. Other firms might charge as much as three to five points—$300 to $500. If the investor could not use all of the capital loss in one tax year, the balance of the capital loss can be carried forward without time limit.

A tax swap only results in a deferral of tax rather than a permanent tax saving. This is because if you hold the bond until it reaches maturity, you will have to report a capital gain equal to the difference between your original purchase price and par. However, you reap a substantial benefit because you have had the use of money for a number of years until the bond comes due at par. The savings are substantial if you do a tax swap on a long-term bond.

Reduction of Maturity Swap—If you are holding long-term bonds and believe interest rates will rise substantially in the near future, you might swap your holdings for shorter-term bonds. This would prevent a substantial price loss because shorter-term debt is not as vulnerable to price changes as are long-term bonds. In this case, you would hold the short-term bonds until maturity.

Improve Rating Swap—You might consider trying to improve the quality of your portfolio if you anticipate the economy turning down. Historically, in bad economic times, the spread between higher-rated and lower-rated bonds increases, sometimes dramatically. If you swap *after* it is apparent that the economy is souring, your losses might be substantial. If you missed the market, and want comfort in a bad economic environment, you might consider portfolio insurance.

b. Cost and Timing of Bond Swap

Tax swapping season is September through December, though a loss taken any time during the year will suffice for tax purposes. Although bonds you swap may be relatively equal, you must understand the costs of having the transactions performed. The broker takes two spreads—one on the bonds you sell and another on the bonds you buy. You must comparison shop to get the best price. Some brokers encourage you to look only at current yield instead of yield-to-maturity in deciding what to swap. We believe that you should focus on the yield-to-maturity that you receive on the bond that you buy from the broker compared to the yield-to-maturity that the broker gets on buying your bond. Be aware of what you are giving up to obtain the tax loss. Although the idea of a swap is tantalizing, calculate all costs of spreads, lower yield, longer maturity, and poorer quality before proceeding.

B. Selection of Bonds for Sale to Raise Cash

Have you decided to sell your bonds instead of borrowing against them? There are a number of factors that should be considered in evaluating the marketability of the bonds you propose to sell.

1. Odd lots of less than $100,000 will receive lower bids than round lots of $100,000; very odd lots (of less than $25,000) will receive the lowest bids for the reasons described above.

2. Sell quality issues in times of economic uncertainty. At those times, people flee from the lower-rated bonds and rush to quality. Accordingly, you will receive a relatively higher price for quality bonds in a climate of uncertainty.

3. Select a well-known issue to sell. Thinly traded bonds from obscure places draw poor bids since it is more difficult for the brokers to resell these bonds.

4. Avoid selling a bond that is coming under selling pressure. When the market is flooded with a particular issue, the bids will be lower.

5. Check with your broker to discover if the brokerage house has a heavy inventory in a bond you are thinking of selling. If the house inventory is not turning over quickly in that particular issue, the broker will have little incentive to provide you with a good price.

6. A market maker in a particular bond may be in a better position to give you an optimum bid than your usual broker, though it is often difficult to discover who the market makers are in a particular issue.

7. Avoid selling an issue that has had bad press, if the only

reason for sale is to raise cash. The negative public attitude toward a particular issue will reduce the seller's bids. For example, Washington Public Power Supply System bonds, which are in default, immediately cast aspersion on all public utility bonds that rely on take-or-pay contracts as revenue sources. The negative impact fades gradually as it becomes apparent that similar bonds are financially stable.

8. Sell to a broker with whom you have developed a good relationship. If the broker believes you are a good customer or a potential source of additional business, then the bid might be better. The expected spread between bids of different brokers may be between one and seven points.

9. Call a number of brokers to get their bids before approaching the broker with whom you deal. It is always wise to have information on the value of the bond before agreeing to sell.

Remember that you are selling your bond in an auction *market*. The price you are offered is based upon the supply of similar bonds and the market demand for them. *The final judge of the value of the bond is the marketplace*. If you are dissatisfied with the bids you receive, withdraw your bond from the market and wait a while. Market circumstances change, and you may do better or worse at another time.

C. Procedure for Selling a Bond

First, be sure to have complete and accurate information about your bonds. Have written out the number of bonds you wish to sell, the coupon, the complete name of the bond, the maturity month and year, and the call date with the price at call. It is also handy to have the CUSIP number, which is available from the purchase confirmation slip. This enables the broker to precisely identify your bond and verify your information.

Like a used car, your bond will be valued differently by the various brokers to whom you offer it. You must try to get the best bid possible. If you offer your bond to a broker and his trader does not wish to acquire the bond for his firm, the broker may put your bond on the wire—offer it to other brokers who may have an interest. As the brokers to whom you offered the bonds try to sell it to each other, it may seem that there are many bonds of your particular issue on the market. In fact, it may only be the activity you have generated in trying to sell your bonds. The appearance of a lot of supply may depress the price of your bonds making the bids you receiver lower than otherwise expected. Thus, don't oversell your bonds by too much shopping.

CHAPTER XII

Market Strategies

A. The Effect of Ratings on the Spread between Bond Prices
B. The Reasons for the Spread between Revenue and General Obligation Bonds
    1. Perception of the Security of Revenue and General Obligation Bonds
    2. Unrated Nature of Many Revenue Bonds
    3. Preference for General Obligation Bonds by Commercial Banks
    4. Quantity of Revenue Bonds Offered for Sale, Compared with General Obligation Bonds
C. The Relationship Between Yield and Bond Maturities
D. Market View of Discount and Premium Bonds
E. Ratio of Treasury Bonds to Municipal Bonds
F. Market View of Interest Rates
G. The Effect of Investor Buying Patterns on Trading Strategies
    1. Commercial Banks
    2. Casualty Insurance Companies
    3. Individual Investors
    4. Mutual Funds and Unit Investment Trusts
    5. Brokerage Houses
H. Market Reaction to Change in Registration

The timing of purchases requires ready cash and a knowledge of market responses to various kinds of situations. This chapter will review market strategies and historic performance as they relate to ratings, kinds of municipal bond issuers, bond maturities, interest rates, bond registration, and discount versus par and premium bonds.

A. The Effect of Ratings on the Spread between Bond Prices

The impact of credit ratings on bond prices varies from time to time. The yield spread between Baa and Aaa rated bonds varies with the economic mood of the times. In periods of prosperity, the premium paid by issuers of lower-rated bonds is small. However, in times of substantial economic uncertainty, the spread between bonds rated Aaa and Baa increases. For example, until the early 1970s, Moody's Baa rated bonds usually paid 60 basis points more interest than Aaa rated bonds. However, in 1976, during the New York City fiscal crisis, the spread between Baa and Aaa bonds increased to 200 basis points. By 1978, the spread between Baa and Aaa bonds had been reduced to about 90 basis points. While Baa bonds are of investment quality, they are generally avoided by money managers during times of fiscal stress because the Baa rating is defined as having "speculative characteristics." Thus, an A rating is realistically, though not actually, the bottom investment grade for conservative investors.

B. The Reasons for the Spread Between Revenue and General Obligation Bonds

A useful basis for comparing general obligation bonds and revenue bonds can be found in *The Bond Buyer* indexes. One *Bond Buyer* index tracks the performance of selected general obligation bonds that have 20-year maturities and another tracks selected revenue bonds that have 30-year maturities. The ratings of both the general obligation bonds and the revenue bonds are between A and Aa.*

The indexes are limited in certain respects. They only track the new-issue market as opposed to bonds traded in the secondary market, which might trade quite differently. Also, the indexes tend to lag behind the market. Another limitation is that the revenue bond index, which has been in existence since 1980, lumps together all categories of revenue bonds, blurring the trading distributions of various kinds. As we discussed in Chapter VI, some revenue bonds have a broader market appeal than others and are considered more desirable.

Bearing these limitations in mind, let's look at a comparison of the two indexes.

Traditionally, the market has valued general obligation bonds more than revenue bonds, as illustrated below in the chart, which was reproduced from *The New York Times*.

In July 1983, the spread between general obligation and revenue bonds was 58 basis points, while in January of the same year, it was 150 basis points. In 1986, the spread ranged between 30 to 50 basis points.

There are four factors that affect the relationship between the yields and prices of revenue bonds in relation to general obligation bonds. They are perception of bond security, the unrated nature of revenue bonds, preferences for general obligation bonds by commercial banks, and the sheer quantity of revenue bonds available for purchase, compared with the number of general obligation bonds available.

---

*There is also an 11 Bond Index, which includes an average Moody's rating of Aa, and a new Futures Index, which tracks 50 most recent term issues rated A or better.

Tax-Exempt Yields

Average weekly yields for 20 general obligation bonds and 25 revenue bonds, in percent

Source: The Bond Buyer

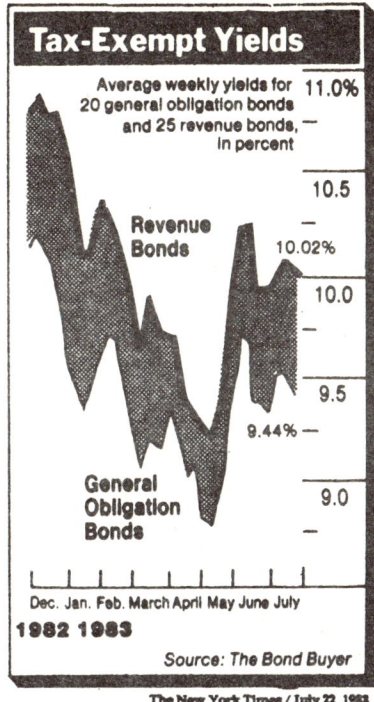

The New York Times / July 22, 1983

1. Perception of the Security of Revenue and General Obligation Bonds

Because of the perception of revenue bonds as riskier than general obligation issues during periods of economic uncertainty, the spread between the yield of G.O.s and revenue bonds increases in troubled times. The higher yield for revenue issues results from their higher default history. If a general obligation bond is in financial trouble, the full faith and credit of the issuer can often avoid a default as funds are shifted from one municipal pocket to another. Although this ability has been limited by ceilings on taxes and the creation of special funds in certain states, general obligation bonds are still considered a more secure investment. Moreover, if a default occurs, a general obligation bond issuer may be better able to reorganize and cure the default than a revenue bond issuer.

2. Unrated Nature of Many Revenue Bonds

Many revenue bond issues are unrated. As a result, revenue bonds tend to yield more than general obligation bonds because unrated bonds generally yield more than rated ones. All the bonds in The Bond Buyer Index are rated bonds.

3. Preference for General Obligation Bonds by Commercial Banks

Commercial banks, which traditionally had been large purchasers of municipal bonds, underwrite general obligation bonds but are restricted from underwriting revenue bonds. They purchase some of their own underwritten general obligation bonds and other similar issues for investment purposes because of their greater knowledge about the nature of these issues. In the past, commercial banks' earnings were strongest during unstable market conditions, at which times they substantially increased their purchase of general obligation bonds. The increased demand raised the price of general obligation bonds relative to revenue bonds. The Tax Reform Act of 1986 will substantially reduce commercial banks' reason for purchasing municipal bonds because of the disallowance of interest expense if a bank owns municipals.

4. Quantity of Revenue Bonds Offered for Sale, Compared with General Obligation Bonds

Municipal borrowers sometimes issue revenue bonds because they cannot issue general obligation bonds for a particular purpose. There has been a substantial increase in the amount of revenue bond issues and a corresponding decline in the number of general obligation bonds issued because new state laws restrict the issuance of G.O.s.

The large number of revenue bond issues contribute to destabilizing the balance between revenue and general obligation bonds, resulting in yield spreads of 25 to 150 basis points or more for revenue bonds, an extra bonus for the alert investor.

C. The Relationship between Yield and Bond Maturities

As a rule, long-term bonds usually yield more than short-term bonds. There are many explanations as to why this is so. The simplest is that investors demand a premium for increasing the maturity of their bond holdings in the face of possible inflation over the lives of their investments.

When the interest rates of bonds of various maturities are drawn on a graph, it is generally illustrated as an upward-sloping yield curve. The term upward-sloping yield curve means that short-term bonds usually pay less interest than long-term debt. An example of that kind of yield curve is drawn below.

Traditionally, long-term municipal bonds continue to yield more than short-term municipal securities even when long-term corporate yields are turning down. In November 1979, however, the yield curve became an inverted yield curve because short-term municipal bonds yielded more than long-term issues. This sometimes occurs when the economy is at its peak rate of growth and

FIGURE 8-6. Yield Curve for Municipal Securities*

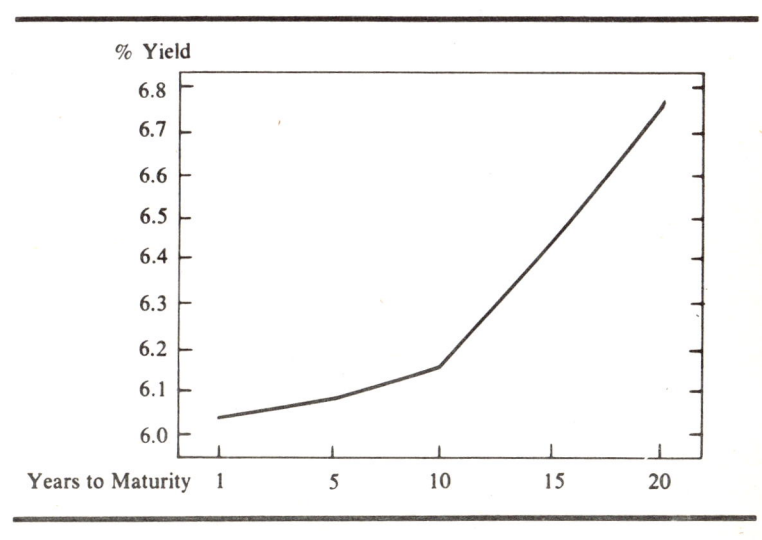

Chart reprinted courtesy of the Public Securities Association

*Moody's Aa-rated general obligation securities, average new-issue reoffering yields, October 1979.

credit tightens, driving interest rates up. If the expectation is that interest rates will drop in the future, more investors want to invest their money long-term to lock in the high rates. The flood of money going into longer-term maturities results in a drop of interest rates in those bonds and an increase in shorter-term maturities.

15 years ago, the purchase of long-term municipal bonds with maturities of 20 to 30 years was not considered risky because interest rates were fairly stable and long-term bonds had a higher yield than the short-term securities. As long as inflation was under control, it was reasonable to invest in long-term bonds to get the extra yield. In today's market, however, as inflation or the anticipation of inflation fuels higher interest rates, long-term bond prices may drop substantially in a short time.

In an inflationary period, the purchasing power of money declines, resulting in higher costs of bonds and higher interest rates. Inflation generally encourages borrowing in the hope that the loans can be repaid with cheaper inflated dollars. The borrower benefits, but the purchaser of long-term bonds suffers a loss. For example, even at a modest 4% inflation rate, the purchasing power of $1,000 in current dollars drops to $456 in 20 years.

Investing in long-term bonds is not for the fainthearted. Below is a table listing the highs and lows of a composite index of 20-year general obligation bonds of all ratings, which reveals the volatility of long-term bonds.

Volatility of Long-Term General Obligation Bonds*

Year	Low for Year	High for Year	% of Change
1986	6.78%	8.33%	22.9%
1981	9.49%	13.30%	40.1%
1980	7.11%	10.56%	48.5%
1977	5.45%	5.93%	8.8%
1973	4.99%	5.59%	12.0%
1968	4.07%	4.85%	19.2%
1964	3.12%	3.32%	6.4%
1961	3.26%	3.55%	8.9%

Source: U.S. Trust Co. 1983—As Amended

*The Bond Buyer Index, which is a composite of index selected 20-year Baa, A, Aa and Aaa general obligation municipal bonds.

In their promotional literature, U.S. Trust Company notes that if you invested $100,000 in May 1980 in a 20-year bond with a 7.11% coupon (which was representative at the time), you could have realized a paper loss of $30,000 or 30%, because there was a 48.5% increase in interest rates in that year. It is interesting to note how the volatility increased as the interest rates rose over the years.

In our view, an investment in any long-term bond is an interest-rate play. Such an investment should be made only if you wish to speculate that rates will drop, and you are trying to achieve a capital gain. The extra 1% or so yield on long-term bonds does not generally merit the risk, unless you are knowingly speculating on interest rates. Refer to the chart in Section F of this chapter and note the constantly rising interest rates between 1951 and 1981. Based upon past history, investing in long-term bonds is very risky for an investor with a buy-and-hold strategy.

D. Market View of Discount and Premium Bonds

Discount bonds are more vulnerable to shifts in the municipal bond market than par or premium bonds. One reason is that discount bonds start with a smaller price base. Thus, a 100 basis point change in yield would have a greater effect on the price of a discount bond than on a par or premium bond. This is a disadvantage when interest rates are rising and bond prices are dropping because the proportional decline is greater for the discounts. However, when interest rates are falling, long-term discount bonds have greater upside potential because of the smaller price base and because there is a much smaller possibility of the bonds being called. Thus, discount bonds have often sold at lower yields-to-maturity than callable par or premium bonds, indicating their greater desirability in this circumstance.

The yield-to-maturity on premium bonds may sometimes be higher than average because the price of the bonds is depressed in anticipation of a possible early call. Thus, the bond may be trading on a yield-to-the call date instead of a yield-to-maturity. This type of offering is called a cushion bond because the call price acts as a cushion against upward price movement. However, there is no downside cushion softening the decline in value of these bonds.

E. Ratio of Treasury Bonds to Municipal Bonds

Municipal bond yields are most often compared to yields on Treasury bonds. Treasuries are exempt from state and local taxes, but they are subject to federal income tax. The Treasuries are compared to municipal bonds through ratios. For example, a statement in the paper might read "yields on long high-grade G.O.s are now almost 90% of yields on long-term Treasury bonds, while the ratio in the 10-year area is 76%."[2] This is translated into standard English as: If you invested $1,000 in a 10%, 30-year Treasury bond, you would receive a 10% pretax yield. By comparison, a 30-year secure general obligation bond would yield 9%. Comparing the 9% yield to the 10% yield equals a 90% ratio of municipal yield to yield on taxable Treasury bonds. The ratios between municipals and Treasuries are generally in the 65% to 70% range. Analysts often consider municipals a good buy when the ratio of municipal bond yield to Treasury bond yield is in the 80%- to 90%-range.

Sometimes a deluge of new municipal bond offerings may drive the yields on municipals up to Treasury bond rates. For example, in January 1982, 30-year Treasury bonds yielded 13.6, and 30-year Connecticut Housing Finance Authority bonds rated AAA were yielding 13.7% Without taking into account yield-to-call, the effective rate of interest after tax for someone in the 33% bracket would be 50% higher on the municipal bond, making it a much better buy. In the summer of 1986, the yield of long-term municipal bonds again exceeded the yield of long-term Treasury bonds.

F. Market View of Interest Rates

Which way are the interest rates moving? Consult the experts, check whether the money supply is expanding or contracting and then . . . Flip a coin! No one can accurately predict which way interest rates are going, though many try. A lot of paper and ink is spent theorizing or guessing the direction of rates, but there are no good predictive measures to consistently indicate the future. When economists are asked about the direction of interest rates, they are fond of saying that interest rates will move in a sawtooth pattern. Is that helpful? Some people might consult soothsayers and fortune tellers. Others examine their gut. James Lebenthal, chairman of Lebenthal and Company is quoted as saying "My belly tells me that interest rates on municipals are going to fluctuate between 9 and 10 percent for a while and that we are right now on the high end of the band."[3] In another example of crystal ball gazing, Larry Speakes, the White House spokesman, said that President Reagan's "prediction earlier today that interest rates will decline is based on 'intuition.' The President and his staff have no specific way of knowing which direction interest rates will go." P.S.—they bounded upward![4]

Rising Interest Rates Reflected in *Corporate Borrowing Costs**

Corporate Borrowing Costs

Year	Rate (%)	Year	Rate (%)
1950	3.75	1967	6.93
1951	3.22	1968	7.28
1952	3.04	1969	9.22
1953	3.23	1970	8.13
1954	2.87	1971	7.54
1955	3.27	1972	7.50
1956	4.26	1973	8.09
1957	4.04	1974	9.47
1958	4.44	1975	9.59
1959	5.27	1976	7.90
1960	4.94	1977	8.39
1961	4.58	1978	9.30
1962	4.28	1979	11.30
1963	4.49	1980	14.38
1964	4.49	1981	15.55
1965	4.92	1982	12.15
1966	5.98	1983 (May)	11.10
		1986	8.5

Source: Wall Street Journal[5]

*Figures are monthly averages for the last month of each year through 1982, and for May 1983—As Amended.

RISING INTEREST RATES REFLECTED IN CORPORATE BORROWING COSTS

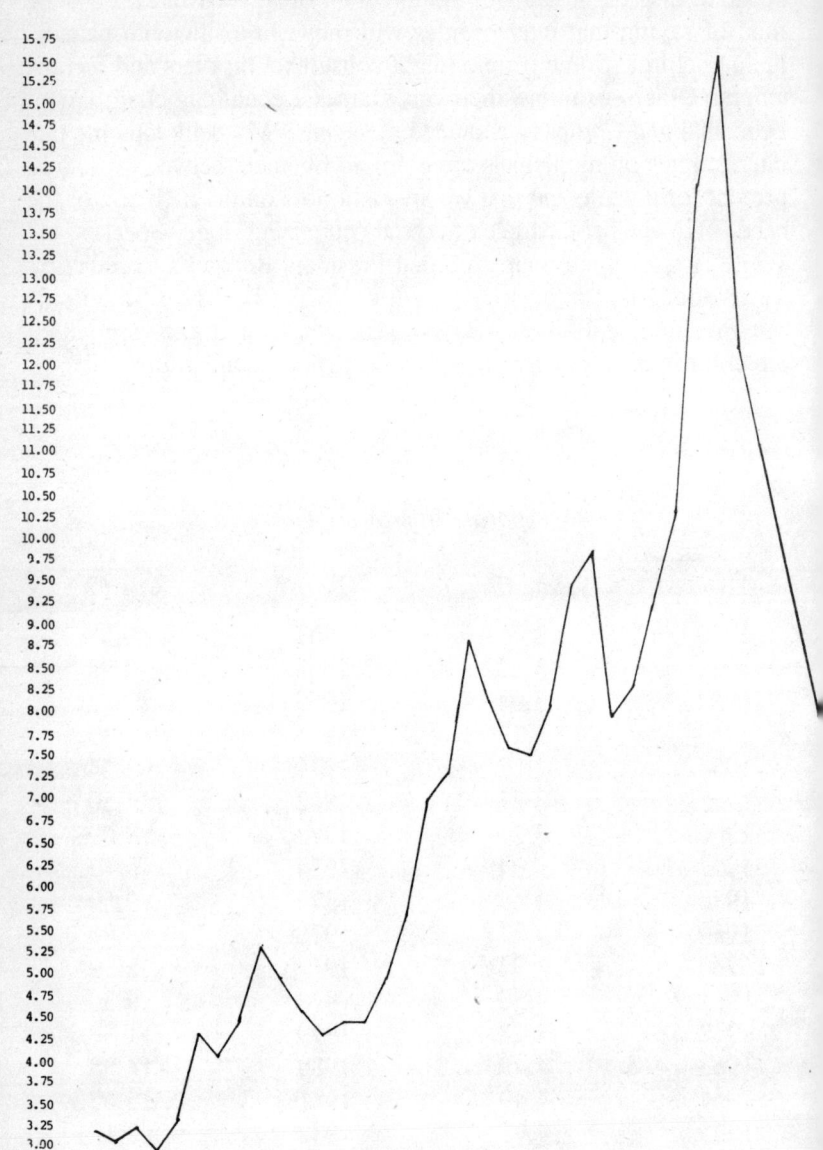

Between 1951 and 1981, interest rates have generally risen. Interest rates rose from 1900 to 1920. Then they dropped substantially during the depression years of 1920 and 1921 and again in 1929. The interest rates bottomed out in 1946 and have been increasing at an accelerating pace since that time until 1981, as illustrated in the table and the graph on the following pages. Since 1981 there has been a substantial drop in interest rates beginning in 1982 and continuing into 1986.

One cause of high interest rates is the anticipation of inflation. Whether inflation is actually rampant or not, the expectation that it will be means that it is only a matter of time before it will heat up again, boosting the demand for compensating interest on loans. In fact there has been a correlation between increasing inflation and rising interest rates. In the 1950s, interest rates, as shown on the preceding table, ranged between 2.87% and 5.27%, while the inflation rate ranged from 1.2% to 6.6%. By comparison, in the 1970s, interest ranges ranged from 7.5% to 11.3%, while the inflation rate ranged from 5.0% to 8.8%.

Real interest rates, (the difference between nominal interest rates and the inflation rate) are at an all-time high. In February 1984, we asked a savvy Merrill Lynch investment banker why three-year Treasury bonds were yielding 11% while the inflation rate was below 5%. He smiled and said that the big moneylenders were saying something very clearly. They did not believe inflation would stay at a low rate and expected interest rates to rise, based upon the recent past. Although the yield on long-term Treasury bonds fell to 7.5% in 1986, real interest rates continued to stay high.

G. The Effect of Investor Buying Patterns on Trading Strategies

Some individual investors follow the purchases of the large institutions to gauge the proper time to enter the market. Historically, there have been three primary purchasers of municipal bonds: commercial banks, casualty insurance companies, and individuals. In general when either the casualty insurance companies or the banks were not in the market, the lack of buyers resulted in increased yields. Although banks and casualty insurance companies traditionally have been heavy purchasers of municipal bonds, their current share has declined, as shown in the table below:

Net Purchases of Municipals
(Billions of dollars)

	1978	1979	1980	1981	1982*
Commercial Banks	$ 9.6	$ 9.5	$13.6	$ 5.0	$ 2.0
Casualty Ins. Cos.	13.5	9.9	7.7	4.0	3.0
Individuals	4.1	9.8	12.2	20.4	36.0
Mutual Funds	0.5	1.4	2.0	2.9	14.0
Others	0.7	(0.8)	0.4	0.6	1.0
Totals	$28.4	$29.8	$35.9	$32.9	$56.0

* Estimates
Source: Flow of Funds Accounts;
  Federal Reserve Board of Governors.

Their share will continue to decline as a result of the new tax law.

1. Commercial Banks

Commercial banks have been heavy buyers of municipal bonds in a cyclical pattern. Traditionally, when interest rates are low and demand for loans are limited, commercial banks have purchased short-and medium-term municipal bonds. As demand for loans increases, the banks slow their purchases or liquidate parts of their portfolios. Commercial banks also buy municipal bonds as collateral for public deposits or for discounting at the Federal Reserve.[6]

Though this pattern of bank purchases has been in effect since World War II, recent changes in taxation are expected to change these patterns. Because of the Tax Reform Act of 1986 change mentioned above in Section B.3., the commercial banks should not be major buyers of municipals in the future. As of 1986 banks own 30% of outstanding municipal bonds.

2. Casualty Insurance Companies

Another traditionally large purchaser of municipal bonds has been the casualty insurance industry. The companies favored long-term revenue bonds that produced the highest returns on their investments. They bought municipal bonds when their profits were comparatively high, to shelter their income. Regulation of the insurance industry produces cycles in profits because rate adjustments for inflation lag behind the companies' actual costs.

There is another reason insurance companies also favored municipal bonds. Unlike stocks, which must be carried on an insurance company's balance sheet at current market value, bonds are recorded on the balance sheet at the cost at which they were purchased. Thus, the insurance company is able to know how much insurance the company can write without regard to market fluctuations. When the current market value of a bond declines, the insurance company does not have to record a loss unless the bond is sold.

Beginning in 1981, casualty insurance companies have not been major purchasers of municipal bonds due to their low earnings. Profits are strongest when inflation is stable or after regulatory commissions grant rate increases. Inflation raises the value of the claims thereby squeezing insurance company profits.

As a result of the Tax Reform Act of 1986, property and casualty insurance companies will have to reduce their deductions for loss reserves by the total of 15% of their municipal bond income. As a result of this change in the tax law, these companies will be less aggressive buyers of municipal bonds than in the past. As of 1986, property and casualty insurance companies owned 12% of all outstanding municipal bonds.

3. Individual Investors

Individual investors also purchase municipal bonds cyclically. They tend to enter the bond market when interest rates are high. For example, small investors were heavy purchasers of bonds in 1981 and 1982, when interest rates were at their peak. In 1981 and 1982, individuals directly and indirectly through funds and trusts accounted for 71% and 89% of the net purchases of municipal bonds, respectively, compared to only 16% in 1978.

The individual investors' current heavy participation in the municipal bond market is attributed in part to the inflationary push of large numbers of people into higher tax brackets. As people are faced with increasingly large tax bites, they seek ways to shelter their income. Anyone with a marginal tax rate of 28% or more benefits substantially from an investment in municipal bonds at current interest rates.

4. Mutual Funds and Unit Investment Trusts

As noted previously, mutual funds and unit investment trusts are increasing their purchases of municipal bonds. These entities are large buyers of bonds of all maturities that are of investment quality. Small investors own most of the mutual fund shares and trust units.

5. Brokerage Houses

Though not usually listed as purchasers of municipal bonds, the brokerage houses buy new issues for resale and maintain large inventories of municipal bonds. As such, they are market makers and important intermediaries in the sales chain. When interest rates are high, the brokerage houses prefer to reduce their inventories because they cannot deduct the interest paid on the money borrowed to purchase municipal bonds. Thus, if you decide to sell your bonds in the face of rising interest rates, you will find a sharply increased spread between the bids and offerings in the secondary market.

H. Market Reaction to Changes in Registration

As of July 1, 1983, all newly issued bonds must be registered as a result of the 1982 Tax Equity and Fiscal Responsibility Act (TEFRA). Exempt from registration are bonds due in one year or less, issued by individuals, not offered to the public, or issued and held by foreigners.

Coupon bonds were expected to yield less than registered bonds because it was assumed that many investors would prefer the anonymity and ease of ownership of the unregistered bonds. However, at the present (January 1985) coupon bonds are selling at only a slight premium. It could be expected that as the supply of coupon bonds diminishes, the premium for coupon bonds will increase.

notes

Chapter XII

[1] PSA Municipal Data Base, Public Security Association, *Fundamentals of Municipal Bonds*, New York: Public Securities Association, 1983. p. 150

[2] Merrill Lynch, Pierce, Fenner & Smith, Inc., *Fixed Income Strategy*, New York: Merrill Lynch, Pierce, Fenner & Smith, Inc. Fixed Income Research Department, January, 1983.

[3] Jack Egan, "Short Bonds: Reading the Interest Rates," *New York Times*, (June 20, 1983), pp. 16–18.

[4] James Grant, "Correct Yield," *Barrons*, (May 16, 1983), p. 76.

[5] Lindley H. Clark, Jr. "A Remembrance of Interest Rates—and an Editor-Past," *Wall Street Journal*, (July 5, 1983), p. 23.

[6] Public Securities Association, *supra.*, p. 146.

CHAPTER XIII

Tax Aspects of Municipal Bonds

A. Federal Income Tax Treatment of Municipal Bonds
   1. The Source of the Federal Exemption
   2. Four Categories of Municipal Bonds
      a. Public-Purpose Bonds
      b. Private-Activity Bonds
      c. Taxable Municipal Bonds
      d. Municipal Bonds Issued Before August 8, 1986
   3. Tax Treatment of Capital Gains and Losses
      a. Basic Definitions and Rules
      b. Taxation of Capital Gains and Losses for 1987 and Future Years
   4. Tax Treatment of Premium Bonds
   5. Tax Treatment of Discount Bonds
   6. Deductibility of Interest Expense Incurred to Carry Municipal Bonds
   7. Estate and Gift Tax
   8. Social Security Tax
B. State Taxes
   1. Types of Taxes Levied
      a. Property Tax
      b. Capital Gains Tax
      c. Income Tax
   2. Effective State Tax Rates
   3. State Taxes and Investment Strategy

A chapter on taxes in a book on tax-exempt bonds? We are afraid so. Although the federal government does not tax interest income from most municipal bonds, it does tax the capital gain resulting from the sale or redemption of a bond at a price higher than the purchase price. In addition, the new tax on Social Security income takes into account municipal bond interest in calculating the base income, which is subject to tax. This is an indirect tax on municipal bond interest.

Tax on coupon interest and capital gains from municipal bonds is collected by some states. Most states tax municipal interest and capital gains earned from bonds issued by other states. This adds up to a lot of information you need to know to take maximum advantage of investments in municipal bonds.

A. Federal Income Tax Treatment of Municipal Bonds

1. The Source of the Federal Exemption

The basis of the exemption of municipal interest income from federal income tax is found in Section 103(a) of the Internal Revenue Code.

In describing precisely which bonds give rise to tax-exempt interest, the Internal Revenue Code goes on for more than 25 pages of fine print and the income tax Regulations interpreting the Code are 92 pages of very fine print.

2. Four Categories of Municipal Bonds

As a result of the Tax Reform Act of 1986, there are now four major categories of municipal bonds:

a. Public-Purpose Bonds

The first category is the so-called public-purpose bonds. These bonds include municipal securities issued directly by state or local governments (e.g., State of New York or City of New York) or their agencies to meet essential government functions, such as financing schools and highway construction funding. Interest income from public-purpose bonds is tax free for federal income tax purposes.

b. Private-Activity Bonds

The second category consists of recent municipal bonds (generally those issued after August 8, 1986) that are used to finance activities that primarily benefit individuals or companies.

In general an issue is a private-activity bond if more than 10% of the proceeds of the issue is to be used directly or indirectly in any trade or business carried on by any person. Private activity bonds include, with many limitations and restrictions, categories of municipal bonds: (a) multifamily rental housing, (b) airports, (c) docks and wharves, (d) mass commuting facilities, (e) local furnishing of electricity or gas, (f) local district heating or cooling, (g) facilities for furnishing of water, (h) hydroelectric facilities, (i) hazardous waste disposal facilities, and (j) sewage and solid waste disposal facilities.

Interest payments from the private-activity bonds enumerated above are tax-exempt from the regular computation of federal income tax, but as a result of the Tax Reform Act of 1986 are considered a preference item that is subject to the alternative minimum tax. Other items of tax preference for individuals include accelerated depreciation on real estate and personal property, intangible drilling costs, expensing of mining exploration and development costs, percentage depletion, incentive stock options and net loss from passive trade or business activities.

Taxpayers are subject to the alternative minimum tax if that tax exceeds their regular federal income tax. Although the general structure of the alternative minimum tax will be the same as it was prior to the Tax Reform Act of 1986, the new law expands the reach of the alternative minimum tax. The alternative minimum tax rate has been raised from 20% to 21%. In addition, the exemption amount of $40,000 for married couples ($30,000 for single people and $20,000 for married persons filing separately) will be reduced by 25 cents for each dollar that minimum taxable income exceeds $150,000 for married couples ($112,500 for singles and $75,000 for married persons filing separately).

Many investors will still not be subject to the alternative minimum tax. For investors not subject to the alternative minimum tax, the fact that private-activity bonds are a tax preference item will be an opportunity rather than a burden because such bonds will yield more than public-purpose bonds. In October 1986, such private-purpose bonds were yielding about 50 basis points more than public-purpose bonds to compensate the holders for this potential adverse possibility.

c. Taxable Municipal Bonds

The third category is made up of municipal bonds, the income of which is not exempt from federal income tax (although it may be exempt from state and local tax in the state in which they are issued). These bonds were viewed by Congress as nonessential to the functioning of state and local governments. Such bonds include certain industrial development bonds, pollution control bonds, bonds for sports, convention and trade show facilities, parking facility bonds and bonds to fund industrial parks. Securities Data Corp. reported that $2.74 billion of taxable municipal bonds came to market in the first nine months of 1986.

In September 1986, these taxable bonds were offering a generous advantage over taxable Treasury bonds. Yields for taxable municipal bonds in maturities of seven to 15 years ranged between 7.6% to 8.5%, almost 90 basis points over comparable returns on Treasury bonds. These taxable municipal bonds would be excellent investments to fund your pension and individual retirement accounts since interest received by these entities is tax-exempt.

Apparently, these generous yields are necessary until such bonds gain greater market acceptance.

One problem with these taxable municipals is that because of their novelty (in late 1986), an investor who wishes to sell a small amount of these bonds before maturity may face a limited market and thus pay a larger spread on the sale.

d. Municipal Bonds Issued Before August 8, 1986

Municipal bonds issued before August 8, 1986 will generally not be subject to the regular federal income tax nor the alternative minimum tax.

A provision of the Tax Reform Act of 1986 allows the Internal Revenue Service to declare bonds *retroactively* taxable from their date of issue if the issuer violates certain technical rules relating to (a) the types of instruments in which issuers may invest bond proceeds and (b) the amount of earnings that may be retained. These are the so-called "arbitrage" rules. This is a dramatic change from prior law, which protected bondholders by preventing the IRS from retroactively declaring an issue taxable once bond counsel certified that it was tax-exempt. Issuers will face a complex task in monitoring their bonds in order to comply with these technical rules. However, issuers will not be able to reclaim the interest paid to investors, meaning they would have to pay the tax themselves. If they did violate the rules and subject the bonds to taxation, they would face low ratings on new issues, forcing them to pay top interest rates on new bonds.

3. Tax Treatment of Capital Gains and Losses

a. Basic Definitions and Rules

The sale by an investor of a municipal bond or his collection of the bond proceed at maturity may give rise to a capital gain or capital loss. However, each sale is not taxed separately. At the end of a taxpayer's fiscal year, gains and losses recognized on capital transactions (including sales of stock, personal property, and real estate) are netted.

b. Taxation of Capital Gains and Losses for 1987 and Future Years

The Tax Reform Act of 1986 has changed the federal income tax treatment of net capital gains. The Act has repealed the 60% deduction for long-term capital gains for 1987 and future years. For 1988 and future years, net capital gains will be taxed at the same rate as ordinary income, i.e., either at a 15% or 28% tax rate depending on a taxpayer's income level. However, see Part I, Chapter I for a description of the 5% surcharge in certain tax brackets that might result in a 33% *marginal* tax rate for certain taxpayers. For 1987 only, net capital gains will be subject to a maximum tax rate of 28%.

For 1987 and future years, there is a $3,000 limitation on the deduction of net capital losses. A dollar of capital loss will be able to offset a full dollar of ordinary income up to the $3,000 limit. Any excess capital loss may be carried forward (but not back) indefinitely until it is used.

4. Tax Treatment of Premium Bonds

A bond is purchased at a premium if it is purchased at a price greater than its face value at maturity. A bond sells at a premium when the coupon interest is greater than the prevailing effective interest rate on similar bonds. When a taxpayer sells a bond and is calculating the capital gain or loss, the premium on a municipal bond *must* be amortized, (written off over the remaining life of the bond.) The amortization period extends from the date of acquisition to the date of maturity or earliest call date. It is usually preferable to elect straight-line amortization since the basis of the bond would be reduced at a slower pace, thus making a capital loss more likely. If you keep your premium bond until maturity, your basis will equal the face value of the bond so that no capital loss will result on redemption or repayment. The amount amortized each year is not a deductible expense, since the coupon interest is tax-exempt. However, the amount amortized reduces the taxpayer's basis, or cost, of the bond.

For example, if a taxpayer buys a $1,000 face 10-year municipal bond for $1,100, there is a premium of $100, and $10 must be amortized each year for the 10-year period, reducing the taxpayer's basis for his bond. If the bond is sold after five years, the taxpayer's basis in the bond for computing gain or loss is $1,050 ($1,100–$50). No tax deduction or capital loss is allowed for this $50 of amortized premium.

5. Tax Treatment of Discount Bonds

A discount bond is purchased at a price less than its face value at maturity. A bond sells at a discount when the coupon interest rate is less than the prevailing effective interest rate on similar bonds. The tax treatment of discount depends upon whether the discount represents original issue discount or secondary market discount.

The original issue discount on bonds purchased directly from a state or local government unit is treated as municipal interest and thus is tax free. For example, all municipal interest on zero-coupon bonds is original issue discount and thus tax free. The original issue discount is apportioned over the bond's life. For holders of municipal bonds issued after September 3, 1982, and acquired after March 1, 1984, the apportionment is not made evenly over the life of the bond but is made pursuant to a formula that uses compound interest concepts (i.e., a smaller addition to basis in the early years and a larger addition in the later years). This apportioned amount is added to the bond's purchase price to arrive at an adjusted cost basis for determining future capital gains or losses for income tax purposes if the bond is sold before its maturity date. The original issue discount is also apportioned among the original holder of the bond and any subsequent purchasers.

For municipal bonds issued at a discount prior to September 3, 1982, the holders can accrue such discount proportionally over the life of a bond and adjust the basis of the bond to reflect such accrual.

The holders of municipal obligations with maturities of one year or less that are issued at a discount can either accrue the discount proportionally (days held divided by days from acquisition through maturity) or use a constant interest basis (compounding daily).

All discount that is not original issue discount is treated as secondary market discount. The tax basis of a bond is its original cost to the taxpayer unless the bond has been acquired by gift or inheritance. Thus, the difference between the original cost and the proceeds received when the bond is sold usually determines the amount of the taxable gain or loss.

For example, assuming a bond has no original issue discount, if a taxpayer buys a previously issued bond in the market for $800 and resells it for $900 two years later, he must report a capital gain of $100 for federal income tax purposes.

6. Deductibility of Interest Expense Incurred to Carry Municipal Bonds

With limited exceptions, the Internal Revenue Service will attempt to disallow a taxpayer's interest expense in a case where borrowed money is used to purchase or carry municipal bonds.

Section 265(2) of the Internal Revenue Code provides:

> "No deduction shall be allowed for interest on indebtedness incurred on or *continued* to purchase or *carry* obligations the interest of which is wholly exempt from tax." [*Emphasis added*].

Thus, if you borrow $10,000 from a bank at 12% interest and use that $10,000 to buy a municipal bond, you will not be permitted to deduct the $1,200 of annual interest ($10,000 × 12%) that you pay the bank. The same rule would apply if you used the $10,000 borrowed from the bank to purchase an interest in a unit trust or bond fund that holds municipal bonds.

The rationale behind this rule can be illustrated by an example. Assume that an investor who is in the 33% tax bracket borrows $10,000 at 10% interest and uses the money to buy an 8% municipal bond. The investor's real interest cost after taking into account the benefit of an interest deduction is 6.7% because the investor is in the 33% tax bracket. However, the 8% coupon income is received tax free. Thus, the investor would make an after-tax profit of 1.3% (8% − 6.7%) on this borrowed money solely at the expense of Uncle Sam.

While it is clear that interest expense is disallowed when loan proceeds are used directly to buy municipal bonds, the rules become more complex when we seek to understand the meaning of when indebtedness is "continued to purchase or carry" municipal bonds as stated in Section 265(2) of the Code. Some actual cases might help to explain the meaning of these terms.

In *Bernard P. McDonough*,[1] affirmed by the 4th Circuit Court of Appeals, a taxpayer purchased municipal bonds for cash in one brokerage account and bought taxable securities on margin in another brokerage account. (When securities are purchased on margin, an investor borrows money from his broker to finance part of the purchase cost.) Despite the separate brokerage accounts and the fact that the municipal bonds were purchased for cash, the court disallowed the interest expense in the margin account. The burden of proof is on the taxpayer to show that he did not incur or *continue* the debt to purchase municipal bonds. The court pointed out that the taxpayer had advanced no reason for not selling his municipal bonds to reduce his margin debt. The court did not accept the argument that the relationship between his margin debt and his municipal bonds was merely happenstance.

It is not necessary to trace the loan to the municipals, but merely to show that a sufficiently direct relationship existed between the borrowing and the municipal holdings.[2] Once a direct relationship is shown, the interest expense will be disallowed even if it exceeds the municipal income.[3]

It is the position of the Internal Revenue Service that if you own municipal bonds, the interest deduction should be disallowed if you borrow money to acquire nonbusiness portfolio assets such as securities (other than a substantial ownership interest such as 80% control of a corporation), or a limited partnership interest in real estate, or oil and gas syndications.[4]

There are five cases where I.R.S. agrees that an investor may deduct interest expenses although he also holds municipal bonds:

(1) The interest deduction is allowed where one spouse incurs an interest expense and the other spouse purchases municipal bonds with his or her own funds. The necessary direct relationship between the municipal bond and interest expense does not exist here.

(2) The interest deduction is allowed when a taxpayer owns

municipal bonds and his closely held corporation has loans outstanding.

(3) The interest deduction is allowed in connection with debt incurred by an active trade or business.

(4) Prior to the 1986 Tax Reform Act an interest deduction was allowed in full where borrowing was for personal purposes only, such as for the purchase of a home or car, since such borrowing does not have a sufficiently direct relationship.[5] Such interest deduction will be phased out between 1987 and 1990. However, if the taxpayer puts a mortgage on his house and uses the proceeds to buy municipal bonds, the I.R.S.'s position is that the interest deduction should be disallowed.

(5) Where an individual's investment in municipal bonds is insubstantial (municipals do not exceed 2% of total portfolio) and no direct relationship exists between the municipal bonds and the borrowing, there will be no disallowance of interest expense.[6]

7. Estate and Gift Tax

Municipal bonds are included in the gross estate for purposes of computing the federal estate tax. Similarly, a gift of municipal bonds is subject to federal gift tax. Thus, the federal gift and estate tax rules relating to municipal bonds are the same as those relating to taxable bonds.

8. Social Security Tax

Beginning in 1984, up to one-half of an individual's Social Security benefits may be included in his taxable income and be subject to federal income tax. However, none of an individual's Social Security benefits will be included in his taxable income unless his adjusted gross income exceeds a base amount. This base is $25,000 for single taxpayers and $32,000 for married couples filing jointly. For this purpose, adjusted gross income comprises half of Social Security benefits plus *interest income or municipal bonds* plus all other income. This is the only way that interest on municipal bonds would increase your federal income tax.

Three examples may be helpful in understanding the new taxation of Social Security benefits.

Example 1—Single Taxpayer

1984 Adjusted gross income	$12,000
Plus: One-half of $6,000 (1984 Social Security benefit)	3,000
Plus: Total amount of interest on municipal bonds	3,000
Total Income	$18,000
Minus: Base Amount	(25,000)
Excess:	-0-

In this case, none of the $6,000 benefit is subject to federal income tax.

Example 2—Single Taxpayer

1984 Adjusted gross income	$18,000
Plus: One-half of $6,000 (1984 Social Security benefit)	3,000 (A)
Plus: Total amount of interest on municipal bonds	5,000
Total Income	$26,000
Minus: Base Amount	25,000
Excess:	$ 1,000
One-half of Excess	500 (B)
The lesser of (A) or (B) is added to taxable income	$ 500

In Example 2, $500 of the $6,000 Social Security benefit would be subject to federal income tax as ordinary income.

Example 3—Single Taxpayer

1984 Adjusted Gross Income	$30,000
Plus: One-half of $6,000 (1984 Social Security Benefit)	3,000(A)
Plus: Total amount of interest on municipal bonds	11,000
Total Income	$44,000
Minus: Base Amount	25,000
Excess	$19,000
One-half of Excess	9,500 (B)
The Lesser of (A) or (B) is added to taxable income	$ 3,000

In Example 3, half of the $6,000 Social Security benefit would be subject to federal income tax as ordinary income.

For married taxpayers, the computations would be the same except that the base amount would be $32,000 rather than $25,000. Thus, for a married couple, the conclusions would be as follows:

Example 1 would have the same result. None of the Social Security benefit received by a married couple would be subject to tax.

Example 2 would have a different result for a married couple. Because of the higher base amount ($32,000), none of the Social Security benefit would be subject to tax.

Example 3 would have the same result, half of the Social Security benefit ($3,000) received by the married couple would be subject to federal income tax as ordinary income.

B. State Taxes

1. Types of Taxes Levied

Depending on where you live and whether or not you purchase bonds sold by an issuer in your state, you may be subject to state and/or local taxes. These may be in the form of income tax, property tax, or capital gains tax.

a. Property Tax

According to the *Guide to State and Local Taxation of Municipal Bonds* published by Gabriele, Hueglin & Cashman, Inc. as of 1983, 11 states subject out-of-state municipal bonds to personal property taxes, but only Ohio taxes some in-state issues. Though the territorial bonds described below cannot be subject to state income taxes, they may be subject to a state's personal property tax.

b. Capital Gains Tax

State capital gains taxes generally follow the same principle described above with respect to federal capital gains taxes and require a taxpayer to report as state taxable income the net capital gain on municipal bonds reported for federal income tax purposes. Thus, both in-state and out-of-state net capital gains may be subject to state income taxes. To the extent that a state follows federal law, the 60% capital gains deduction will be repealed for state tax purposes as well as federal purposes. In addition, since the federal tax rate has been decreased, the benefit of a federal deduction for state taxes paid will decrease. Thus, in high-tax states, the state tax burden on capital gains will be substantially increased.

c. Income Tax

As of September 1985, the table below indicates whether municipal bond income received by individuals and corporations is subject to state income tax. If income from municipal bonds in a state is subject to state income tax, it is marked by an X; municipal income in all other states is either specifically exempted from tax or there is no state income.

The table indicates that 37 states and the District of Columbia currently subject out-of-state municipal bond income of individuals to tax and five states subject municipal income from bonds issued by in-state issuers to tax. Under the doctrine of reciprocal immunity, the states do not tax obligations of the federal government and the federal government does not tax certain state and other municipal debt. This principle extends to territorial bonds. As a consequence, income from bonds issued by the District of Columbia when it was a territory. Guam Puerto Rico, the Virgin Islands and American Samoa are exempt from federal, state, and local taxes. The same rule applies to Alaska bonds issued before 1959 and Hawaii bonds issued before 1960.

2. Effective State Tax Rates

In order to understand the impact of state taxes on an investor's return, the nominal or dollar amount of state taxes must be distinguished from the effective tax rate. The distinguishing point is based

Tax Aspects of Municipal Bonds

State	Individuals State's Own Bonds	Individuals Other States' Bonds	Corporations State's Own Bonds	Corporations Other States' Bonds	State	Individuals State's Own Bonds	Individuals Other States' Bonds	Corporations State's Own Bonds	Corporations Other States' Bonds
Ala.		X		X	Mo.		X		X
Alas.					Mont.		X	X	X
Ariz.		X		X	Nebr.				
Ark.		X		X	Nev.				
Ca. Franchise			X	X	N. H.		X		
Cal. Income		X		X	N. J.		X	X	X
Colo.		X		X	N.M.				
Conn.		X	X	X	N. Y.		X	X	X
Del.		X		X	N. C.		X		X
D. C.		X[1]		X	N. Dak.		X[3]		X
Fla.			X	X	Ohio		X		
Ga.		X		X	Okla.	X	X	X	X
Haw.		X		X	Ore.		X	X	X
Ida.			X	X	Pa.		X		
Ill.	X	X	X	X	R. I.		X		X
Ind.				X[2]	S. C.		X		X
Iowa	X	X	X	X	S. Dak.				
Kan.	X	X	X	X	Tenn.		X	X	X
Ky.		X		X	Tex.				
La.		X		X	Utah			X	X
Me.		X			Vt.				
Md.		X		X	Va.		X		X
Mass.		X	X	X	Wash.				
Mich.		X		X	W. Va.		X		X
Minn.		X	X	X	Wis.	X	X	X	X
Miss.		X		X	Wyo.				

[1]Taxable if purchased after 1991 (exempt until then).
[2]Taxable only for gross income tax purposes.
[3]Taxable only if long form is used.

Source: Commerce Clearing House, *State Tax Review*, Vol. 46, no. 38 (September 17, 1985).

on the fact that the amount of state taxes paid may be deducted on a taxpayer's federal income tax return. For example, if a taxpayer is in the 28% federal income tax bracket and pays a state tax of $100, he would deduct that $100 on his federal income tax return and receive a tax benefit of $28 ($100 × 28%). If the taxpayer in this example is in the 10% state tax bracket, the effective rate of state tax would be 7.2% rather than 10%, taking into account the federal tax benefit.

The formula to reduce the nominal rate to the effective rate is as follows: Effective rate = nominal state rate × (1.00 − marginal federal income tax rate).

For example, if the taxpayer is in the 28% federal tax bracket and pays a 10% nominal state tax rate, his effective rate of state tax would be 7.2% rather than 10%, computed by the above formula as follows:

Effective state tax rate = 10% × (1.00 − .28)
= 10% × .72
= 7.2%

3. State Taxes and Investment Strategy

Your initial reaction to the realization of the high in-state taxes you may have to pay may be to make a mental note to purchase only in-state bonds, (bonds sold by an issuer in your state of residence). The lure of double or triple tax-exemption is a strong drawing card. However, you may be doing yourself a disservice if you do not compare out-of-state bond yields to in-state yields each time you purchase bonds. If bonds are in relatively short supply or there is a large demand for bonds in your state, the yield on bonds in your state may decline when compared to out-of-state bonds.

As a general rule, if you live in a high tax state such as New York or California and you are in the 28% federal tax bracket, out-of-state bonds will be desirable if they yield at least ¾ of 1% more than in-state bonds. Because of the great demand for in-state bonds in high-tax states like New York and California, it may be desirable for investors to buy out-of-state bonds when out-of-state bonds yield more than ¾ of 1% more than in-state bonds. In addition, if you have a substantial portfolio, you may want out-of-state bonds to enable you to achieve geographic diversification, even if in-state bonds would be desirable strictly from a tax viewpoint.

notes

Chapter XIII

[1]*Bernard P. McDonough*, Tax Court Memo, 1977–50.
[2]*Wisconsin Cheeseman, Inc.*, 388 F2d. 420 (CA-7, 1968).
[3]*J. S. Wynn, Jr.*, 411 F2d 615 (CA-3, 1969), Cert. Den. 396 U.S. 1008.
[4]Rev. Proc. 72–18, 1972-1 CB 740.
[5]Section 4.02 of Rev. Proc. 72–18.
[6]Section 3.05 of Rev. Proc. 72–18.

CHAPTER XIV

The New York City Story

A. Moratorium and Technical Default—The Small Investors Takes the Bait
B. Warning Signs of Financial Weakness
    1. Rapid Increases in Short-Term Debt
    2. Fiscal Monkey Business
    3. Declining Revenues
    4. Increased Welfare and Pension Costs
    5. Layoffs of Municipal Employees
C. Who is to Blame for the Default?
    1. City Administration
    2. Underwriters
    3. Bond Counsel
    4. Rating Agencies
D. New York City is Saved
E. Results of New York City's Financial Disarray
F. Recommendations to Investors

This chapter will summarize the story of how and why a moratorium was declared on New York City's short-term debt on November 15, 1975. The story is long and complicated—it was in the making for many years and is laced with ineptitude, punctuated by greed, and sprinkled with deceit. The story is the cause for both pessimism and optimism. Yes, there was a default on $100 million bond anticipation notes in March 1975, but it lasted only 24 hours. There was a suspension of payments on New York City's short-term debt, but it was declared unconstitutional by the New York State Court of Appeals on November 19, 1975, and no principal was lost.

Though this was called a moratorium, to holders of New York City debt who could not sell their bonds and who *had* to exchange short-term high-coupon debt issues for long-term low coupon bonds, this was a default! Could such a major default happen again? Yes! Would knowledgeable investors be completely taken by surprise? No! The New York City story provides a piece of vital history and warning signals to municipal bond investors.

A. Moratorium and Technical Default—The Small Investors Take the Bait

On November 15, 1975, the New York State Legislature passed the Moratorium Act, which suspended the requirement that New York City redeem short-term obligations that had reached maturity. This meant the city had cash-flow problems and was unofficially bankrupt because it could not pay its bills. Thousands of small investors had purchased New York City's securities between October 1, 1974, and April 15, 1975, absorbing a substantial part of the $4 billion worth of securities sold during that time. Ten days before the passage of the Moratorium Act, New York City's short-term obligations were selling at only 35% to 45% of their face value. What a return! Who would have believed the nation's largest city could not pay its bills?

Ironically, but not by chance, small investors had been denied access to the city notes before the default because the debt required a minimum investment of $100,000. However, to help keep the sinking ship afloat, the city and its underwriters reduced the face value of new issues from $100,000 to $10,000 to make them attractive to small investors. City bonds were sold with high interest coupons and high yields to attract the small individual investor. The city's securities were also placed with the city's pension funds and with bond sinking funds. City officials were presumably prudently managing those funds on behalf of the beneficiaries, the retired employees of the City of New York.

B. Warning Signs of Financial Weakness

The financial disarray of New York City flashed warning signs to investors long before the city actually was unable to meet its debt. The warning signs included rapid increases in short-term debt, reports of fiscal monkey business including attempts to circumvent legal debt limits, reports of declining revenue, increased welfare costs and pension benefits, and actual or threatened layoffs of municipal employees.

1. Rapid Increases in Short-Term Debt

New York City has a capital budget, which funds public works, such as bridges and roads, and an expense budget, which funds annually recurring costs. In the early 1970s, New York City used the capital budget funds to pay some of its recurring costs and, in addition, borrowed short-term funds to pay current expenses. Thus, the city's short-term debt grew enormously in a short period of time. Although many municipalities borrow in anticipation of revenues, a rapid increase in short-term debt is one of the clearest indications of pending financial difficulties.

On June 20, 1975, New York had outstanding debt in excess of $14 billion. $4.54 billion consisted of short-term debt, more than double the amount owed in 1973. Only a little more than half of the total New York City short-term debt was secured with specified revenue to redeem the notes. Tax anticipation notes (TANs) were to be paid from expected collection of city real estate taxes. In selling the TANs, the city assumed that all real estate taxes owed to New York would be collected, an unreasonable expectation. Bond anticipation notes (BANs) were to be paid from the proceeds of new bonds, which were to be floated to retire the BANs; that is, if new bonds could be sold. Revenue anticipation notes (RANs) were to be paid by unspecified revenues.

2. Fiscal Monkey Business

Since the mayoralty of Robert Wagner in 1965, borrowing against anticipated revenues without repayment in the subsequent year, had become a general practice of the New York City administration. This meant the city would borrow against revenue that it expected to receive in the unspecified future by floating TANs, BANs, and RANs. Put more simply, in many cases, this was borrowing without much collateral.

The city's employees used budgetary, accounting, and financing practices that created an unrealistically favorable picture of New York's financial condition. These practices included floating bonds backed by future revenues that officials knew would never be received. The city's books carried forward revenue expected from the federal government that had been formally disavowed. As stated above, New York City also used monies set aside for capital improvements to meet daily operating expenses. This practice resulted in the deterioration of the city's roads, bridges, tunnels, and public buildings. It was most graphically illustrated by the collapse of the West Side Highway in Manhattan. Such "creative financing" by city officials attempted to make New York City appear financially solvent when it was on the brink of bankruptcy.

A Stabilization Revenue Corporation (SRC) was established by the city, charged with the responsibility of changing short-term debt into long-term debt without putting a ceiling on New York City's ability to borrow. A lawsuit was brought against the city, claiming the SRC was illegal because it tried to circumvent New York City's legal debt limit. Though the suit was not substantiated, it further reduced investors' confidence and restricted the ability of the city to borrow, intensifying cash-flow problems.

3. Declining Revenues

The exodus of large businesses from New York City resulted in a loss of tax revenue from both the businesses and its employees. The outflow of the middle class to the suburbs, in addition, weakened the city's tax base. Despite the weakening real estate market, the city did not downgrade its expectations of real estate and income taxes, and it maintained delinquent taxes on the books as expected revenues. In that way, it borrowed against money officials knew would never be received.

4. Increased Welfare and Pension Costs

The influx of poor people from the South and Puerto Rico resulted in the swelling of the welfare roles. New York State tried to provide an adequate stipend for those unable to work, thus attracting the nation's poor. Hard bargaining by the unions and ineptitude on the part of the city's administration resulted in large wage increases and pension benefits. As wages increased, amounts to be paid to the union pension funds also automatically inflated beyond the city's ability to pay.

5. Layoffs of Municipal Employees

In order to balance the budget and pressure the state and federal governments, layoffs were always threatened and sometimes carried out. The layoffs were always in essential services where they would be least acceptable to the general public. Mayor Abraham Beame would then rescind the layoffs completely, confusing everyone.

C. Who Is to Blame for the Default?

Where were the protections that should have prevented a major default from occurring? Why was New York City able to continue to sell bonds in the face of this public disaster?

1. City Administration

The Security and Exchange Commission placed major blame for the disaster at the feet of Mayor Abraham Beame and Comptroller Harrison Goldin, both of whom had knowledge of and perpetuated the system of financial excesses.[1] New York City officials knew there was an ever-growing disparity between revenues and expenditures. However, they wrote reports and made public statements that did not accurately reflect the city's deplorable financial condition. Beame's fiscal flip-flopping created a sense that his cries of insolvency only reflected attempts to decrease union pressures at the bargaining table, and force the state and federal governments to come to the city's assistance. Federal guarantees of New York City's bonds were especially sought to make city debt issues salable, but to no avail. New York was a Democratic city pleading for aid from Republican President Gerald Ford in an election year. The city was used as a whipping post to illustrate uncontrollable Democratic Party spending. The fiscal mirrors used by Beame and Goldin made the city's bankruptcy appear to be more ill-conceived politics than dire economic need.

2. Underwriters

What of the other investor safeguards? The underwriters were major banks who helped the City sell the bonds.[2] They included Chase Manhattan Bank, First National City Bank, Morgan Guaranty Trust Company of New York, Manufacturer's Hanover Trust Company, Bankers Trust Company, Merrill Lynch, Pierce, Fenner and Smith, Inc. and Chemical Bank.

According to a questionnaire circulated by the Securities and Exchange Commission, they did not view it as their responsibility to verify the facts in the city's disclosure documents. The underwriters tended to rely on the managing underwriter to conduct the inquiry. The most important factors in deciding to underwrite an issue were profitability, favorable ratings, customer demand, and the general market conditions, including the resalability of the bonds. Also of importance was the historical relationship the city had with the major underwriting syndicate to sell New York City bonds.

Although between October and April of 1975 the underwriters had detailed information about the financial crisis of the city, they still represented New York City's bonds as safe investments and sold them to the public. At the same time, certain underwriters were in the process of reducing or eliminating their own holdings of the city's securities. Some banks refused to purchase additional New York City debt for their own accounts or for the accounts of investors for which they were responsible. Though the underwriters tried to liquidate their holdings, in March 1975 they had notes exceeding $1 billion or 20% of their net worth. Deputy Mayor Cavanagh stated: "The banks and us are in a community of interests. If we go down, they go down." The city sank slowly as the credit market for its debt shrank because New York City was unable to demonstrate that it could resolve its fiscal crisis. In effect, the underwriters were finally forcing the city to take remedial action because the market for its bonds was so saturated and they could not or would not absorb any more New York City debt.

On March 23, 1984, a federal judge approved partial settlements totaling $2,850,000 from six defendants in the litigation. The book is still not closed on those who were accused of major violations.

3. Bond Counsel

Bond counsel opinions are supposed to assure investors that legal risks as to the validity of the bonds are negligible. The legal opinion on a bond addresses two matters: the authority of the municipality to issue the securities and the tax-exempt nature of the securities. Like the underwriters, the bond lawyers did little independent investigation and relied almost exclusively on city officials and the rating agencies. As such, they allowed themselves to be duped by the city into misleading the investing public. Like the underwriters, bond counsel for the city had developed long-term relationships with New York. From the period January 1973 through March 1975 four firms acted as bond counsel: Wood Dawson Love & Sabatine; Sykes, Galloway & Dikeman; Hawkens, Delafield & Wood, and White & Case. In the sale of these city securities, bond counsel was retained by the underwriters to approve sales that had already been agreed to by the city and the underwriters. The lawyers would send the city forms to complete and use the information obtained without further verification or investigation. Even when there was a question of fiscal solvency, the lawyers did not take steps to verify the information.[3]

4. Rating Agencies

The rating agencies represent key safeguards in bond investing. Based upon their ratings, interest rates and bond prices are set. According to a Securities and Exchange Commission report written in August 1977, the bonds that were rated by the two prime agencies, Standard & Poor's and Moody's, were based largely upon unverified data and information furnished by the city. The history of the ratings is not reassuring to the investor. In July 1965, Moody's lowered the New York City rating from A to Baa, the lowest investment grade. Standard & Poor's followed suit in 1966, reducing the City's bond rating to BBB from A, a rating comparable to Moody's, due to rising municipal expenditures and deteriorating economic conditions.

In 1968, Moody's raised its rating of New York City bonds to Baa1. On December 18, 1972, Moody's raised its ratings of city bonds from Baa1 to A. The rating increase, according to Dr. Jackson Phillips, executive vice president of Moody's, was due to an increase in the market value of taxable real estate and other current sources of revenue in relation to the deficit.[4] This rating was endorsed despite negative indications, including congressional testimony in 1972 by Comptroller Goldin that the city's tax base was eroding and New York City had not been successful in closing major budget gaps. In December 1973, Standard & Poor's raised its ratings as well, citing steady improvement in the city's financial picture based on the financial report issued by the city. Though they were aware of the fiscal gimmickry, states the 1977 SEC report, they accepted assurances that steps were being taken to correct the abuses.

During the fiscal year 1973–1974, the city increased the amount of its short-term debt outstanding. The state Legislature authorized the establishment of the Stabilization Reserve Corporation, which would incur long-term debt without endangering the city's ability to borrow further. Standard & Poor's and Moody's still did not change their ratings.

A smaller rating agency, Fitch Investors Service, issued an analysis of the city's declining economic situation. After the publication of the city's June 1974 annual report, Fitch downgraded New York's bond rating from A to medium grade on all bonds maturing prior to January 1, 1980, and to fair grade on all bonds maturing thereafter, citing the "further deterioration of the city's financial operations." Moody's and Standard & Poor's, after a visit with Comptroller Goldin, waited to see if steps would be taken to remedy the situation. Both agencies, however, issued reports to their subscribers describing the city's plight, while sustaining the A ratings.

In January 1975, Moody's decided to drop its rating on the city's BAN's from MIG 1 (its highest rating on short-term debt) to MIG 2. The SEC report states that in a meeting with Comptroller Goldin, upon hearing the news, he regarded that a drop in rating could be a "very nearly fatal blow" to the city. He asked Moody's to defer its decision.

In April 1975, seven months before New York's default, Standard & Poor's finally suspended the ratings of New York City bonds based upon two pieces of information: New York State could not aid the city if the city was unable to meet its principal and interest payments on its outstanding debt, and the city, which had increasing difficulty borrowing, would default if it could not borrow. Moody's rejected Standard & Poor's evaluation and maintained its rating. It was not until October 2, 1975, (one month before default) that Moody's dropped its New York City bond rating from A (upper-medium) to B (marginally speculative) and finally to Caa (very speculative) as city officials acknowledged publicly that New York would default without federal aid, which did not appear to be forthcoming.

D. New York City Is Saved

New York City teetered on the brink of disaster until it was rescued by the state and federal governments. Short-term debts were converted into long-term debt by the Municipal Assistance Corporation, a state agency commonly referred to as Big M.A.C. M.A.C. issued its own bonds, which are secured by the city's stock transfer taxes and sales taxes. Although this money is generated in the city, it never passes through the hands of New York City's financial managers. For the small investor, this meant that $1.6 billion of city notes held by the public was exchanged for 10-year 8% M.A.C. bonds. Although M.A.C. bonds stretched out the payments of the city's short-term debt at lower interest, they also assured their payment. Despite the fact that the city's anticipation notes (BANs, RANs and TANs) were sold as if they had first lien (call) on the city's revenues, in fact they did not. Representations were made by the comptroller's office that all bonds and notes issued by the city were to be paid before other debts, salaries, or other obligations. In fact, "the first lien so called" did not apply to payment of the principal of the various anticipation notes issued by the city but only to the interest due at maturity. *Five years* after the issue date, holders of TANs and RANs had the right to have revenues set aside for redemption of the bonds according to the state's Constitution. For BANs, there was *no establishment of first lien* even after five years. No clear representations of these facts were given to noteholders. The issue was sidestepped through conversion of the notes into M.A.C. bonds. However, the lesson is clear to educated purchasers of high-coupon short-term paper.

In order to strengthen the M.A.C. bonds, the federal government authorized $4 billion in guarantees of new state securities in order to enable the state to further assist the city to prevent a more substantial New York City default. These guaranteed securities were to be phased out over a four-year period between 1976 and 1980. The federal guarantees required restructuring of the city's debt, an exchange of short-term securities for long-term securities with lower interest rates, and the state control of city finances. It was not until February 15, 1984, that New York City was able to float bonds in its own name at an investment-grade level. Before that date, it relied on the Municipal Assistance Corporation to raise its money.

E. Results of New York City's Financial Disarray

The impact of the declining solvency of the city was felt by investors, large and small, including other municipalities and states, underwriters and the nation.

Small investors took the brunt of New York City's debt moratorium. According to the SEC report, individual investors were not told of the risks involved in buying New York City debt. Of 500 individual investors who responded to a questionnaire, 60% had not previously invested in municipal bonds. Furthermore, they were almost totally unaware of the city's financial condition. Other investors bought New York City securities when things looked gloomiest, counting on a federal bail-out.

As a result of the moratorium on New York City debt, other municipalities had to pay much higher interest rates in order to borrow. Municipalities in the same geographic area were particularly affected, though all municipalities with weak credit ratings were hurt by higher interest rates.

Underwriters demanded more information on new bond offerings as a result of the moratorium. The Municipal Finance Officers Association published voluntary guidelines, which the underwriters have followed to protect themselves against lawsuits and to forestall the establishment of federal guidelines. Voluntary guidelines enable the underwriters to tailor the degree of disclosure to the situation of the issuer. Uniform reporting would increase the costs of floating new securities uniformly even if creditworthiness were not in doubt.

In a questionnaire sent to investment advisers at banks and insurance companies to ascertain what kind of additional information they would like to have to encourage purchases of municipal bonds, an accounting firm found that there was no great demand for additional information. They found that the most important considerations in purchasing bonds were interest rates and to some extent maturity dates. They required concisely stated financial disclosures to make investing easy.

If a more substantial default had occurred, a disastrous ripple effect was anticipated in the entire country. The effects of default would have included increased interest rates translated into higher state and local taxes, small bank failures, disruption of the bond market, and closure of the bond market to municipalities with weak issues. The possible results on New York City alone would have been catastrophic: payrolls unmet, massive layoff of city workers, school closings, city vendors driven to bankruptcy, prisons and hospitals unfunded, abandoned construction, defaults of New York City pension plans, and general capital decay.

F. Recommendations to Investors

Based on the New York City experience, the following are warning signs:

1. Be wary of purchasing bonds when there appears to be many bond issues based on the same credit. Every new issue dilutes the pre-existing credit unless the bonds are secured by a particular source of revenue.

2. Bad publicity, while not necessarily justified, affects the ability of the municipality to cover short-term borrowing needs.

3. Fiscal weakness stems from floating bonds in anticipation of revenue that may never be received and from creative bookkeeping, which gives only the *appearance* of declining debt.

4. Heed the warnings. Indicators in the media of a weakening economy and hence a decline in expected revenue include: increased unemployment, increased welfare roles, middle-class flight to the suburbs, escalating union contracts with emphasis on increases in fringe benefits, and a declining real estate tax base. These factors can ultimately lower the rating of an issue and cost you money by reducing the value of your bonds.

5. Rating agencies are not always in agreement on the ability of a debtor to pay. When there is a discrepancy among the rating agencies, it is safer to assume that the lowest rating is the proper one.

6. Do not count on a federal government bail-out. It must be politically expedient as well as fiscally possible.

7. When purchasing notes and bonds, ask if and when they have first lien.

G. The City: 1986

New York City has balanced its books for six consecutive years in accordance with generally accepted accounting principles (GAAP). On June 30, 1986, the city satisfied the statutory conditions for termination of the control period during which the city had to submit four-year budgets to the Financial Control Board and the Municipal Assistance Corporation. The city has refinanced all but $1 million of federally guaranteed city general obligation bonds, which Messrs. Koch and Golden was indicative of the city's financial revival.[5] The refinancing removed the federal guarantee and stretched out the lifetime of the debt.

Though the city has reclaimed its independence, not everyone anticipates a rosy future. The problems of the past remain intrinsically the same. According to Edward V. Regan, New York State comptroller and a member of the State Financial Control Board, the city is once again relying too heavily on "one-shot revenues and one-time savings" to close anticipated budget deficits.[6] The city faces a $1 billion dollar deficit in three years. Though the refinancings reduce the city's debt payments immediately, they increase the amount the city will have to pay over the long term. In addition, the anticipated elimination of $270 million of federal general revenue sharing funds in 1987 will not enhance the city's ability to balance its budget.

notes

Chapter XIV

[1] Understanding the City and its Officials," *Securities and Exchange Commission Staff Report on Transactions in Securities of The City of New York* (August 26, 1977).
[2] "The Rise of the Underwriter," *SEC Staff Report, supra.*
[3] "The Role of Bond Counsel," *SEC Staff Report, supra.*
[4] "The Role of the Rating Agencies, *SEC Staff Report, supra.*
[5] Joseph Laura, "State warns 1.5 billion city deficit loans," *Crain's New York Business,* (July 8, 1985), p 5.
[6] *Ibid.*

CHAPTER XV

The Washington Public Power Supply System (WPPSS)

A. The Rise and Fall of WPPSS
B. Warning Signs of Financial Weakness
C. Who Is to Blame?
    1. Bonneville Power Administration
    2. Utilities
    3. Board of Directors of WPPSS
    4. Underwriters
    5. Brokers
    6. Rating Agencies
D. Benefits from WPPSS
E. Financial Fallout from WPPSS
F. Alternative Conclusions to the Tale
G. WPPSS 1986 Update

"Municipal bonds? You wouldn't want to invest in those. You know about WHOOPS don't you?"

This is a line used by hucksters who wish to steer you into other investments that are risky for you and lucrative for them. For those of you who bought defaulted Washington Public Power Supply System plants 4 and 5 bonds and felt the sting, the hucksters' words ring true. However, the rate of default on municipal bonds has always been very low, and most defaults are quickly corrected.

A. The Rise and Fall of WPPSS

WPPSS, as the system is known, is a joint-action agency comprising a number of electric utilities in the Pacific Northwest. The five WPPSS nuclear power plants are grouped into two units, based upon the kinds of financial security backing them. Plants 1, 2, and 3 are secured by a debt-service guarantee of the federal Bonneville Power Administration. Plants 4 and 5 were supported by participating WPPSS utilities that agreed to accept financial responsibility for the projects whether or not they ever received any electricity from the plants. WPPSS plants 4 and 5 were canceled and the utilities that were building them defaulted on $2.5 billion of municipal bonds. This was the largest default in history. the contracts securing the bonds were held to be invalid by the highest court in the State of Washington.

WPPSS was originally created to oversee the construction and management of electrical power plants for 23 municipal utilities and rural electric power cooperatives in the Pacific Northwest in 1957. It was not until the early 1970's, however, that contracts between these utilities and the Bonneville Power Administration (BPA) were negotiated and executed for the construction of nuclear power plants 1, 2, and 3. BPA is a federal agency that sets rates and markets power from federal hydroelectric dams. BPA agreed to purchase all the electricity from plants 1 and 2, 70% of the output of plant 3 and to guarantee debt service on bonds issued to finance these projects. All of the WPPSS utilities participating in plants 1, 2 and 3 are customers of BPA, which is buying their shares of the three units by reducing its bills to the utilities—a process called net billing. The 30% of plant 3 in which BPA does not have an interest belongs to four private utilities.

WPPSS was empowered by the Washington State Legislature to issue municipal bonds to finance the plants. The bonds for plants 1, 2 and 3 were rated triple-A by Moody's and Standard & Poor's because of their backing by BPA. Since the utilities would be unable to use all of the 1,200 megawatts produced by plants 1, 2 and 3 (which would be enough energy to power Seattle), the utilities offered shares in the plants to other public and investor owned utilities in Oregon, Idaho, Montana, and Washington. More than 100 utilities initially signed up for a "riskless" venture in nuclear power.

In 1976, contracts were signed by 88 utilities for the construction of plants 4 and 5. Bonneville did not agree to purchase the electricity from plants 4 and 5 as it had done for the first three units. The utilities signed "take-or pay, come hell or high water" contracts with WPPSS, which obligated them to pay for the plants even if no electricity was ever generated by them. In the first half of 1976, a number of municipal utilities that had originally agreed to participate in plants 4 and 5 withdrew from the project, citing lack of need for additional power. The utilities claim Bonneville notified them that power could not be guaranteed to them beyond 1982 if they did not participate in the two WPPSS projects. As a result, many utilities that decided not to participate signed contracts on July 14, 1976, which obligated them to help fund plants 4 and 5. Bonds were sold with a legal opinion that verified the binding nature of the take-or-pay contracts. The bonds issued for plants 4 and 5 were initially rated A1 by Moody's and A+ by Standard & Poor's.

Revised budget estimates for plants 4 and 5 sent the cost of the five plants soaring from an original estimate of $3.4 billion in July 1976 to a total of $7.8 billion in February 1981. Additional bonds were sold in April 1981 for an outstanding total of $2.25 billion for plants 4 and 5 alone. The escalation in costs was attributed to mismanagement, labor strife, regulatory delays, and construction delays. Inflation boosted the overall costs of the construction of the plants and the costs of borrowing. Moreover, additional interest costs arose because of the difficulty of finding purchasers for bonds of plants 4 and 5 due to the saturation of the market with WPPSS bonds.

In mid-October 1981, WPPSS had exhausted its construction funds for plants 4 and 5, which were then only 19% complete. Soon thereafter, construction was suspended on plants 4 and 5, along with the A1 rating by Moody's. However, it was not until May 1983 that WPPSS defaulted on its $15.6 million monthly payment to Chemical Bank, the trustee for the WPPSS bondholders.

Chemical Bank, as trustee, sued the utilities to force them to make timely payment pursuant to the take-or-pay contracts. The June 15, 1983 decision of the Washington State Supreme Court was that the utilities were not authorized under Washington State law to enter into the take or pay contracts relating to plants 4 and 5 because they lacked an "ownership interest," or sufficient control over the plants to constitute the equivalent of an ownership interest.[1] In July 1983, WPPSS admitted that plants 4 and 5 were in default, and their remaining assets were transferred to Chemical Bank.

The current status of plants 1, 2, and 3 is: Construction on plant 1 has stopped and the unit has been mothballed due to a reduced need for electricity. Plant 2 is finished and began commercial operation in October 1984. Plant 3 is mothballed and requires substantial additional financing if it is to be completed. Federal District Court Judge Richard Bilby ruled that neither WPPSS nor BPA had the legal authority to halt construction on plant 3; however, it remains mothballed.

In summary, there are $8.3 billion of WPPSS bonds currently outstanding, constituting approximately 2.4% of the outstanding United States municipal debt, and one of the five plants is completed.

B. Warning Signs of Financial Weakness

How could investors have known that this danger awaited, like shoals hidden right beneath a calm sea? There were warning signs which could have steered them away from the danger:

1. Though revenue bonds usually do not need voter approval, they ultimately require public support for repayment of the debt. There were vocal segments of the population strenuously opposed to nuclear power. Their opposition was not the cause of default, but they did prevent, in part, the problem from being cured.

2. There were too many WPPSS bonds outstanding. Some eye-opening facts were recounted by attorney James E. Spiotto.[2] WPPSS bonds constituted more than 50% of the electric utility municipal bonds issued in 1975. In 1978, WPPSS issued $1.2 billion in revenue bonds, equivalent to 20% of all gas and electric municipal bonds issued that year. In the six-month period between September 1981 and March 1982, a total of $2.25 billion of WPPSS bonds were sold with a coupon of 13.93%. Total outstanding debt for all five plants was $8.33 billion in 1982. Of that, $2.25 billion was for plants 4 and 5. Though you may not know the number of outstanding bonds of a particular issue, you should be able to get a sense of the general availability. You can ask the seller whether there are many bonds for sale by a particular issuer. If everyone seems to have a particular bond, its familiarity might make it appealing. But you should remember that you are buying a promissory note. The more promises to pay that are outstanding, the more difficult it might be for the promises to be kept.

3. By way of comparison, when New York City defaulted it had $14 billion of debt outstanding, $6 billion of which was short-term. Though WPPSS' debt was much less, there was no stream of income to pay its obligation. On the other hand, New York City is supported by a substantial tax base. WPPSS 4 and 5 revenue bonds were riskier because there was no income to pay off the debt until the plant, were completed and operational.

C. Who Is to Blame?

Looking for a villain? There are multiple causes of the problem called Whoops. The entire story has not yet been written, though a pointing finger has moved in the direction of the participants described below.

1. Bonneville Power Administration

The Bonneville Power Administration is an agency of the federal government that has control over the hydroelectric power produced in the Pacific Northwest. Federal legislation favored the distribution of this cheap power to the publicly and cooperatively owned utilities, called the preference customers. However, nonpreference customers such as the investor-owned utilities and aluminum companies also had some legal rights to this power. The bargain rates of hydroelectric power were boosting consumption by about 7% per year. As a result, BPA facilitated the building of nuclear and coal burning power plants in the region to forestall a power shortage based upon a projected continuing increase in demand for power at a 7% annual growth rate.

The method employed by BPA to support the construction of WPPSS plants 1, 2, and 3 was net-billing. Net-billing enabled the preference utilities to enter into construction agreements for coal and nuclear power either alone or in combination with publicly owned utilities. It allowed the preference utilities to charge BPA for power from the WPPSS plants that BPA would receive in the future. The net effect of this arrangement is that BPA is obligated to pay the participants, and the participants are obligated to pay WPPSS their pro rata shares of the total annual costs of the plants, whether or not the plants are completed.

Construction of plants 1, 2, and 3 began in the 1970s with BPA backing, for an estimated cost of $3.1 billion. In 1973, WPPSS began to construct plants 4 and 5 and budgeted $3.5 billion for them. Plants 4 and 5 did not receive BPA backing because the Internal Revenue Service revised its regulations, denying municipal bond tax exemption to a corporation issuing municipal bonds with the guarantee of a federal agency. BPA was active in planning plants 4 and 5, and it encouraged utility participation in the financing. Utilities were told that if they needed additional power in the 1980s they should enter into participant agreements.

Not all utilities took the bait, however. Seattle, the largest city in the Northwest, voted 5 to 4 against participation in July 1976. To meet any increases in electricity, a 12-volume report recommended energy conservation and alternative energy sources rather than building plants 4 and 5. That same month an architectural engineering firm, Skidmore, Owings and Merrill, completed a report for BPA reiterating those points. This advice as well as other negative reports were rejected, and plans for construction proceeded.

2. Utilities

Why did WPPSS default on plants 4 and 5? The immediate reason was that the 88 public utilities backed out of the take-or-pay come hell or high water contracts that they signed for plants 4 and 5. You may ask, how could they renege on signed contracts?

This is the very question that the WPPSS attorneys at the law firm of Wood and Dawson are asking themselves, in light of the Washington State Supreme Court's rejection of the responsibility of the 88 utilities to meet their obligations.

There was a question of the legality of the take-or-pay contracts. Eleven utilities located in Oregon were barred by an Oregon Court from paying their share because the court decided that they did not have the authority to enter into the take-or-pay agreements with WPPSS in the first place. However, the Oregon Supreme Court subsequently reversed the lower court and decided that the Oregon utilities did have authority to enter into the take-or-pay contracts.

On October 15, 1982, the judge from the King County Superior Court ruled participants in plants 4 and 5 did have legal authority to repay the debt, but the judge did not rule on the validity of the take-or-pay contracts. On June 15, 1983, the Washington State Supreme Court decided that the utilities located in Washington did not have the authority to enter into the take-or-pay agreements. Given the fact that a minimum of 70% of the participants were excused from their responsibilities, the court decided that the remaining participants would not have entered into the contract if they had known the burden of payment rested solely on them; therefore, the judge also excused them.

Chemical Bank, in its class-action suit, counter-attacked. It charged that if the local municipal utilities did indeed sign contracts without authority then they committed fraud, misrepresentations, and security violations. That issue is yet to be decided.

3. Board of Directors of WPPSS

Ultimately, blame comes to rest on those people who authorized and were supposed to oversee the construction of the five nuclear power plants. The WPPSS directors were drawn from the small towns of Washington state. Though accomplished small businessmen, they were unprepared to deal with the mammoth operation of five nuclear power plants. One director is quoted as having thought the decision to construct five plants was conservative because at one time 25 plants were under consideration.

Spending the money raised on Wall Street proved to be very difficult. As a quasigovernmental body, WPPSS was required to approve any expenditure over $15,000. This created hours of paperwork. In addition, all contracts were to be by competitive bidding. This resulted in the additional horror of three different construction designs for plants 1, 2, and 3.

Since plant designs were continually modified, the contractors were able to jack up their prices after they were awarded the building contracts. A case in point is the bill presented by Morrison-Knudsen Company for pouring concrete for plants 3 and 5. The cost skyrocketed from an expected $40.2 million to $214.4 million three years after the work was to have been completed.

Due to a little log rolling, between 45 and 65 general contractors were employed at each site, instead of the traditional three. The board of directors tried to spread the work around to reward local constituencies.

Additional problems included delays caused by improper construction, and labor strikes that affected three of the plants for five months. The cost of construction of the plants was revised up to $26.6 billion by 1982. Too much time and money was squandered to enable the completion of all five plants. The Washington State Senate inquiry concluded that "WPPSS mismanagement has been the most significant cause of schedule delays and cost overruns on the WPPSS projects."

4. Underwriters

Since WPPSS plants 1, 2, and 3 were backed by a federal agency, BPA, the bonds were greeted with open arms on Wall Street. The bonds were syndicated by some of the premier names in public finance—Merrill Lynch, Goldman Sachs, Salomon Bros., Smith Barney, Blyth Eastman Dillon, and Paine Webber. Virtually every brokerage house of any consequence participated in these huge offerings.

Initially, the bonds of plants 1, 2, and 3 were rated triple-A and had a modest average coupon of 7% due to the backing of BPA, a federal agency. The bonds sold well until 1979, when a study by Blyth Eastman Dillon, the WPPSS financial adviser, indicated that the institutional buyers were almost saturated with WPPSS bonds. This warning was ignored. One of the WPPSS directors, C. Stanford Olsen, recalled that "Whenever cash was low, we would just toddle down to Wall Street."[3] In the fall of 1981, $750 million more was raised, with Merrill Lynch as the lead underwriter. The fees for that sale totaled $22.5 million. Small investors bought 70% of the bonds, biting at the 15% coupon offered as bait.

A legal question that will be considered by the courts is whether the underwriters diligently investigated the risks associated with the WPPSS bonds. Charles Wolf, a finance professor at The Columbia University Business School, noted that 99.8% of all municipal bonds issued since 1940 have been paid back in full or are current in their payments indicating a good enough track recorded by the investment concerns. Those who have suffered from WPPSS default will argue that 2% default is significant, focusing on their own losses rather than on the comparative safety of municipal bonds.

In 1978, T. Rowe Price removed plants 4 and 5 bonds from its tax-exempt municipal bond portfolio because of concerns over management and construction schedules. Because this institutional investor was unloading its WPPSS bonds due to the perceived risk, an issue that will be considered by the courts is whether the underwriters might have knowingly ignored the substantial possibility of default.

Another key issue to be considered is just what the investment houses knew about the viability of 4 and 5 when they sold the last $200 million in bonds, shortly before a construction moratorium was declared in March 1981. The offering prospectus, which is supposed to reveal the financial condition of the plant, was prepared by WPPSS, not the underwriters. It contained only sporadic warnings of problems in its 99 pages of text.[4] Three months after the bonds were sold, WPPSS Managing Director Robert Ferguson announced the system had estimated the project's cost at $23.9 billion, up from $15.9 billion. Work was stopped on plants 4 and 5 soon after, never to resume.

5. Brokers

Did you buy WPPSS bonds and feel that you were misled? Your broker might not have known any more about the financial condition of WPPSS than you did. Though prospectuses are provided by the underwriters, most brokers do not have the time to read them. Most bond buyers look at the rating and the interest rate and do not inquire further. Is that the fault of the buyer or the seller? Caveat emptor—let the buyer beware.

Many individuals own WPPSS bonds as part of a portfolio of shares of a unit investment trust or a municipal bond fund. If those bonds are part of an insured portfolio, the American Municipal Bond Assurance Corporation will be paying the tab. $23.7 million face value of bonds has been insured, for a total of $76.4 million to be paid out in principal and interest payments over 35 years.

6. Rating Agencies

The rating agencies analyze information that is given to them. They do not investigate hunches or look to make a story. The staffs employed to analyze the bonds is relatively small compared to the number of issues they rate.

From the investors' perspective, the ratings did not forecast the WPPSS default; however, the rating services do not purport to foretell what will happen. They only state the financial condition of the issuer at particular moments in time, the time the bonds are issued or when they are reviewed. This is a hard lesson to learn but essential to remember in buying bonds. The history of the bonds speaks for itself.[5]

Plants 1, 2, and 3 were originally rated triple-A by Standard

& Poor's and Moody's. In May 1983, after intermediate downgradings, Standard & Poor's suspended its ratings of WPPSS when the newly appointed WPPSS bond counsel, the New York firm of Wilkie Farr & Gallagher, could not guarantee that revenues generated by plants 1, 2, and 3 would be secure from plants 4 and 5 bondholders. Moody's Investors Service followed suit in June 1983.

Plants 4 and 5 bonds came to market rated A1 by Moody's and A+ by Standard & Poor's. Standard & Poor's downgraded plants 4 and 5 bonds from A+ to BBB in January 1982. This rating was suspended in August 1983. Moody's lowered the ratings for plants 4 and 5 to Baa1 until the rating suspension in January 1982.

D. Benefits of WPPSS

In any catastrophe, there are always some who benefit. You might immediately think of lawyers reaping the harvest from the WPPSS default and providing long-term employment for some 83 law firms. The lawyers represent the injured parties and those who are accused of causing the injuries including the utilities, the cities, law firms, rating agencies, underwriters, engineers, consultants, and individual defendants. Robert Greening, manager of the Public Power Council in Seattle, a group that represents the region's consumer-owned utilities on planning and rate making issues, said that "Quite frankly, many (law) firms are on a gravy train that they have never seen the likes of or ever will again."[6]

Another category of people marginally benefitting from WPPSS are the journalists who have interesting press to report. Perhaps the most enterprising journalist is Cyrus Noe, the Seattle freelance writer and consultant. He initiated a weekly newsletter in the spring of 1983 with the sole purpose of covering the policy debate and litigation swirling around WPPSS.

Other beneficiaries are the brokerage houses, which earn spreads on the buying and selling of defaulted WPPSS bonds. Wary investors might also choose to dump their WPPSS bonds, take their losses and be rid of the entanglement. Risk-oriented institutions or individual investors may buy them to hold for possible capital appreciation. When the Oregon Supreme Court decided that the Oregon utilities were bound by their take-or-pay contracts, certain WPPSS bonds appreciated by 30 basis points. The WPPSS default is also an opportunity to snag new clients through seminars, reports, and telephone hotlines with knowledgeable specialists.

Construction companies are also tried to turn bad news into good fortune. Two major contractors—Ebasco Services Inc. and Bechtel Group, Inc. proposed to finish plant 1 (65% complete) and plant 3 (76% complete) for a relatively fixed price. However, the quoted figure did not guarantee the number of hours needed to complete the project or costs of alterations ordered by the Nuclear Regulatory Commission. The contractors were seeking funding for the projects in an attempt to remain employed in a virtually moribund nuclear market, where more than 100 plants have been canceled in the last 10 years.

Another positive result from the WPPSS fallout has been to force those responsible for nuclear plants in other parts of the country to take a hard look at their projected plans and semi-completed projects. The difficult decision of plant completion versus abandonment is somewhat easier because of the financial morass of WPPSS.

E. Financial Fallout from WPPSS

Some kind of federal bail-out for WPPSS is repeatedly discussed in the media. However, the media states that a bail-out is highly unlikely because the bondholders are probably high-income people seeking to shelter their income. Therefore, little sympathy can be generated by their plight. What these statements fail to take into account is that municipal bonds, through the vehicles of trusts and funds, are the tax shelters of the masses. It is the only tax haven that a middle-class person can participate in for only $1,000. Moreover, it is these tax-sheltered dollars that enable publicly supported projects for public welfare to be financed for the low interest rates available in the tax-exempt market.

On the other side are angry consumers who rail against the spiraling costs of electricity in what used to be the lowest electric rate district in the country. BPA has increased the average retail cost of a kilowatt hour for 138 Northwest utilities to 3.4 cents from less than 2 cents between 1982 and 1983, and the fear is that rates will rise again. Customers of the 88 utilities involved in plants 4 and 5 would have seen rates climb to 3.7 cents if the utilities had been required to pay off the debt. This is still well below the national average of 6.6 cents and the 15.8 cents charged residential customers by Con Edison in New York.

The unknown future of electric utility rates has led some home owners to install wood stoves to escape the mounting rates. Alumax, Inc. canceled plans to build an aluminum smelter and Boeing Co. shut two electric boilers burning natural gas in the Pacific Northwest. The aluminum industry has shifted its production capacity from the Pacific Northwest to plants in other regions due to the rapid increases in electric costs. As less energy is used, the cost to the remaining consumers mount.

It is unclear even if projects 1, 2, and 3 are completed if a market will be found for their output. Falling demand, weakening oil prices, and competition from cheaper plants have made the WPPSS nuclear cones into white elephants. Moreover since the cones were built to withstand a nuclear attack, they will probably last as long as the pyramids of Egypt.

The fallout from WPPSS has made it more difficult and expensive for other public power borrowers to bring their bond issues to market. North Carolina Municipal Power Agency No. 1. indefinitely postponed a $350 million bond issue connected with the construction of the Catawba nuclear power plant in North Carolina. Soon after the default, Washington State general obligation bonds paid a half percentage point, or 50 basis points, more than comparable A/AA rated bonds. At the last sale in October 1983, however, the penalty was only 20 basis points due to good market responses. The Port of Tacoma, however, claimed it had to accept a higher interest rate for bonds issued to build new shipping facilities simply because it is located in Washington.

The WPPSS default has heavily burdened insurance companies, which hold a total of $1.85 billion of the WPPSS bonds, according to figures compiled by A.M. Best & Company, an Oldwick, N. J. research firm. The State Farm Group of Bloomington, Ind., holds the largest block of WPPSS bonds at $257.2 million. Other companies holding more than $100 million include Crum & Forster, Continental Insurance, Fireman's Fund, and Hartford Insurance. Other large WPPSS bond holders include The Fidelity Guaranty, Aetna Life & Casualty, Kemper Insurance, CIGNA and CNA.

The WPPSS default has caused a reevaluation of whether to build or complete mammoth plants with ballooning construction costs. Closer evaluation of nuclear power plants has led to discussions about the termination of construction at the Shoreham plant, which is owned by the Long Island Lighting Company, the Zimmer plant in Cincinnati, the Seabrook plant in New Hampshire and the Midland plant in Michigan.

Finally, it has forced the prospectuses of utility bond issues to be carefully drawn as prospective institutional buyers try to avoid the difficulties of another WPPSS.[5] The first joint-action power agency to sell bonds after the WPPSS default was the Michigan Public Power Agency. It came to market with an exhaustive 233-page document, which set a record for length and was for longer than the usual 130 pages. Whether this will be the beginning of a trend of strict disclosure is yet to be seen, but the question remains as to who will read it.

F. Alternative Conclusions to the Tale

Writing about what may happen to complete the story of WPPSS is comparable to composing a novel with alternative endings. Since the script is not finished, you can select the ending you like—for the time being.

1. WPPSS declares voluntary bankruptcy. WPPSS must voluntarily file because it cannot be forced into bankruptcy even though it defaulted. In that event, the "Chinese Wall," which separates plants 1, 2 and 3 from plants 4 and 5, might collapse, resulting in placing all assets in one pool. WPPSS has sought legislation to allow it to separate plants 4 and 5 from plants 1, 2, and 3.

2. WPPSS does not declare bankruptcy, but the trustee, Chemical Bank, files suit against WPPSS as a whole and if successful uses the assets of plants 1, 2, and 3 to pay back the $2.25 billion debt in default plus the accrued interest, which might total as much as $7 billion.

3. The 88 utilities who agreed to pay for plants 4 and 5 might be found guilty of fraud and misrepresentation. Then they may be obliged to pay for outstanding debt.

4. The United States Supreme Court might require the utilities to pay for plants 4 and 5 pursuant to the take-or-pay contracts.

Though this course of action seems unlikely, there is the possibility of its occurrence. On March 26, 1984, *Credit Markets* reported that the Oregon Supreme Court reversed a lower court decision that annulled the contract with WPPSS. This judgment, affecting only 11 of the participants, has no practical immediate effect. On October 2, 1984, the U.S. Supreme Court refused to review the opinion of the Idaho Supreme Court that municipalities of the state did not have the legal authority to sign the WPPSS Participants' Agreement.

5. WPPSS debt might be restructed through a refinancing agency that would have additional state or federal guarantees. The agency would either pay off the old debt in full, make tender offers to purchase bonds, or recall outstanding bonds after issuing refunding bonds.

6. The assets of plants 4 and 5 would be placed under state court supervision. The assets would be liquidated and the proceeds would be paid out to creditors on an agreed upon schedule.

7. The federal government might gallop to the rescue to renew investor confidence in municipal bonds. This is the most unlikely scenario of all.

8. The State of Washington might be forced to assume the burden of payment of interest and principal on the defaulted bonds. The National WPPSS 4 and 5 Bondholders Committee filed a billion dollar lawsuit against Washington State in November 1984. The action against the state claims that Washington has a "moral obligation" to the bondholders and "a contract implied in the law" to repay the debt.

According to Mark C. Ruzick, a special litigation counsel in the Civil Division's Federal Programs Branch, nuclear power engineers deal in "known unknowns" and "unknown unknowns." He added, 'I've only given you the known unknowns in this litigation. I don't know what the unknown unknowns are.'"[7]

G. WPPSS 1986 Update

Though no settlement has yet been reached on all the outstanding law suits, there have been new developments. WPPSS projects 4 & 5 continue to be in default, and projects 1, 2, & 3 continue to be solvent. In fact, as interest rates have declined, the value of 1, 2, & 3 bonds had soared into the premium ranges of $1,250 for each $1,000 face value bond, due to the hefty 14¾% and 15% coupons.

New proposals have been placed on the bargaining table. One idea involves establishing an agency to refinance projects 1, 2, & 3 bonds at lower rates, which would reduce the debt burden of the agency and improve its financial position. A major problem in the refinance project is the pending litigation of $2.25 billion of bonds sold for projects 4 and 5. Though this might sound like good news, holders of projects 1, 2, and 3 bonds might not think so as the value of the bonds dropped in anticipation of the proposed redemption of the bonds at par.

The other proposal is that the Department of Energy is considering converting partially completed projects 1 or 4 to the production of nuclear weapons materials. The Department of Energy is currently using the Hanford nuclear reactor in eastern Washington state. It is scheduled to be phased out in 1995, or it could be revamped at a cost of $1.5 billion.

notes

Chapter XV

[1] James E. Spiotto, "Washington Public Power Supply System," *Current Municipal Defaults and Bankruptcy,* 1983, James E. Spiotta, Chairman. New York Practicing Law Institute, N4 -4915, p. 152.
[2] Spiotto, pp. 154–155.
[3] Michael Blumstein, "The Lessons of a Bond Failure," *The New York Times,* (August 14, 1983).
[4] *Ibid.*
[5] "WPPSS Bond Rating Threatens Financing in Northwest Region," *Wall Street Journal,* (June 17, 1983).
[6] Rich Arthur, "Justice Steps Up WPPSS Defense Effort," *Legal Times,* (Feb. 13, 1984), Vol. VI, No. 36, pp. 28.
[7] *Ibid.*

Postscript—How to Begin

Here we are at the end of the book. Did you read the whole thing or are you starting at the end to see if you can get the jist without having to read the book? Sorry to say, you will have to start at the beginning and work your way through if you want to have a good grasp of municipals, though we will give you a few handy guidelines to speed you on your way. If you have already read the book, read it again! It is one of a few books from which you can benefit by close reading. If you still have questions, you can write to us at the following address: The Scarsdale Investment Group, Ltd. P.O. Box 454, Scarsdale, New York, 10583, and we will answer your questions.

Having decided to proceed with municipals, call a couple of brokers and ask for their informational packets on municipal bonds. They will also give you some up-to-date information on their bond offerings.

You should also begin reading the financial publications for current articles pertaining to municipal bonds. Especially recommended is the Bond Market page of the *Wall Street Journal*, which includes current information on interest rates, new-issue tombstones, notices of redemption, and occasional incisive reporting of newsworthy events. *The New York Times* provides similar information with occasional topical overviews by Michael Quint. *Forbes* is one financial magazine with an abiding concern for the activities of the bond market. It provides a regular review of interest rate movements and recommendations for caution or purchase. A special favorite of ours is the column of Ben Weberman who always has timely and thoughtful comments about current events. *Business Week* also provides information to bond buyers in the form of background on financial affairs.

Having keyed yourself into the information viaducts on bonds, decide for yourself with what degree of risk you feel comfortable. Do you want to purchase only solid AAA bonds or would you feel comfortable seeking a higher return and less security. Consider also what your future needs may be. How soon will you need your principal returned? Can you anticipate any family needs for capital within the time period you are considering investing your dollars? Remember, if you decide to sell your municipals you may not be able to earn as much as if you held them to maturity. Can you anticipate that your income will remain sufficiently high to take advantage of the tax-exempt interest you will be paid? If you can foresee a decline in your income due to job loss, retirement, or some other factor, adjust your maturity dates accordingly.

Now that you have done all your research, decide upon the type and maturity of bond you are seeking. Before you pick up your phone to call your seller of bonds write the following information across the top of a piece of paper.

Rating & No. of Bonds	Coupon	Issuer	Date	Yield-to-Maturity	Yield After-Tax	Current Yield	Unit Price

Now you are ready to proceed. Call your seller.

Did you buy a bond? Hurrah for you! You have taken the first step in receiving tax-free income. April 15th is already looking better than before. You say it is not exactly what you wanted? Do you have second thoughts? Don't worry! The good part about bonds is that they come due at 100. You get your money back and you can start all over again.

Set up a separate file to store your confimrations. You will need these if you plan to sell one of your bonds. Make a note in a place you will remember when the interest payments on the bonds are due and when your principal will be returned. Place your bond in a secure location for safekeeping and enjoy your added income!

GLOSSARY

ACCRUED INTEREST—Interest due the seller or buyer of a bond. It is interest which has accumulated since the last interest payment to the date of sale.
ALL OR NOTHING (AON)—The seller will sell the bonds only if all the bonds in that particular lot are purchased.
AMORTIZE—To amortize the premium on a bond is to reduce the premium equally over the life of the bond.
BASIS POINT—The yield on a municipal bond is usually given in terms of basis points. One basis point is equal to $1/100$ of 1 percent.
BEARER BOND—A bond that is not registered and thus has no identification as to owner. A bearer bond is assumed to be owned by the person who possesses Bearer bonds are easily negotiable since ownership can be quickly transferred from seller to buyer.
BLIND POOL—Bonds sold for a purpose to be decided *after* the sale of the bonds.
BOND—Written evidence of an issuer's promise to repay a loan to a bondholder, with interest, at a specified time.
BOND BANK—A special bank established by some states to purchase the bonds issued by municipalities, and pay the municipalities with money raised by the bond bank on sales of its own bonds.
BOND FUND or FUND—A mutual fund which holds a diversified portfolio of bonds.
CALL DATE—A specified time when an issuer can redeem (i.e., repurchase), all or part of an issue before its maturity date.
CALLABLE BONDS—Bonds that the issuer can redeem (i.e. repurchase) at its option before the bond's maturity date at a specified price which is often above its face value.
CONFIRMATION—A written document which confirms an oral agreement to buy or sell bonds.
COUPON—The amount of interest (e.g. 6% of the bond's face value) which the issuer will pay the bondholder annually.
CURRENT YIELD—The amount of annual interest divided by the amount paid for the bond.
CUSIP NUMBER—An acronym for The Committee on Uniform Security Identification Procedures. Each bond issue has a separate identification number.
DATED DATE—The date of issue of a municipal bond.
DEFAULT—The failure to pay interest or principal payments promptly when due.
DOUBLE-BARRELED BOND—A bond secured by the pledge of two or more sources of repayment.
DISCOUNT BOND—A bond sold at less than face value.
FACE AMOUNT—The par value or the amount that the issuer will pay when the bond matures; the amount appearing on the face of the bond.
GENERAL OBLIGATION BOND—A bond secured by the issuer's full faith, credit and taxing power.
GO TO THE WIRE—Use the computer retrieval services to find the bonds meeting a customer's specifications.

GUARANTEE—The promise to aid aefaulted bond issue at a specified time if certain criteria have been met.

INDUSTRIAL REVENUE BOND (IDB)—A municipal bond generally issued by a state or state agency to construct or purchase industrial facilities which are leased to a private corporation. This bond is secured by the credit of the private corporation rather than by the state or state agency.

INSURANCE—Provided by private insurance companies, a promise to pay interest and principal in the event of a default.

LETTER OF CREDIT (LOC)—A bank's promise to pay either principal and/or interest in the event of a default during a specified period of time.

LOAD—Sales charge collected upon the sale or redemption of some trust units or fund shares.

MANDATORY CALL—The requirement that the issuer repurchase its bonds from the bond holder before maturity if specified conditions are met.

MARKETABILITY—The ease with which a municipal bond can be sold at a reasonable price in the secondary market.

MATURITY DATE—Date when the principal amount of a bond is payable.

MORAL OBLIGATION—Revenue bond feature which implies that the state will support the bonds in the event of a default, although the state is not legally liable to do so.

MUNICIPAL BOND—A bond issued by a state, a state agency, or a subdivision of a state, like a city or county; or a bond having an accepted legal opinion that it is tax-exempt due to municipal support.

NON-CALLABLE BOND—A bond that the issuer cannot repurchase from the bondholder before its specified maturity date.

OFFERING PRICE—The price at which sellers offer to sell bonds to buyers.

PAR VALUE BONDS—The principal amount of a bond at maturity.

PREMIUM BOND—A bond sold at a price in excess of its face value.

PUT—A bond feature providing the bondholder the right to sell the bond back to the issuer at a specified price at a specified time.

RATING—An estimation by a rating agency of an issuer's ability to pay interest and principal when due.

REAL INTEREST RATE—The actual interest rate of a bond less the inflation rate.

RED HERRING—Trade name for the prospectus describing a newly issued bond.

REFUNDING—The purchase of a bond issue from the bondholders by the issuer and the sale of a new bond issue by the issuer at more favorable terms.

REGISTERED BOND—A nonnegotiable instrument, the ownership of which is recorded in the name of the bondholder.

REVENUE BOND—A municipal bond payable solely from the revenues derived from operating a project acquired or constructed with the proceeds of the bonds.

SECONDARY MARKET—The trading market for outstanding bonds and notes.

SINKING FUND—A fund set aside by an issuer on a periodic basis to retire bonds at or prior to maturity.

SPREAD—The difference between the bid and asked prices of bonds.

SWAP—The exchange of one bond for another, generally done to establish a tax loss.

TOMBSTONE—An announcement in the newspaper describing the features of a new bond issue, but not the offering prices.

TENDER OFFER—An offer, by an issuer, to buy back a certain amount of an outstanding bond issue at either a negotiated or set price.

TENDER OPTION PUTS (TOPs)—Low coupon, long-term bonds with the put insured by a letter of credit from a bank.

YIELD-TO-MATURITY—A computation which takes into account the time value of money. It is used as the basis of comparing municipal bonds to one another.

YIELD-TO-MATURITY AFTER TAX—The yield to maturity reduced by the tax on the difference between the purchase price and redemption price on a discount bond.

UNIT INVESTMENT TRUST (or TRUST)—A fixed portfolio of municipal bonds usually sold in undivided interests of $1000.

INDEX

Accrued interest charges, (*see* Interest)
After-tax yields of investments, *see* Yield computations
Alternative minimum tax—*see* Tax aspects of municipal bonds
AMBAC (American Mutual Bond Assurance Co.), 64, 141–145, 259

Baldwin United,—*see* AMBAC
Bankruptcies, *see* Default
Banks:
  letters-of-credit, 64, 141–145
  municipal bond trading by, 178, 212
  trustee, 163
  as underwriters, 204
"Basis book," 50
Basis point, 42
Bearer bonds, *see* Unregistered bonds
Bid and asked prices of dealers, spread in, 195–196
Bond anticipation notes (BANs), 41, 239, 245
Bond banks, state, 65, 138–139
Bond Buyer, The, 61, 129
Bond Buyer indexes, 202
Bonneville Power Administration (BPA), 251–253, 255–256
Borrowing with municipal bonds as collateral, 225–227
Brokerage firms, 23, 33, 163, 177–178, 214
  discount, 177–178
  funds purchased through, 92
  purchasing municipal bonds from, 177–179
Buying municipal bonds, *see* Purchasing municipal bonds

Call and redemption options, 45–46, 186
  early call risk, 164–165
Capital gains tax, 222–223
  on municipal bond funds, 93–94
  state, 229–234
  yield-to-maturity after, 50, 186
Cash, raising, 171
  selecting bonds to sell, 195–196
  selling bonds as way of, 195–196
Cash-management type accounts, 163

borrowing against funds in, 170
Cleveland default, *see* Default
Collateral for a loan, municipal bonds as, 33, 170–171, 192
College and university bonds, 122
Commercial paper and short-term notes, tax-free, 41, 158
  rating of, 134–135
Compound interest, 48–51
Confidentiality and investing in municipal bonds, 172–173
Confirmation of purchases, 185–186, 267–268
Consolidation of your portfolio, 192–193
Corporate uses of municipal bonds, 173
Coupons, 42–43
Current yield, *see* Yield computations
Cushion bond, 207
CUSIP (Committee on Uniform Identification Procedures) number, 186, 196
Custodianship and recordkeeping, 86, 100

Damaged bonds, 163–164
Deep discount trusts, 82–83
Default:
  Cleveland, 23, 156
  risk of, 149–150
  defaults and the ratings, 155–156, 159
  the historical record, 150–155, 203
  how to minimize, 158–160
  if a bond issuer defaults, 155–156
  swapping defaulted bonds, 193–194, 260–261
  see also New York City default; Washington Public Power Supply Systems (WPPSS) bonds
Definition of municipal bonds, 39
Discount bonds, 24, 42–43, 207
  federal tax treatment of, 224–225
Discount brokers, 178
Diversification, 85–86

Early call risk, *see* Risks
Education expenses, 172
Electric utility public power bonds, 120–121
  see also Washington Public Power Supply Systems (WPPSS) bonds

271

Index

Estate tax, 227
Exchange privileges among a family of funds, 101

Federal guarantees for municipal bonds, 59–60, 140–141
Federal income taxes, *see* Tax aspects of municipal bonds
Fees, management, *see* Management fees
FGIC (Financial Guarantee Insurance Company), 64, 141–145
Financial Guarantee Insurance Company (*see* FGIC)
Financial security, 15–16, 169–170
Fitch Investors Service Inc., 46, 244
Floating or variable-rate bonds, 57–58
Floating-rate trusts. *See* Unit investment trusts
Front-end fees for funds, 70–71
Funds, *see* Municipal bond funds
Futures contracts, 95

General obligation bonds, 40, 111–113
  spread between revenue bonds and, reasons for, 203–204
General Reinsurance Corporation, 142
Gifts to minors, 11
Gift tax, 172, 227

Health Industry Bond Insurance, *see* HIBI
Hedging by municipal bond funds, 95
HIBI (Health Industry Bond Insurance), 64
High-yield funds, bond selected for, *see* Municipal bond funds
Historical record of municipal bond defaults, *see* Defaults
Hospital bonds, 118–119, 141
Housing bonds, 63–64, 117–118
  call options of, 45–46, 164–165

Income taxes, *see* Tax aspects of municipal bonds
Industrial development bonds (IDBs), 122–123
Industrial Indemnity Company, 64
Information sources on municipal bonds, 33–34, 179–181, 267–268
Insurance:
  FDIC and FSLIC, 59–60
  insured trusts, 83–84
  private, 23, 64, 141–145, 159
Insured trusts, 83–84
Interest, accrued, 87, 190
Interest expense incurred to carry municipal bonds, 224–227
Interest-free loans, 171–172
Interest rate(s), 160–161
  floating or variable, 57–58
  market view of, 208–211
  paid by bonds, 43–45
    long-term bonds, 205–207
  real, 211
Investment philosophy, 15–16
Investment strategy of funds versus trusts, 69–70
IRA, 174

Kenny & Co., J. J., 181
Kenny Wire, 181
Keogh plan, 174

Legal opinion on bonds, 47, 242–243
Letter-of-credit (LOC), 65, 83, 145
  trust issues backed by, 83
Liquidity of the investment, 23–24, 30, 35, 39, 84–85
  liquidity risk, 162–163
Load funds, 92
Loans:
  interest-free, 171
  to minors, 11
  see also Borrowing with municipal bonds as collateral
Long-term bond funds, 96–97, 104
Long-term bond maturity, 205–206
  negative aspects of, 75, 87, 161, 208–211
Lost bonds, 163–164

Management fees, 28, 72–73, 93
Market price decline, risk of, 160–162
Market strategies, 201–215
  effect of investor buying patterns on trading strategies, 213–214
  effect of ratings on spread between bond prices, 201
  market reactions to changes in registration, 214–215
  market view of discount and premium bonds, 207
  market view of interest rates, 208–211
  ratio of taxable bonds to tax-free bonds, 208
  reasons for spread between revenue and general obligation bonds, 202–204
  relationship between yield and bond maturities, 205–207
Massachusetts, Proposition 2½, 113
Maturity date of bond, 42
  in municipal bond funds, 96–98
  negative aspects of going long-term, 75, 87, 161
  relationship of yield to, 205–207

Index

MBIA (Municipal Bond Investors Assurance Corp.), 64, 141–145
Minicoupon bonds, 58–59
Money market municipal bond funds, 29, 98, 105
Moody's Investor Service, 64
   rating of bonds by, 46–47, 129, 131–135, 142, 155, 244
   New York City, 244
   WPPSS, 259–260
   rating of short-term notes and commercial paper by, 131, 133–135, 244
Moral obligation security, 66, 117–118
Municipal Assistance Corp., see New York State Municipal Assistance Corp.
Municipal bond funds, 28, 29, 69–75, 89–107
   comparison with unit investment trusts and, 69–75
   determining the price, 71
   high-yield funds, bonds selected for, 94–96
   investment strategy, 69–70
   management fees and sales charge, 70–71, 93
   method of purchase, 70
   quality, 73–74
   reading the prospectus, 74–75
   redemption—hidden costs, 72–73
   reinvesting, 73
   evaluation of, 89–107
      analysis of yields, 102–103
      the costs, 92–94
      maturity, 96–98
      quality of portfolios, 94–96
      sampling of issuers of intermediate funds, 106–107
      special features and services of, 99–101
Municipal Bond Insurance Association (See MBIA)
Municipal bonds:
   common features of, 41–48
   comparison to other tax-favored investments, 8–11
   defaults, see Default
   definition of, 39–40
   desirable features of, 21–25
   examples of financial solutions using, 25–29
   funds, see Municipal bonds funds
   how and from whom to buy, 106–107, 177–179
   market strategies, 201–215
   misconception about, 29–30
   preliminary steps before purchasing, 35–36, 267–268
   proper and improper uses of, 169–174
   ratings, see Rating of a municipal bond
   reasons to buy, 5–8
   risks of investing in, (see risks)
   short-term tax-free instruments, 41
   special features of, 55–66
   tax aspects of, 219–234
   trusts, See Unit investment trusts
   types of, 40
Municipal Bond Securities Rulemaking Board, 59, 185

New York City default, 22, 131, 137, 156, 158, 162, 237–248
New York State, 237
   moral obligation bonds, 66, 117–118, 139–140
New York State Dormitory Authority Bonds, 140–141
New York State Municipal Assistance, Corp. (MAC), 57, 157–158, 180, 245
New York State Urban Development Corporation, 117, 131, 138, 153
No-load funds, 72, 92

Odd lots, 187, 195
Open-ended mutual funds, see Municipal bond funds

Pension plans, 10, 174
Pollution control bonds
Premium bonds, 42–43, 203–204
   federal tax treatment of, 223
Pricing of bonds, 42–43
   effect of ratings on, 201
Primary (new issue) market, 181–184
Principal amount of the bond, 186
Profit, selling bonds to make a, 191
Profit-sharing plans, 10, 174
Property tax, 229
Proposition 13, 111, 113, 157
Purchasing municipal bonds:
   confirmation and payments, 185–186
   guidelines for talking with the seller, 186–188
   preliminary steps, 33–34, 267–268
   the primary (new issue) market, 181–184
   the secondary market, 184
   sellers of municipal bonds, 177–179
Put bonds, 24, 55–56, 95, 161

Rating agencies, see Rating of a municipal bond
Rating of a municipal bond, 46–47, 145
   defaults and, 155–156, 157–160, 246–247

Rating of a municipal bond *(continued)*
　effect of, on the spread between bond
　　prices, 201
　methods used by issuers to improve the,
　　138–145
　　federal guarantees, 140–141
　　private insurance, 64, 83–84, 141–145
　rating agencies:
　　beginning of, 129
　　comparison of rating systems,
　　　135–136
　　duplicating the ratings, 130
　　a guide to the ratings of, 131–135
　　limitations of the ratings, 137–138
　　methods used to establish ratings,
　　　129–130
　　unrated bonds, 94–95, 136–137
Reciprocal immunity from taxes, states
　sharing, 231
Recordkeeping, 86, 100–101
Redemption options, *see* Call or
　redemption options
Refunding, 61–62
Registered bonds, 45, 163–164
　market reaction to changes in
　　registration, 216
Revenue anticipation notes (RANs), 41,
　238–239, 245, 248
Revenue bonds, 40, 114–125, 153
　description of, 114–115
　spread between general obligation bonds
　　and, reasons for, 202–204
　strengths and weaknesses of, 115–116
　types of, 116–125
　user fees to pay back, 115–116
Richelsons' Investment Rules, 16–18
Risks, 16–18, 22, 83–84, 149–162
　of default, 149–162
　early call, 164–165
　of general obligation versus revenue
　　bonds, 203–204
　liquidity,
　　of price decline, 160–162
　　of theft, loss, or damage, 163–164

Safety of municipal bonds, 22–23, 30
San Jose Unified School District, bonds of,
　154–155
(The) Scarsdale Investment Group, Ltd.,
　xii
School building authorities, state, 138–139
Secondary market, 184
Securities and Exchange Commission, 74,
　241
Sellers of municipal bonds, 177–179
　guidelines for talking with, 188–188
　see also Banks; Brokerage firms

Selling strategies and techniques, 191–197
　procedure for selling a bond, 196–197
　reasons for selling, 191–195
　selection of bonds to sell to raise cash,
　　195–196
Short-term notes (*see* commercial paper)
Sinking fund, 62–63
Social Security tax (*see* taxes)
Standard & Poor's, 46–47, 64
　rating of bonds by, 131–133, 134,
　　135–136
　　key to, 143, 154
　　New York City, 244
　　WPPSS, 259–260
　rating of commercial paper by, 131,
　　133, 135
Stolen bonds, 163–164
Student loan bonds, 121–122
Supersinkers, 63–64
Swapping bonds, 193–195

Taxable bonds, 22–23
Tax Allocation Bonds, 124–125
Tax anticipation notes (TANs), 41, 239,
　245
Tax aspects of municipal bonds, 219-254
　federal income tax treatment:
　　alternative minimum tax, 220–221
　　of capital gains and losses, 222–223
　　deductibility of interest expense
　　　incurred to carry bonds, 225–227
　　of discount bonds, 224–225
　　estate and gift tax, 227
　　of premium bonds, 223–224
　　Social Security tax, 227–229
　state taxes, 229–234
Tax shelters, 8–9
Tax swaps, *see* swapping bonds
Tender Option Puts (TOPs), 56
"Tombstone," 182–183
Treasury bonds, 61–62, 208
Trusts:
　for high tax bracket beneficiary, 172
　to support dependent or needy relative,
　　171–172
　see also Unit investment trusts

Underwriters, 181, 184
　New York City default and the, 241–242
　WPPSS default and, 258–259
U.S. Department of Housing and Urban
　Development (HUD), 118
U.S. Government agency-backed municipal
　bonds, 22, 59–60
Unit investment trusts, 78–88
　see also Municipal bond funds
　calculations of yield on a unit, 81

Index

Unit investment trusts *(continued)*
  comparison of owning individual municipal bonds versus trust units, 79–87
  costs of owning a unit, 79–80
  sampling of issuers of, 87–88
  special types of, 82–84
University bonds, *see* College and university bonds
Unrated bonds, 94–95, 136, 137, 204
Unregistered bonds, 45, 214–215
Urban Development Corporation, New York State, 117, 138, 140, 154
Utility bonds, *see* Electric utility public power bonds

Warrants, 56–57

Washington Public Power Supply Systems (WPPSS) bonds, 85–86, 121, 141, 143, 150, 156, 159, 162, 196, 251–265
Water and sewer bonds, 119–120

Yield computations, 48–51
  current yield, 48–49
  for municipal bond trusts or funds, 81, 98
  yield-to-call, 50–51, 168
  yield-to-maturity, 49–50, 66, 190, 205–207
  yield-to-maturity after capital gains tax, 50, 187–188

Zero-coupon bonds, 25, 58–59

CARROLL & GRAF
FINE WORKS OF NON-FICTION AVAILABLE IN QUALITY PAPERBACK EDITIONS FROM CARROLL & GRAF

- [ ] Anderson, Nancy/WORK WITH PASSION $8.95
- [ ] Asprey, Robert/THE PANTHER'S FEAST $9.95
- [ ] Athill, Diana/INSTEAD OF A LETTER $7.95
- [ ] Bedford, Sybille/ALDOUS HUXLEY $14.95
- [ ] Berton, Pierre/KLONDIKE FEVER $10.95
- [ ] Blanch, Lesley/PIERRE LOTI $10.95
- [ ] Blanch, Lesley/THE WILDER SHORES OF LOVE $8.95
- [ ] Bowers, John/IN THE LAND OF NYX $7.95
- [ ] Buchan, John/PILGRIM'S WAY $10.95
- [ ] Carr, Virginia Spencer/THE LONELY HUNTER: A BIOGRAPHY OF CARSON McCULLERS $12.95
- [ ] Conot, Robert/JUSTICE AT NUREMBURG $10.95
- [ ] Cooper, Lady Diana/AUTOBIOGRAPHY $12.95
- [ ] Edwards, Anne/SONYA: THE LIFE OF COUNTESS TOLSTOY $8.95
- [ ] Elkington, John/THE GENE FACTORY Cloth $16.95
- [ ] Farson, Negley/THE WAY OF A TRANSGRESSOR $9.95
- [ ] Goldin, Stephen & Sky, Kathleen/THE BUSINESS OF BEING A WRITER $8.95
- [ ] Green, Julian/DIARIES 1928–1957 $9.95
- [ ] Haycraft, Howard (ed.)/THE ART OF THE MYSTERY STORY $9.95
- [ ] Lansing, Alfred/ENDURANCE: SHACKLETON'S INCREDIBLE VOYAGE $8.95
- [ ] Leech, Margaret/REVEILLE IN WASHINGTON $11.95
- [ ] McCarthy, Barry & Emily/SEXUAL AWARENESS $9.95
- [ ] Mizener, Arthur/THE SADDEST STORY: A BIOGRAPHY OF FORD MADOX FORD $12.95
- [ ] Montyn, Jan & Kooiman, Dirk Ayelt/A LAMB TO SLAUGHTER $8.95

- ☐ Mullins, Edwin/THE PAINTED WITCH
  Cloth $25.00
- ☐ Munthe, Axel/THE STORY OF SAN MICHELE
  $8.95
- ☐ O'Casey, Sean/AUTOBIOGRAPHIES I
  $10.95 Cloth $21.95
- ☐ O'Casey, Sean/AUTOBIOGRAPHIES II
  $10.95 Cloth $21.95
- ☐ Poncins, Gontran de/KABLOONA $9.95
- ☐ Pringle, David/SCIENCE FICTION: THE 100 BEST NOVELS $15.95
- ☐ Proust, Marcel/ON ART AND LITERATURE $8.95
- ☐ Rowse, A.L./HOMOSEXUALS IN HISTORY $9.95
- ☐ Roy, Jules/THE BATTLE OF DIENBIENPHU $8.95
- ☐ Russel, Robert A./WINNING THE FUTURE
  Cloth $16.95
- ☐ Salisbury, Harrison/A JOURNEY FOR OUR TIMES
  $10.95
- ☐ Service, William/OWL $8.95
- ☐ Sloan, Allan/THREE PLUS ONE EQUALS BILLIONS $8.95
- ☐ Werth, Alexander/RUSSIA AT WAR: 1941–1945
  $15.95
- ☐ Wilmot, Chester/STRUGGLE FOR EUROPE $12.95
- ☐ Zuckmayer, Carl/A PART OF MYSELF $9.95

Available from fine bookstores everywhere or use this coupon for ordering:

Caroll & Graf Publishers, Inc., 260 Fifth Avenue, N.Y., N.Y. 10001

Please send me the books I have checked above. I am enclosing $_____ (please add 1.75 per title to cover postage and handling.) Send check or money order—no cash or C.O.D.'s please. N.Y. residents please add 8¼% sales tax.

Mr/Mrs/Miss _____
Address _____
City _____ State/Zip _____

Please allow four to six weeks for delivery.